MUSTANG PERFORMANCE
H A N D B O O K

Engine and drivetrain modifications for street, drag strip or road racing use. Covers all models of the Ford Mustang, 1979 to present.

WILLIAM R. MATHIS

HPBooks

HPBooks
are published by
The Berkley Publishing Group
200 Madison Avenue
New York, New York 10016

First edition: November 1994

© 1994 William Mathis
10 9 8 7 6 5 4 3 2 1
Printed in U.S.A.

Library of Congress Cataloging-in-Publication Data

Mathis, William R.
    Mustang performance handbook / William R. Mathis.
            p.   cm.
    Includes index.
    ISBN 1-55788-193-6 (paper)
        1. Mustang automobile—Motors—Modification. 2. Mustang
automobile—Performance.   I. Title.
TL215.M8M3   1994   94-18029
629.25'04—dc20   CIP

Book design & production by Bird Studios
Front cover photo by Charlie Rathbun
Interior photos and drawings by William Mathis unless otherwise noted

CONTENTS

ACKNOWLEDGEMENTS

Thanks to the following individuals and companies for their support. Without it, this book would have been much more difficult to put together:

Jim Bell of Kenne-Bell
Joe Rivera of EFI Hyperformance
Chris Marvel
Howard Duffy
Richard Pederson
Ford Motor Company
Bruce Griggs of Griggs Racing
Alyse Borla of Borla Performance Industries
Todd at Baer Racing
Dan Phelps of Ford SVT
Dorothy Thomas and Angelo Giampetroni at Ford Motor Company
Sam Guido, Hank Dertian and John Vermeersch of Ford SVO
Bob Franzke of N.O.S.
Steve Esslinger of Esslinger Turbo Products
Edelbrock Performance
Dario Orlando of Steeda Motorsports
Mary at SuperFlow
John Coleman of Suspension Techniques
Dennis Hilliard of Central Coast Mustangs
Autotronic Controls Corporation (MSD)
Joy Laschober at Bondurant School of High Performance Driving
Cari Southworth of Kenny Brown Performance Parts
Elizabeth of Saleen Performance Parts
John Chaney, the aviator
Tom Wilson of Super Ford magazine
Donald Farr of Dobbs Publishing

Special thanks to Roger for supporting me through this venture, Bob for being a good friend while I struggled, and Michael Lutfy of HPBooks for taking the chance.

A very special thanks to Glenda, for removing the multiple "howevers," correcting the country boy grammar and most of all for being there. . .

. . .and to Major and Alexis. An extra special thanks for tolerating my absence. You know Dad loves you.

INTRODUCTION

The third-generation Mustang is the most popular high-performance car on the road today. Many a former "Brand X" driver has transferred his loyalty to the Blue Oval because of the Mustang. Great ride and handling combined with a real V8 engine have made this the #1 car among the street performance crowd. However, to bring the Mustang to its full potential requires specific modifications. There are many qualified race car and performance shops that will be happy to modify your car for you. However, banks only loan money in that quantity to real businesses. The cost of the parts to achieve a high level of success at the drag strip or on a road course is pretty unreal to the average racer. When you add on the cost to assemble or modify the car so that the parts actually work, the price generally becomes prohibitive. That is why this series of books was written.

Yes, I said series. This handbook was originally written as one book to provide the Mustang enthusiast with a good basis for modifying his car. However, due to the sheer volume of material required to cover the entire subject of modifying the Fox Mustang for all levels of performance, from mild street to all-out competitive racing, it was deemed best that our customers would be better served to cover this enormous subject in two separate volumes. This volume, *Mustang Performance Handbook,* is directed at making horsepower and putting it to the axles with bolt-on type modifications. The stock Ford 5.0 shortblock can take considerable abuse before internal upgrades are necessary. The second volume, *Mustang Performance Handbook 2,* is directed at putting the power to the ground for optimum acceleration and handling for the street enthusiast, quarter-miler and road racer. That book deals with extensive chassis and suspension modifications, ranging from popular bolt-on kits to full roll cage construction. Both of these books cover the important basics and advanced procedures for building a competitive and reliable performance car.

The modifications in this handbook are designed to specifically address the '79 to '93 Fox Mustang. However, the new Fox-4 Mustang engine is essentially the same as its predecessors. Other than pulley, intake and transmission/bellhousing changes, the drivetrains are virtually identical, so the modifications provided in this volume will also apply to the Fox-4 cars.

However, I've narrowed the subject down to only the post-'86 fuel-injected cars. The Ford computer-controlled fuel-injection is state of the art technology. A carburetor cannot compare to the perfect fuel metering produced by the EFI systems. For those of you with a carbureted engine, there are several excellent books on how to modify the Holley carburetor for performance, including one from HPBooks. Or, you can convert to EFI with a Ford Motorsport wiring harness and kit. Given the modest price of this kit, retro-fitting an EFI engine into the older Fox cars should be a primary consideration.

Value—If you have a rare car such as the SVO, ASC McLaren, '84-1/2 Anniversary Mustang, Saleen, SAAC, '93 Cobra or the '79 Indy Pace Car, then be aware that these modifications will generally have a significantly negative impact on the value of your investment. Yes, I know it's hard to believe how anyone could find a stock Mustang more appealing than your 11-second doorslammer. However, a Sunday's outing to one of the many car shows will set you straight. Original equipment, rare Mustangs with anemic stock engines fetch premiums that one could almost retire on. A Mustang chopped up to accommodate a supercharged 800 hp engine and a trick four-link Pro Stock suspension can only hope to sell for a small portion of the original vehicle's price—even though the cost of making these modifications exceeds that same price. Think about it before you begin. Remember that the modifications you make, you make mainly for your own enjoyment.

Economy—Modifications to your engine to increase horsepower will cause your fuel consumption to increase. Don't believe the feldagarb published in some magazines bragging about 20+ miles to the gallon fuel economy from that trick-looking 450 hp 11-second machine. Horsepower equates to burned fuel. Even a very efficient high-performance racing engine with a low brake-specific still requires a minimum number of pounds of fuel per hour to generate one horsepower. Unfortunately that high efficiency is subject to multiplication by the number of horses involved, not to mention the typical higher rear axle ratios necessary to harness all that power. The problem is further exacerbated by the frequency with which we find our right foot planted to the floor.

Legality—Loud obnoxious cars serve only to anger the voting public, "voting" being the key word here. Many of the limitations you are experiencing in high-performance motoring are the direct result of pressure put on our legislators and Congressmen by the voting public. Even if you vote, and a significant portion of you don't, you're outnumbered, so keep that in mind. With today's advancements in muffler technology, there is no need to wake up the neighbors with a blast down the street with glass-pack mufflers.

Modifications to the emission systems of most cars in this country are not only a violation of state law but also a federal no-no that can result in a mind-numbing fine. We are constantly bombarded by the media about the very real danger to our environment from pollution. Building a high-performance engine, sporting an efficient low fuel brake-specific that does not meet the operating emissions equipment requirements of your state, will only contribute to the demise of this sport and possibly your bank account. As with the advances in muffler technology, advances in cam design, headers, catalytic converters and of course, the Ford ECU computer (the god of Ford hot rodding that made it all possible), have given us the ability to make cubic horsepower without destroying our environment. Please think and act responsibly. ■

GETTING STARTED

Before you start ripping things apart and ordering all those neat go-fast goodies, it is necessary to evaluate your limits and determine exactly what you intend to accomplish. This is the most important aspect to modifying your powertrain. You must consider your budget, the ancillary modifications associated with elevated horsepower, and the proper combination of options if you are to achieve the optimum results. One of the many lessons I learned the hard way concerned racing the same car I depended on to get me to work. If you modify your only means of transportation, you can count on walking a great deal. The portion of time spent walking versus driving skews toward walking as the horsepower levels increase. This is real world. You are going to break parts and others will wear out more rapidly as you bump the horsepower upward. If this is a problem for you, then limit the modifications to those that will keep the horsepower below 300. Beyond this point, Murphy, (of Murphy's Law fame), will start to take an active interest in your car. Obviously, your racing budget will also require additional maintenance when Murphy joins your team.

COST

Every hot rodder has read the many testimonials in various high-performance

The first body series of the Fox Mustang ran from '79 through '82. This '79 Mustang of Mark Jenkins is typical of the modifications seen on these earlier cars. Headers, cam, 4:10 gears and a big Holley propel this machine to the mid-12's.

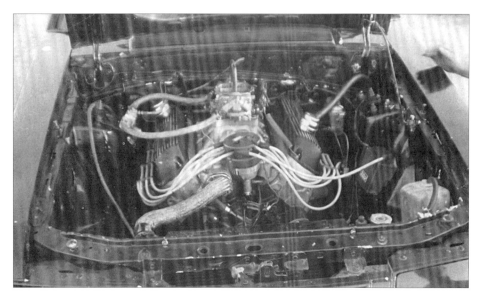

This fast '83 Mustang of Bobby Gagne represents the second body series of the Fox Mustangs (1983/84). It has had a new heart installed to replace the tired old 5.0. The heavily massaged 351W fitted to Bobby's car is basically a bolt in. Lightweight and simple engine controls have made these pre-EFI cars a favorite with hardcore drag racers.

calculate the total cost. Now double whatever you came up with. This will put you somewhere in the ballpark. Remember, Murphy grew up in a hot rod shop and has a complete working knowledge of how to increase the costs of any racing engine, no matter how well planned.

You probably will never recover what you spend on your machine. Although this book is geared to the average person with average means, somehow we always end up spending more than we expect to. Anyone who believes they will be able to sell their car and recover all the bucks spent on those neat go-fast modifications is probably half a bubble off.

magazines boasting about the 11-second racer with only "$814.27" invested in it. If you believe this then you probably also own several acres of beautiful swamp land in the Florida everglades. The truth of the matter is: speed costs money. The more money—the faster you go. Building an engine to produce the horsepower for a 12-second run can be accomplished without major cash outlays. However, making the 400+ horsepower necessary to see the 11s or faster will require you come up with a suitcase full of money, large bills, of course. It is very important to understand this before you start. Trying to build a mega-horsepower engine, without assessing the true costs before you begin, will only lead to disaster. Too often, engines are started with expensive trick pieces and then have to be compromised with inferior quality to finish as the bucks run out. The end result is the wrong combination of expensive parts that add up to a poorly performing engine.

Before you start, know exactly what you can afford to spend. Make a list of the pieces that work in combination and

PARTS

Building high-horsepower engines to go fast will not mean much if you can not get the power to the ground. The stock Mustang equipment is pretty rugged, but when subject to the abuse given by the average leadfoot, things start to break as horsepower is elevated. Obviously, to go fast, modifications to the engine must be accompanied by modifications to other parts of the powertrain. Don't kid yourself into thinking things will be OK. You will find yourself watching a lot of races from the sidelines or walking home

Probably the most popular body style of the Fox Mustangs is the third body series of the 1985 GT. Last of the carbureted engines and 7.5 axles, these cars came with the first roller cam engines. This popular torque arm-equipped 1985 GT of professional racing driver Howard Duffy runs the fast E/SP class in the SCCA Solo II category.

a great deal if you don't combine the engine modifications with other powertrain modifications. This gets back to the first section of this chapter: know your budget limits and plan for the total package. Upgrades to clutches, transmissions, driveshafts, differentials and axles all have to be considered along with the engine mods.

Balanced Combinations

Probably the most abused area in hot rodding is the lack of balanced combinations of engine modifications. Everyone wants the wild idle sounds of a radical camshaft. To the racer, this is pure heaven. Unfortunately, without the other pieces that are necessary to provide adequate fuel, intake and exhaust flows, not to mention sufficient compression to make it work, a wild sound is all you'll end up with.

Do not make the mistake of buying different pieces without considering the manufacturer's recommended modifications. This is particularly true when selecting a camshaft. All the major camshaft grinders (Crane, Lunati, Comp Cams, Crower, Ultradyne, etc.) have tremendous experience grinding camshafts for Ford and people like Jack Roush. They use that experience to improve their products and they know what combinations work. You may be one of the smartest humans on this planet, but there is no substitute for experience.

GET ORGANIZED

If you are building your car to run in a specific class, get a rule book first. Read the rules for allowed and disallowed modifications. Go to the races and check out race cars in your class. Look for subtle changes, take good notes and always be a good listener, especially to the conversation of the mechanics. They

don't get the attention the hot shoe drivers get but they invariably love to tell you how they made it fast.

Keep in mind your findings as you make the modifications provided in this book. Write them down! Before you start, get a three-ring binder. Include ruled paper, graph paper, and blank sheets in this binder. As you modify your car, you will be adding data sheets provided in this book for specific recordkeeping. Keep this with you whenever you work on the car or go to a racing event. Note any changes made to the car before, during and after a race or car show. At an event, take notes about competitor's cars and anything interesting they may be trying. Always be mindful that everyone is constantly looking for an edge so keep a sharp eye.

DRIVETRAIN HISTORY

Since the introduction of the Fox Mustang in 1979, there has been

The rare SVO Mustang is a super car to build a high-performance racer from. Excellent suspension and brakes, these cars make great autocrossers. Shown here is the author's 2,500 lb., 450 hp four-banger '85 SVO. The rush from a full-bore blast is incredible!

Beginning in 1987, the 5.0 engines that are the basis for the GT engines through 1993 went into production. Shown here is the Speed Density controlled 1988 LX of Larry Sample. Equipped with an assortment of the trick go-fast goodies manufactured by Larry's company (Auto Specialties), this pony consistently travels the quarter in the 11-second zone.

continuous development of the entire drivetrain for the V8-powered cars. Camshafts, intakes, heads, blocks, transmissions and rear axles have all been tweaked, tuned, and changed. It is important to know these differences before you start modifying or purchasing a Mustang. Armed with the correct information, you will be able to better determine what parts to replace and the best salvage items to seek, as well as determine if the engine has the potential to satisfy your performance needs. The rest of this chapter will provide you with a basic understanding of those differences.

Engines

1979 5.0—This engine was the basic 28-oz/in. imbalance 1978 version and the last of the old-style thick-block 302s. A good performance block, the leak-prone two-piece rear main seal means an ever-present oil leak. Unfortunately, this engine had 8.4:1 compression cast pistons, an economy cam, a 369 cfm two-barrel carburetor with a mechanical fuel delivery system and junk heads that together produced a mind-boggling 140 horsepower. The cast-iron exhaust

manifolds and single two-inch exhaust system does not allow for much improvement either. Other than a heavy and strong block (by comparison to 5.0 blocks), this engine has very little performance potential. However, if you're going to stay with this engine for some reason, there are some upgrades

that will help. Install an '86 or newer water pump; the latest head gaskets; 1983-'85 4V carburetor and intake; '86 or newer roller block; a two-piece marine rear main seal; a roller timing chain; and an '82 D30E marine cam.

1980-1981 4.2-liter—The 4.2-liter (255 cid) V8 found in this series of Mustangs is totally worthless for high-performance modification. Do not waste the time or the money trying to modify this engine.

1982 5.0 H.O.—Things got much better this year. This engine came with the standard '79-style 302 heads, the flat-tappet marine camshaft (D3OE-AA) with .416 In./.444 Ex. lift, 260 In./278 Ex. duration, 8.4:1 compression cast pistons, a roller timing chain, and a 369 cfm Motorcraft two-barrel carburetor. The internal balance was changed to utilize 50 oz. imbalance components and a thin-cast 302 block (15 lbs. lighter). In its best state of tune this engine produced 157 horsepower. Although this engine ushered in the new era of high performance for the Mustang, it has very little performance potential. The heads

Generally considered to run harder at the drag strip, the Speed Density controlled fuel systems found on the '87 & '88 (non-California '88) Mustangs do not use a Mass Air meter. This Speed Density controlled 11-second '87 of John Crawford sports a custom-built upper intake fabricated from a truck induction system. This intake really flows some serious air!

have tiny ports and small valves, the pistons are cast and low compression, and the block is pretty weak. This engine is also the last 302 5.0 with the two-piece rear main seal, so the rear main oil leak has to be tolerated. The flat-tappet camshaft has less performance potential than the later roller versions, especially where the exhaust sniffer is used for inspection. The best bet is to replace it with a 1987 or newer roller block engine.

1983 5.0 H.O.—This series of engines were basically the same as the 1982 engine with a few minor changes. The heads, camshaft, exhaust manifolds and pistons were all carryovers from 1982. A 600 cfm Holley four-barrel replaced the Motorcraft two-barrel, and the crankshaft and block were altered to

use a one-piece main seal. Horsepower increased to 175. Again, these engines have limited performance potential due to the cast low-compression pistons, flat-tappet cam, tiny head ports and weak block.

1984 5.0 H.O.—The 1984 engine was a carryover from 1983 and shared the same performance limitations. This was the first year fuel injection was offered in the Mustang. All Mustangs manufactured with the A.O.D. transmission got the Low Pressure Central Fuel Injection. Equipped with two 52-lbs.-hr. injectors, this system has no performance potential.

1985 5.0 H.O.—Beginning in 1985 the 5.0 block utilized a hydraulic roller tappet camshaft, forged 8.4:1

compression pistons and tubular exhaust manifolds with 2 1/2" exits, as well as improved cylinder heads. Due to the improved breathing associated with the roller cam (266 degrees duration and 444" lift, both intake and exhaust) and tubular dual exhaust, horsepower increased to 210. The induction systems sported an improved Holley carburetor, or the Low Pressure Central Fuel Injection found on the A.O.D. (automatic overdrive) equipped cars (early A.O.D. cars with the CFI system may have been flat-tappet equipped). As with previous years, the Holley carbureted model could be improved with the usual modifications, but not so with the central fuel injection system. The unique central fuel injection provided outstanding

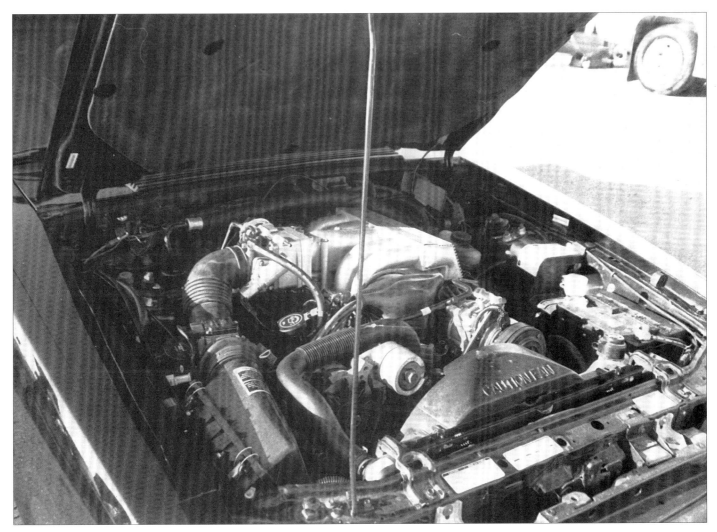

The Mass Air meter controlled fuel systems installed on 1988 California and all 1989 and newer GTs allows significant engine modifications without having to go to a special computer system. This '93 Cobra Mustang has had its cast upper plenum replaced with the tubular GT-40 type.

The limited production '93 Cobra Mustang sported softer suspension, a cast GT-40 type upper intake, GT-40 heads, a special camshaft with more lift but less duration, a 70mm Mass Air, 65mm throttle body and more aggressive computer programming. Rated at 235 horsepower, these cars have considerable potential.

throttle response and fuel economy but no performance potential. This is the first 5.0 engine overall that had some performance potential due to the forged pistons and roller cam. Although a vast improvement over previous years, this roller cam block is weak, has poor heads and has low-compression, limiting its naturally aspirated potential.

1986 5.0 H.O.—A thicker deck and semi-siamesed cylinders make this block considerably stronger than previous 5.0 engines. Compression was increased to 9.2 by eliminating the dish and valve eyebrows in the pistons. This engine had a unique cylinder head with a shrouded intake valve that was designed to improve swirl and the rate of burn. Additionally, this was the first year Ford installed the multi-port fuel injection (Speed Density) in the Mustang. This system came with the standard 19 lbs-hr. injectors. The roller camshaft was a carryover from 1985. The tubular exhaust manifolds were changed to eliminate the cold start exhaust control

valve and the outlet sizes were decreased to 2 1/4". Horsepower was published at 200, with torque increased to 285 lbs-ft.

This engine would appear to have significant performance potential. Unfortunately, the lack of valve eyebrows in the pistons limit the amount of valve lift that can be utilized. This is not the worst. The high swirl combustion chambers are useless for performance and essentially render the heads junk. In addition, the intake manifold has tiny ports and a 58mm throttle body. The Speed Density-controlled fuel injection has trouble handling performance components, especially camshafts, further limiting the performance potential (although you can convert to a mass air system). Replacement heads, intake and throttle body are minimum changes just to bring this engine up to par with the 1987-or-later engines.

1987-1988 5.0 H.O. (Except 1988 Calif.)—Beginning in 1987 Ford switched to the truck head (E7TE

casting) with its larger ports and 1.74/1.46 valves, 9.0 compression forged pistons (with .030" dish and valve eyebrows), a larger runner intake and the now standard 60mm throttle body. Like the 1986 fuel injection, these cars utilized the Speed Density system for fuel management and suffered the same performance limitations. Fortunately, Ford Motorsport offers a kit to upgrade the Speed Density cars to Mass Air. The camshaft, exhaust manifolds and block were carryovers from 1986. These engines offer good performance potential especially when coupled with a power adder.

1989-1992 5.0 H.O. & 1988 5.0 H.O. Calif.—There is no doubt that this series of engines has the greatest performance potential of all the standard 5.0 H.O. engines. Although the block, heads, intake and exhaust manifolds are unchanged from the 1987 engines, the introduction of the 55mm Mass Air meter-controlled fuel injection allows the use of radical camshafts. These engines are the best choice for performance, if a choice exists.

The camshaft in the H.O. engines was changed in August of 1988 to reduce valvetrain rattle. Slight changes to the intake lobe ramps were made to prevent momentary slack occurring between the lifter's roller and the lobe. This change caused a slight reduction in flow efficiency, resulting in a loss of about 3 horsepower. Obviously, the pre-August cam is the better choice.

1993 5.0 H.O.—This series of high output engines was basically identical to the 1989 through 1992 engines except for one very important change. Beginning in 1993, Ford elected to drop the expensive forged pistons in favor of the bean-counter specials, the cast hypereutectic aluminum units. Although excellent pistons, use of a cast piston provides a significant barrier to high performance. Turbo, supercharging or nitrous oxide are pretty much out of the question. The cast pistons can only handle modest power gains before they head south.

1993 5.0 Cobra—The limited edition Cobra Mustang comes equipped with a 235 horsepower version of the standard 5.0 H.O. engine. Ford swapped the standard heads for a set of the cast-iron GT-40 versions, installed the SSC type exhaust manifolds, a unique cast aluminum GT-40 style intake, with 65mm throttle body, 24 lbs-hr. injectors, 70mm mass air meter, a shorter duration higher lift camshaft, 1.72 rockers and a specially programmed EEC-IV computer. Obviously, this engine setup provides a good starting point for developing a performance 5.0. Finding one is another thing altogether. The change to the cast pistons in the 1993 engines was also applicable to the Cobra version. As noted previously, this change seriously limits the performance potential of this engine. The many performance upgrades of the Cobra engine were welcome additions, however, cast pistons just will not hold

up under racing conditions.

Final Advice—If you are shopping around for a Mustang with the intent of building a performance car, stick with the 1989-1992 versions. The mass air fuel injection will greatly simplify modifications. If your budget does not permit upgrading your existing older Fox Mustang with one of the better engines (1987 or newer) then recognize the limitations that a cast piston or flat-tappet cam has. If your engine is a pre-'87, at a minimum you should replace the heads and exhaust manifolds with '87 or later versions. Obviously the two-barrel found on the 1982 H.O. will have to go. The new retro-fit hydraulic roller cam kits that are currently available from several cam grinders make an excellent choice for improving performance in the pre-roller engines and should be seriously considered.

Transmissions

Automatics—There have been only two automatics offered in the 5.0

Mustang, the 1979 C-4 and the automatic overdrive (A.O.D.). Anyone who has been around a drag strip lately knows the C-4 is the transmission of choice for the shiftless group. Although the A.O.D. can be modified to withstand considerable abuse, it will generally not take the abuse of the high horsepower engines. As an alternative, several drag racing Mustangs have switched to the GM700-R4 or the tough and proven small-block C-6 Ford. I prefer the small-block C-6 with its excellent ratios and bullet-proof strength.

The physical size of the small block C-6 will require the judicious use of a large hammer, in the transmission tunnel, in order to fit. Given the excellent crop of racing C-4s that are currently available, use of a C-6 should probably be reserved for 700+ horsepower engines.

Manual—There have been two basic types of gearboxes offered in the 5.0 Mustang. The 1979 to 1982 V8 Mustangs came with the SROD four-speed while all others sported the Borg-Warner T-5. The SROD transmission

One of the best upgrades you can make to a stock EFI Mustang is the installation of the '93 Cobra Mustang 70mm Mass Air meter. Shown here, this meter is significantly larger around the middle and basically has smooth sides. Ford Motorsport offers a complete upgrade kit (M9000-C52) which includes the 70mm Mass Air meter, Cobra computer and 24 lbs-hr. injectors.

If you are searching for a Fox Mustang to race, the Notchback LX is the best choice for drag racing. The coupe is considerably lighter than the GT and prices are generally much more reasonable. If your thing is high speed (Nevada Silver State Classic), stick with the hatchback as they have a smaller drag coefficient.

was basically an aluminum cased T&C toploader that was modified to use a single rail enclosed shifter similar to the T-5 that followed. Unfortunately, the SROD is far more effective as a boat anchor than as a performance transmission. It had poor gear ratios and was generally prone to failure.

The T-5 was first introduced in the 1983 GT Mustang and has constantly been refined since its release. There are essentially five series of T-5s that have been offered in the Mustang. The first was the close ratio version that was installed in the 1983 and 1984 models. These transmissions are useless as performance pieces (refer to above comment about the SROD). They have very small gears and will go south under normal driving conditions. Do not waste your money on one of these.

The second series of T-5s appeared in the 1985 GT Mustang and had significantly improved gearsets as well as a wider ratio (3.35 low gear). This gearbox remained essentially unchanged until 1989. It is an adequate, at best, gearbox for autocrossing and light SCCA class racing. Powershifting is out of the

question. Generally, this gearbox will not withstand high horsepower demands or the continual abuse of drag racing.

Beginning in 1989, the gearsets were upgraded in the T-5 to improve the torque capacity. Of the standard T-5s, these are the strongest and should be the first choice when scrounging the salvage yards for a new tranny.

The fourth series of T-5s can be found in the Cobra and late series '93 H.O. Mustang. This transmission has the World Class T-5 wide ratio gearsets and can stand the abuse of 325 lbs-ft. of torque. The wide ratio gearset makes it ideal for drag racing. Phosphate-coated cluster gears and the use of a tapered roller bearing between the input and output shafts make this T-5 the best production unit available. Obviously, the limited production of these cars makes these gearboxes difficult to find in the salvage yard.

The last series of T-5s to see action in the Mustang are the World Class close-ratio units found in the late-model Saleen Mustangs. These are very tough gearboxes with the 2.95 low gear and evenly spaced ratios. If road racing is

your thing, then this is the best "factory installed" gearbox available in the Mustang.

Clutches

Through 1985, the V8 Mustang used a 10" clutch that is marginal for a stock engine and will require replacement regularly. Beginning in 1986, the Mustang got a larger 10.5" clutch and new flywheel assembly. This is the same clutch that has been installed in all V8 Mustangs since 1985, with some minor changes in pressure plate clamping rates. The larger post-'85 clutch and flywheel will bolt up to the earlier cars (except the 28 oz-in. imbalance 1979 engine) without modification. If your clutch requires replacing, skip the stock stuff. Ford Motorsport offers a complete clutch kit that is generally much cheaper than a stock replacement unit and is considerably stronger.

Rear Axles

There are only two axle assemblies that have been installed in the V8 Mustangs since 1979: The 7.5" ring gear and the 8.8" ring gear varieties. Both came equipped with 28-spline axles and the Ford Traction-Lok differential. The 7.5" version is worthless for performance use. A stock 5.0 175 horse engine will generally destroy this axle assembly with little effort. The 7.5" axle was installed in all 1979 through 1985 V8 Mustangs, all SVO Mustangs, and all non-V8 Mustangs. It was available in 2.73, 3.08, 3.27 (automatic cars), 3.45 (1984 SVO) and 3.73 (1985/86 SVO) ratios.

8.8"—Beginning in 1986, the tough 8.8" axle was standard in all V8 Mustangs. It was available in 2.73, 3.08, 3.27, 3.42, 3.55 (Saleen/special order), and 3.73 (Saleen/special order) ratios. The higher and more desirable ratios are very rare, so do not expect to find one in a salvage yard. These axle assemblies have been used in everything from 9-second drag racers to the Duttweiler built 200 mph Car Craft Cobra Mustang. It is reliable and tough.

When scrounging the salvage yards, it is important to be able to recognize a 7.5 vs. an 8.8. The simplest method is to look at the service cover. The 8.8 assembly has four straight sides with rounded corners where the 7.5 has two

A comparison of the two sizes of clutches that were fitted to the 5.0 Mustangs is shown. The smaller 10" pressure plate (on the right) was installed through 1985. Beginning in 1986, the clutch was upgraded to the 10.5" shown on the left. If your car is equipped with the smaller clutch, you must replace the flywheel to upgrade to the larger pressure plate.

straight sides (top and bottom) with rounded ends. See the accompanying photo for a side by side comparison.

Axles—All Fox Mustangs were built using a 28-spline axle regardless of whether the axle assembly was a 7.5 or 8.8. These axles are fully interchangeable with one another and are identical in length (28.75" flange face to tip of splines). The only exception is the SVO Mustang. The SVO utilized axles from the '82-'83 Lincoln Continental that were 1.25" longer than the standard Mustang axle. The SVO axle will fit in any 7.5 or 8.8 axle assembly, but the stock Mustang drum brakes will not fit. Generally speaking, axles as old as those found in an SVO will probably be worn out and not a good choice anyway. Check the splines closely when buying used axles.

The thrust of this book has been directed at EFI engines. Other than induction differences, the modifications provided are applicable to any of the 5.0 engines. Unfortunately, the low-compression cast pistons of the pre-'85 and the '93 engines will severely limit the type of camshaft as well as level of horsepower that can be tolerated by these engines. Since this volume is geared to bolt-on type performance items, careful consideration should be given to replacing the older engines with an RHO long block or rebuilding your stock short block with forged and higher compression pistons. ∎

All Fox Mustangs through 1985, non-5.0 through 1993, and all SVO Mustangs, were fitted with the useless 7.5" axle assembly. The standard and very tough 8.8" axle (rear of picture) was installed in the 5.0 Mustangs beginning in 1986. The axles can be easily recognized by the inspection covers. The 7.5 has only two straight sides, top and bottom, while the 8.8 is basically a square with rounded corners.

THE *SHORT* BLOCK

2

The first step in making horsepower is to get the short block in order. Since the thrust of this book is directed toward bolt–on type modifications, I will not get into modifications that require complete disassembly of the short block. I will not cover pistons, cranks and rods. I will assume you will be using an assembled short block that is ready to run, whether it is a 5.0 or a 5.8-liter engine.

If your 5.0 engine is tired and needs a complete rebuild, the Ford RHO short blocks are a great bargain. Additionally, there are numerous high–performance engine rebuilders that offer short blocks on an exchange basis. These are priced considerably cheaper than having yours rebuilt. If this is your approach, stick with reputable shops like RHS in Memphis and Ford RHO.

Obviously the 5.8 (351W) block has greater potential than the 5.0 (302) and can be substituted easily for the 5.0 short block. The only changes necessary are long tube headers (the shorty headers will generally work without modifications), lower intake manifold, oil pan and accessory brackets. The following modifications apply to either engine, so swapping is an option.

BOTTOM END MODIFICATIONS

Some of the following modifications can be accomplished with the engine still in the car. To reach the bottom end, you should remove the intake and heads so the engine can be hoisted up high enough to remove the oil pan. If a camshaft or timing gear/chain change is part of the plan (covered in later chapters), do them before re–installing the oil pan.

Main Caps

If you are running a non–four bolt block (stock) and more than 6 lbs. of boost, you should remove the crankshaft main caps and have them machined to utilize the Roush Racing main cap girdles and studs. These have been around for a long time and are the industry standard for this type of modification to the small-block Ford. They will provide considerable rigidity to the block and prevent the main caps from

The cost of elevating the horsepower in your Mustang can be pretty unreal. Fear not. Ford Motorsport has an incredible bargain on a complete fuel-injected 351 engine package (M6007-L58). Designed to use serpentine accessory drives, this package is virtually a bolt-in replacement. (Photo courtesy Ford Motorsport SVO)

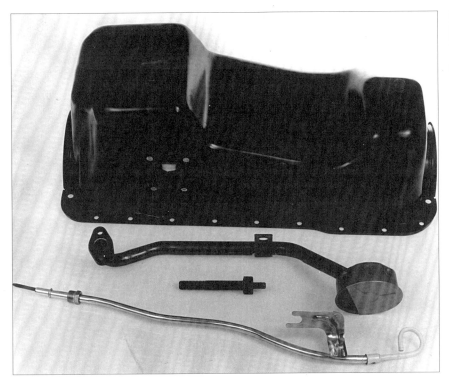

Before you can install a 351W in your Fox Mustang, it is necessary to get the correct oil pan, oil pump pickup tube and dipstick tube. These items were designed for Ford vans and can be purchased from Ford Motorsport in kit form (M6675-A58). (Photo courtesy Ford Motorsport/SVO)

If you are building an engine to withstand the abuses of 450+ horsepower, a four-bolt main block such as the Boss 302 shown is a must. The conventional 5.0 block is too thin, especially around the front main, to withstand regular high horsepower stress.

walking around under high boost/high rpm conditions. The instructions that come with the kits are very clear. Any competent machinist can do the milling. The 302/5.0 kit is PN JR5T–63A33–B and the 351W/5.8L kit is PN JR8T–63A33–A.

Harmonics that develop in a crankshaft in the upper rpm band can eat horsepower and destroy the main bearings. The Vibratech Fluidampr® is the hot ticket to keep your 5.0 crankshaft spinning freely.

Harmonic Balancers

When you plant your foot in the throttle, severe harmonic vibrations along the crankshaft can rob horsepower and shorten crankshaft life. This is why high-performance Ford small-block engines, such as the 289 HiPo, Boss 302 and Boss 351, all have very heavy crankshaft dampeners or harmonic balancers.

However, the 5.0 H.O. engines are not equipped with these units. Considerable horsepower is lost as energy that would normally be transmitted to the gearbox is spent vibrating the crankshaft. Currently, the Vibratech Performance "Fluidampr®" (PN 715221 for EFI engines) is the hot ticket to control this problem. This trick dampener is a direct replacement for the stock unit and does not require rebalancing the engine. Although expensive, it is a worthwhile investment, especially when running your engine beyond 6000 rpm.

Crank Bearings

For engines with more than 50,000 miles on them (25,000 miles if you're a leadfooted hot rodder) the crankshaft bearings must be examined carefully and most likely replaced. If the "Check Engine" light comes on when launching from a light or under severe cornering or braking, then chances are the engine has been run with a momentary loss of oil pressure. This occurs when the oil runs away from the pickup under high *g* loading.

Remove the bearings one pair at time. Wipe them clean and look for spots that might indicate where debris may have become embedded in the bearing. If you see the slightest tint of copper to the bearing replace them. If you have one bad bearing, chances are the rest are probably not far behind. Bearings are inexpensive and simple to replace, so do not take a chance.

For a stock journal crankshaft, several manufacturers sell a .001" oversize Clevite 77 bearing that will provide much needed clearance. These are

The most dependable small block available is the Ford Motorsport M6010-A4 racing block. These blocks regularly see 750 horsepower with complete reliability. You will need a last name like Getty to buy one though.

inexpensive and easy to substitute for the stock bearings with the pan off. All you need is a torque wrench and the bearings. Just loosen the bolts and remove the caps. Rotate the crankshaft slightly to access the upper bearing and pop it out with a screwdriver. Be sure to clean the new bearings with lacquer thinner before installation.

Slip the new oversize bearing in position, being sure to observe the location of the tang (toward camshaft on rods). Use an oil squirt can with a 50/50 mixture of a good synthetic engine oil and GM's EOS (Engine Oil Supplement), PN 1052367, to lubricate the new bearings before re–torquing.

The best insurance for your crankshaft, especially on engines running power adders, are main studs. Studs can be torqued to much higher levels and are far more resistant to failure than bolts.

Although not the thrust of this book, if you have your block apart, be sure to deburr all the sharp edges. Blocks fail when cracks form. Smooth edges are a standard blueprinting procedure for any racing engine.

Oil Pan
Modification

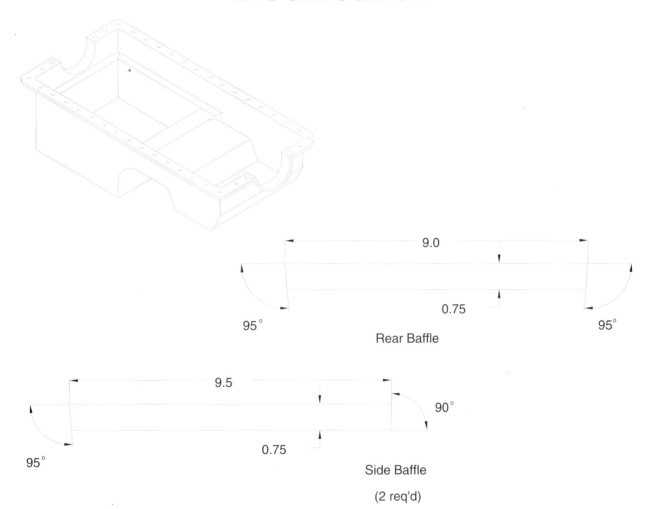

Rear Baffle

9.0

0.75

95°   95°

9.5

95°   90°

0.75

Side Baffle

(2 req'd)

1. Fit narrow (3/4") strips along rear and sides of rear sump.
2. Tack-weld strips in position just below rear main cap sealing area.
3. Fit and tack-weld wide strip at front edge of rear sump.
4. Stitch weld 1" beads along all edges.
5. Bend side and front strips down approximately 10° to 15° and weld corners.

9.0

1.5

Front Baffle

Materials:
(1) 4" x 10" 16 gauge Steel

Fig. 2-1

Oil Pan

If you are a road racer, and your class rules permit, replace your oil pan with either a Canton or Hamburger oil pan. Keeping oil around the pickup is very important when negotiating high *g* turns. When the stock oil pan is required, weld 3/4" wide strips of 18-gauge steel around the forward inside edges of the pan just below the main cap seal area (see Fig. 2-1). Also, weld a strip at the forward edge of the rear sump to prevent oil from running forward under braking. For drag racing, the small strip along the rear inside walls of the pan will prevent oil from flowing up into the block at launch. Weld these so there is a 10°-15° downward slope to the strips. These may not seem like much; however, they will go a long way toward keeping oil pressure in your engine.

Windage Tray—One of the best improvements you can make is to add a *windage tray.* These reduce the parasitic drag on the crankshaft as the oil tries to rotate with the crank. It also helps prevent aeration of the oil. Generally, you can expect an additional 10 to 15 horsepower after installing one. For the 5.0, Ford Motorsport sells the Boss 302-type windage tray kit. Included in the kit are a Boss 302 windage tray, four special main cap bolts and four windage tray attachment bolts. If you want to use the rear sump pickup tube or Roush Racing main cap girdles, some modification will be necessary. For the 351W, you will have to purchase a windage tray from Canton or Hamburger.

Oil Pump

For racing use, the stock oil pump should be replaced if the engine has more than 20,000 miles on it. At a minimum, the stock oil pump shaft should be replaced with a competition piece. When replacing the pump, a high–volume unit should be installed if a turbocharger, supercharger, or remote oil cooler is being installed. However, a normally

If you have the block apart, be sure to radius the oil outlet hole where the oil filter attaches. This will smooth the transition and slightly reduce parasitic horsepower loss.

The cheapest 15 horsepower you can get is by adding a windage tray to the bottom end of your 5.0 engine. Originally designed by Ford for the Boss 302, this tray will prevent the oil from being sucked up around the crankshaft at high rpm.

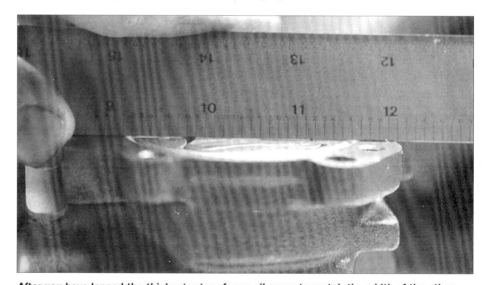

After you have lapped the thickest rotor of your oil pump to match the width of the other, check the rotor-to-housing end clearance. This should be between .002" and .004".

The casting inside the pump body is generally ragged at the machining surfaces so chamfer the edges slightly to remove any loose or rough corners.

aspirated engine without a remote oil cooler does not need a high–volume pump as it will heat the oil as well as pump excess oil to the top end. Additionally, it takes considerably more horsepower to turn a high–volume pump than a regular pump. However, if you are running a normally aspirated engine with flow restrictors in the crankshaft-to-lifter oil feed holes, or if the crank has been clearanced, then you'll need a high-volume pump.

Blueprinting the Pump—A new pump must be disassembled and thoroughly cleaned and inspected for

Inadequate oil supply that occurs when the oil is picked up by the windage of the crankshaft or when it runs away from the oil pickup under severe acceleration (drag racing) will damage the wrist pin holes in the rods. The damage to this new rod occurred on the first lap at Texas World Speedway when the inertia in turn one forced the oil away from the pickup. A windage tray and baffled oil pan are necessary to prevent this.

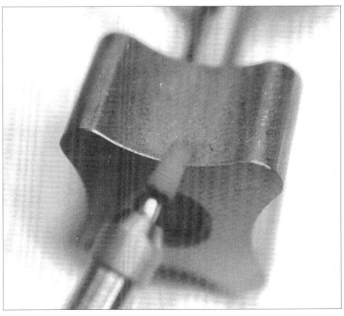

Deburr the edges of the rotors in your oil pump to reduce frictional drag. Rotors will often have dings or burrs in their edges, even new ones.

machining burrs. Never trust a new pump. To ensure that it works properly, use the following steps to blueprint your oil pump:

Step 1

Completely disassemble the pump, inspecting every piece for unusual machining marks, burrs or casting irregularities. This includes the removal of the plug that secures the oil pressure spring (pry it out or drill a small hole and use a slide hammer to remove it).

Step 2

Secure the pump housing in a vise with soft jaws, and carefully radius and blend the oil port with a Dremel or porting tool. The port–to–block exit should be ported out to the diameter of the gasket.

Step 3

Mic the thickness of the two rotors and lap the thickest piece on 180-grit wet/dry sandpaper until the two pieces are matched in thickness.

Step 4

Install the rotors in the housing and check the clearances as follows: rotor to rotor .003" to .006"; rotor to housing end .002" to .004"; rotor to housing, internal .006" to .011".

Use a rotary flapper wheel to increase clearance on the inside of the outside rotor or to increase clearance on housing for the outside rotor. To decrease clearance on rotor to housing end, lap housing on 180-grit wet/dry sandpaper. Do the same to increase clearance except sand the rotors. Take your time, and check the clearance often. It's a lot easier to take more off than to add it back. Be sure the sandpaper is on a flat surface and use generous amounts of water or cutting oil.

Step 5

Once the proper clearances are set, use a Dremel or high–speed rotary file and put a slight chamfer on the edges of the rotors, both top and bottom.

Step 6

If you have the bucks and the time, have the rotors coated with one of the slick processes provided by HPC or

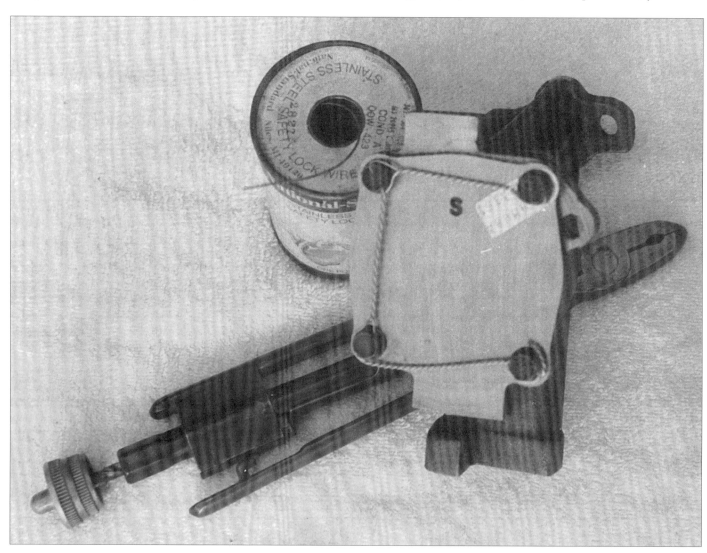

After you have completed deburring and blueprinting your oil pump, drill the bolts and safety-wire them. This is very important on engines that will be used in road racing.

Tired starters on pre-'92 cars should be replaced with the Ford Motorsport M11000-A50 high torque starter. This is a gear-driven Bendix unit that will spin your engine rapidly for instant starts, and it only weighs 7 lbs.

Poly–Dyn. This will significantly improve the life of the pump. If you are a road racer this is particularly important to you.

Step 7

Lap the inside surface of the end plate on 280-grit wet/dry sandpaper secured to a flat surface. Alternately, valve lapping compound on a flat steel plate or thick piece of glass can be used. It is very important to get this piece smooth and flat.

Step 8

Clean all pieces thoroughly with Tide soap and a bottle brush. Flush all pieces with plenty of water, then rinse with clean varsol or spray with a water displacing fluid like WD–40.

Step 9

Reinstall the stock oil pressure spring, shimming the end with two (2) 3/8" SAE washers. This will bring the oil pressure up to 100 psi cold. A new plug should be installed. These are generally available at any auto parts store that carries Dorman freeze plugs.

Step 10

Reassemble the rotors, coating each generously with petroleum jelly. This will insure immediate priming.

Step 11

Install the end plate using grade 12 bolts that have been drilled for safety wire. Safety wire the bolt heads.

Step 12

Clean the pump–to–block mating surfaces with lacquer thinner. Install the pump to the block with a new gasket using grade 12 studs with nuts or bolts that have been drilled for safety wire. When installing the oil pump be sure to include a new competition oil pump driveshaft. This is cheap insurance against high–rpm failure.

The oil pump driveshaft has a retainer disc on the distributor end that prevents the shaft from being pulled out of the pump when the distributor is removed. Failure to observe the correct installation procedure (retainer end into distributor shaft) will become apparent the first time you attempt to remove the distributor and the shaft takes a bath in the oil pan.

When the pump and shaft have been properly fastened, recheck the pump shaft one last time and then safety-wire the pump–to–block nuts or bolts.

STARTERS

If your car is a pre-'92 model, chances are you have one of the conventional direct drive starters. They are generally heavy, require significant current draw to spin, and typically do not respond well to extensive use. Fortunately, the starter currently used on all '92 and newer Ford engines is a very compact gear drive unit. It will spin your modified engine without effort and only weighs 7 lbs. It is sold by Ford Motorsport under the part number M11000–A50. If your starter is in marginal condition or you want to save the weight, this is the hot ticket.

ENGINE MOUNTS

Over the years, Ford has changed the motor mount for the small-block V8 several times. Although any of the '79 or newer Mustang V8 motor mounts will work, the newer mounts ('93 and up) found on the GT Mustang and convertible are the strongest. They will provide considerably less engine rotation and will not break like the earlier versions. If your car is one of the older versions and you are stepping up the horsepower or improving traction (slicks or sticky street tires), you should replace your motor mounts with the newer ones. This is particularly important on the left (driver's side) motor mount.

If you are drag racing, the solid aluminum mounts from Auto Specialties are great additions. Utilization of these mounts should be restricted to engines producing not more than 400 horsepower. Engines producing horsepower beyond the 400 mark will generate tremendous stress on the left side of the block under a typical drag race launch. This stress can destroy the block and cylinder walls, causing blowby or even a blown head gasket. The 5.0

blocks are very thin and flex easily. A torque strap to the front of the block (typically the head) will provide better distribution of the stress.

If you are installing an engine producing over 450 horsepower, consider using the flat aluminum front block plates with the rigid frame mounts. These plates bolt to the front of the block and directly to the frame without any form of insulators. The purpose of this type of engine mount is to spread the twisting torque of the engine over a much wider area. The pulling force on the left side of the block and the compression force on the right side of the block will distort cylinder walls, causing a loss of ring seal and horsepower. The stress placed on the sides of a mega-horsepower engine block, especially during a drag-race launch, can distort the cylinders and cause head gasket failure. The laws of physics come into play, converting energy that you are attempting to put to the rear wheels into heat loss as the block flexes. It doesn't take a rocket scientist to understand this translates into slower E.T.s and engine damage. ■

These solid motor mounts manufactured by Larry Sample at Auto Specialties can improve the torque transfer to the rear wheels, especially during a drag race start. The use of these should probably be limited to those engines producing less than 400 horsepower. The concentrated strain on the left side of the block can distort cylinder walls, causing blowby and horsepower loss.

Unless you are breaking in a new engine or flat-tappet cam, synthetic oil is the only way to go. This stuff typically is worth 7 or 8 horsepower at the rear wheels.

CYLINDER HEADS, VALVES & SPRINGS

3

CYLINDER HEADS

The most important item that determines the horsepower potential on an internal combustion engine, especially the small-block Ford, are the cylinder heads. No matter how much money you spend on headers, cams and intake systems, the flow capacity of the heads will define the efficiency of those items. The internal combustion engine is just a big air pump. Obviously if there is a restriction somewhere in the air path to the combustion chamber, less air is going to go in. Less air, less horsepower. Therefore, improving airflow through the heads will have a dramatic effect on power output. A good set of heads will make up for a lot of average pieces in an engine.

The popularity of the Mustang and the 5.0 engine has produced some very fine aftermarket heads. A well-ported set of the old "C9OE" 351W heads can barely match the flow capability of an unported set of any one of the numerous high–performance Windsor heads on the market today. If your budget permits, spend the bucks and get a set.

When purchasing a set of heads, keep in mind their limitations. Some heads

Adding a set of high-performance cylinder heads can be the best single improvement you can make. Horsepower is largely determined by the efficiency and flow capacity of the heads. Although they can compensate for otherwise average components, proper combinations of cam, intake, headers and valvetrain are necessary to extract the maximum horsepower potential of the heads. (Photo courtesy BBK Performance)

The M6049-K302 aluminum head from Ford Motorsport is essentially a large valve version of the famous GT-40 head of the '60s. This head has large rocker studs and guide plates to use fully adjustable rocker arms. (Photo courtesy Ford Motorsport/SVO)

Any of the aftermarket heads available will greatly improve the performance of your engine. However, experience has demonstrated that certain heads have deck thicknesses that are too thin and consequently will not hold a head gasket when high compression or boost is used to make horsepower. The TFS (iron and new series aluminum), GT-40 (iron) and the DART II (iron) heads have proven to be capable of withstanding boost conditions and still hold the head gaskets. The TFS iron heads have an excellent track record for engines running more than 20 psi of boost. The new Edelbrock "Performer" heads with the 5/8" deck thickness should also hold a gasket, although I have not tried them.

For the normally aspirated engine, the SVO GT-40 heads are a great buy and are excellent heads. They utilize the stock pedestal-mount rocker arms. The Allen Root or SVO J302 aluminum head has excellent exhaust flow characteristics and will save a significant amount of weight over the cast-iron heads. The Edelbrock "Performer" aluminum heads are a great deal like the J302 head. They are offered in a competition version with

have valve spacing that is wider than the stock Windsor heads, which may cause valve–to–piston interference on high–lift cams. The DART II and the Trick Flow Specialties (TFS) heads have these characteristics. Additionally, TFS has recently released a new variation of their head, called the "Pro Stock." This head

has wider valve spacing that permits the installation of a 2.30" intake valve. Because of its extremely high intake ports, it requires a special intake manifold. As TFS claims this head outflows the Yates C3 head, it is obviously for the serious racer.

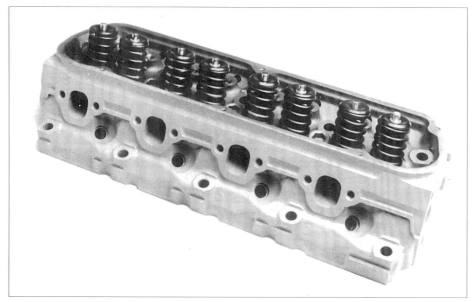

The cast-iron version of the GT-40 cylinder head (M6049-L302) is less expensive and is used as original equipment on the 1993 Cobra. These heads can be ordered bare or fully assembled, polished and with a three-angle valve job. (Photo courtesy BBK Performance)

Pictured here are the new cast-iron Dart Windsor heads. These heads have valve spacing that is wider than the standard Windsor head and may require special machining of the pistons for adequate valve clearance.

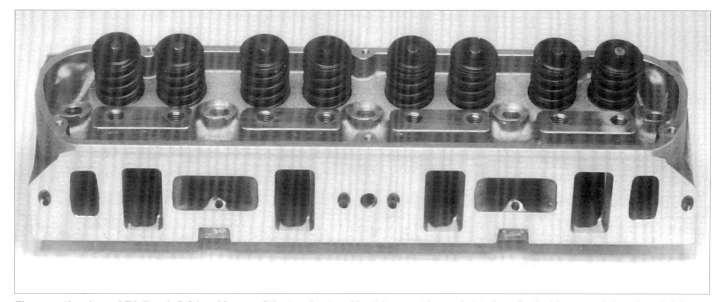

The recently released Edelbrock 5.0 head is one of the toughest and best buys on the market today. Backed by several decades of airflow research and intake design, this head comes with a 5/8" deck, big valves and an E.O. (emissions legal) number. (Photo courtesy Edelbrock Corp.)

3/8" screw–in rocker studs and guide plates, as well as a smog-legal replacement version that uses the pedestal-mount rocker arms. The World Products heads are iron and have two different exhaust bolt patterns, enabling the builder to utilize some very large tube headers. The Yates C3 heads are a canted valve design much like the old Boss 302 head. The combustion chamber and the canted valves require different pistons and consequently will not work well on the standard 5.0 piston. Additionally a special intake and exhaust header are required. Rumor has it that a lower intake that will fit the GT–40 upper intake (on a 5.0 block) is being built to allow this head to utilize the EFI

fuel system. Of course one is reminded of the suitcase of money needed to purchase this setup.

· With the exception of the new "Pro Stock" TFS heads or the canted valve Yates heads, there is not a nickel's worth of difference between any of the high–performance heads on the market today. Several car buff magazines have run comparison tests on the various heads and basically the flow numbers are identical. The only real variation has been when one set of heads had larger valves than another set. Put the same big valves in the other heads and the flow is basically the same. Take the same group of heads and change the camshaft being used for the test and you'll end up with a

new winner in the horsepower race. Essentially when you get past the guts and feathers, the real key to finding top horsepower with a set of heads is finding the right combination of other engine components that best suit those heads. Every engine is different. You can build two engines using identical parts with heads that have been ported by the same person and method and you'll still get different horsepower and torque results.

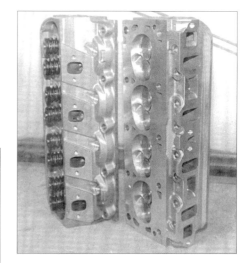

The TFS (Trick Flow Specialties) big-valve aluminum heads are very popular with the supercharger crowd, and will outflow any set of ported 351W heads right out of the box. Manufactured from T-356 aircraft-grade aluminum, these heads have very thick port walls, allowing for significant porting.

CYLINDER HEAD SPECS

	Intake Valve (in.)	Exhaust Valve (in.)	Combustion Chamber (cc's)
Ford GT–40	1.84	1.54	65.5
Ford/AR J302	1.94	1.60	58.0
TFS (iron & alum.)	1.94	1.60	64.0
DART II	2.02	1.60	64.0
Edelbrock Performer	2.02	1.60	60.0

If expense is not an issue, the high-port aluminum head with canted-valves is where the horsepower can be found. These heavily massaged TFS heads are part of what it takes to produce 200 mph speeds from your small-block Ford.

Racing Heads–Basically there are only two questions to answer when purchasing a set of racing heads: (1) how fast do you want to go, and (2) how much can you afford? If you are running in the fast SCCA or IMSA classes or going for the sub-11-second quarter mile, you'll need serious heads from a first-class shop. To do this, money cannot be a factor. A first-class set of Roush or Yates heads will be in the five figure range. The same goes for any of the top-notch drag race sets. For the person running outside these parameters, a set of any of the current high–performance heads will get you there. Just look for the best bargain and go with it.

CYLINDER HEAD PORTING

Deciding whether or not to have your heads ported is strictly a budgetary question. If you can afford it, have it done. Porting equates to horsepower, plain and simple. Many reputable head manufacturers offer fully assembled and ported heads as a package. This is the easiest way to go. Another option is to have a competent head porting shop do the job, and you may even find one that specializes in your type of head.

For the deep-pockets racer, the only way to go is to buy a set of heads from one of the porting geniuses working on the top racers today. You can buy a good set of heads from any of the many Ford-themed high–performance shops advertised in the various magazines. Most shops have someone on staff porting heads. Some have flow benches and can do a pretty good job of wringing out some impressive flow numbers. However, the guys porting the heads for the racers that are winning in the normally aspirated classes are the ones to go to. Make sure you select a head porter that specializes in the type of flow your engine will be using: wet flow for the carbureted engine and dry flow for the EFI. The differences are not much, but there is a difference.

Do not make the mistake of buying a set of trick NASCAR heads for your drag racer because you got a deal. Contrary to common belief, heads are ported for the type of racing and the rpm band they will run most of the time. A trick set of Yates heads that have been ported to run on a restrictor engine can be a formidable force on the high banks. However, they can be very disappointing when used on a drag racing engine, and especially so on a street engine. The same goes for using a set of drag racing carbureted heads on an EFI road racer. If you are going to spend the bucks, make sure the heads you use are ported to suit the application.

If you are running a pressurized engine, supercharger or turbocharger, the porting job on a set of the aftermarket high–performance heads is less critical. This will probably stir some ugly remarks by several head porters. However, unless you are going for the 400+ horsepower range, a basic clean up of the bowls under the valves, and matching the ports, are all you'll need to do. It is only when you move into the high-boost mega-horsepower range, that

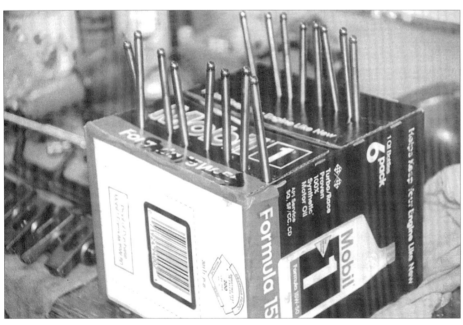

If the original pushrods, rockers arms or cam followers are to be reused, always keep them in the exact order they came out with the lifter or rocker arm end of the pushrods noted. These pieces wear a fit to one another and consequently need to be reassembled in the same relationship and order they came out. Failure to do so can result in premature valvetrain failure.

head flow becomes critical along with all the ancillary parts to make them effective.

Porting Stock Heads

If you can't afford a set of aftermarket heads and the services of a top head porter, you can mildly port and polish your stock heads. This should include a cleanup of the bowls under the valve heads, reworking the valve guides, and matching the ports. To do this you will need the items listed in the chart nearby.

Porting a set of heads, even mildly, is a lot of tedious work. Cleaning up the valve bowls and matching the ports can be accomplished without a great deal of porting. Grinding the ports out to achieve the high flow numbers is a more difficult task. The amateur porter can do it. However, it requires considerable patience. The real key to success is to balance the section widths of the ports. No voodoo, just careful and painstaking grinding and measuring. Essentially, you must look at the port as a series of two–dimensional boxes spaced 1/4" apart. What you will be attempting to do is grind each one of those boxes, blending each to the next, so the area is the same (high school geometry, length times width equals area). This is done to prevent the airflow from having to compress and expand as it travels through the port. Anytime the airflow has to compress or expand, energy is modified and airflow slows. This is particularly important where the intake port is concerned.

Basic Tips

Keep a constant eye on how much you have removed from the walls as you grind the ports. Constantly check the unported head with calipers to insure you haven't taken too much out. How much is too much? Hard to say. Depending on the quality of the casting, some areas of a stock head may be .250" thick while others may only be .100". Listen to the

HEAD
PORTING TOOLS

An inside screw adjustable caliper

vernier caliper

fan

fully enclosed eye protection (goggles preferred)

gloves

hat

respirator mask

duct tape

layout dye

good lighting

auto paste wax or WD–40

Mondello Performance porting kit (Van Nuys, CA.)

high-speed electric rotary grinder that can hold a 1/4" shaft with speed regulator

6-gallon pickle bucket

ear protection

Note: The quality of the rotary grinder will determine how long it takes. With a good grinder you should be able to do a good amateur porting job in about 16 hours. Also, don't waste your money on the cheap porting burrs. They won't stay sharp more than a few minutes and will generally make you frustrated. The Mondello porting kit comes complete with everything you need to port a set of heads. Any of the porting burrs you screw up (and you will) can be purchased from them separately. The Eastwood Co. also sells porting kits and burrs.

Sources:

Mondello Performance
1103 Paso Robles Street
Paso Robles, CA 93446
805/237-8814

The Eastwood Co.
580 Lancaster Ave.
Box 296
Malvern, PA 19355
800/345-1178

Porting heads requires considerable patience, a quality grinder, eye protection and a well-lit work space. To reduce eye injury, a high volume fan should be set up about work height that blows across the cylinder head. The airflow will deflect the slivers as they are thrown from the porting burr. The high vacuum system behind the head is ideal, but obviously beyond the realm of most home garages.

porting burr. As the port wall becomes thin, the sound will become more "tinny." At that point you should carefully evaluate how much more you want to grind. For a head that will see endurance or street action, you should maintain at least an .080" wall thickness in the ports.

By far the best way to port a set of heads is to make a pattern of the ports with flexible silicone mold-making rubber. This will allow you to take exact measurements of the ports and determine how much to grind off of which side.

This is probably overkill for the amateur porter; however, if you want optimum results, this is the way to go. Silicone mold-making rubber can be purchased from most chemical supply houses and is also sold by Manley Performance as part number 40187.

To port a set of heads, you will need a well-lit sturdy table or workbench to set the head. To keep those nasty slivers out of your hair, ears, and out of your back, slip an old t–shirt over your head to your ears, and drape it over your head past your ears and shoulders. Put a cap on over this and you'll keep most of the pieces out. Above all, wear eye protection at all times, something that wraps completely around and seals your eyes, such as a pair of tight-fitting plastic goggles. Wear your prescription eyeglasses only and I can just about guarantee a trip to the emergency room to remove a steel sliver from your eyeball. Not fun. Again, this is the voice of experience speaking.

To insure identical flow characteristics and undistributed airflow, it is very important to map the port volume at 1/4" intervals with a set of calipers before you begin porting as demonstrated by Craig Gallant. You can use Fig. 3-1 to record the measurements and identify where metal should be removed.

Head Porting
Port Volume Mapping

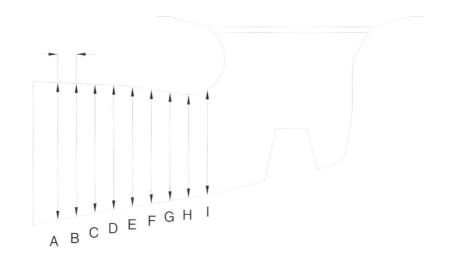

Approx. .250"

A B C D E F G H I

	Intake				Exhaust			
	Width	Height	Area	Correction	Width	Height	Area	Correction
A.								
B.								
C.								
D.								
E.								
F.								
G.								
H.								
I.								
J.								
K.								

Area=Width x Height

Correction=Largest Area - Current Area

Fig. 3-1

Make copies of this chart and use it to record the volume of each port at 1/4" intervals.

When porting the bowl area below the valve, it is important to center the guide in the bowl (see Fig. 3-2). Taper the guide to a cone. Then take careful measurements for grinding the bowl to center the guide.

Step 1: Cleaning & Inspection

Before you begin, you must disassemble and thoroughly clean the heads. This is especially important for the ports and the combustion chamber. Be sure to get all the ugly stuff out of the exhaust port. Carefully inspect them for cracks. If the heads were from a nitrous, supercharged or turbocharged engine, have them Magnaflux inspected before you begin. It's a real bummer to spend a weekend porting a set of heads only to find out one or both are cracked.

Step 2: Sanding

Use a sanding block or wrap 180-grit sandpaper around a short 2" x 2" board, and cleanly sand the intake, exhaust and block faces of the heads. This is done to provide a clean surface to lay out the port and combustion chamber limits.

Step 3: Layout

With machinist's layout dye or equivalent, swab around the port openings and the left and right extremes of the combustion chambers, where the head gasket comes closest to the chamber. When scribing the combustion chambers, insert the block dowels in the heads to center the head gaskets.

Step 4

Carefully lay the intake gasket over the intake ports, being sure to align the mounting holes correctly. Lightly scribe around the inside edge of the gasket at each port to define the outer limits of the port. Do the same for the exhaust and the combustion chamber.

Step 5

Align a straight-edge along the lower and upper marks made in Step 4 and scribe a heavy line to provide a more exact definition to the ports. Do the same for the sides, except take care to make the ports exactly the same width. Do this for the intake and the exhaust. This may seem like overkill. However, gaskets will sometimes be slightly warped between cylinders. By using a straight-edge, you will be able to lay out the ports so they will all start at the same height and width. Once the porting is complete and the engine is being assembled, you will glue the new intake gaskets in position.

Step 6

Locate the head so the combustion

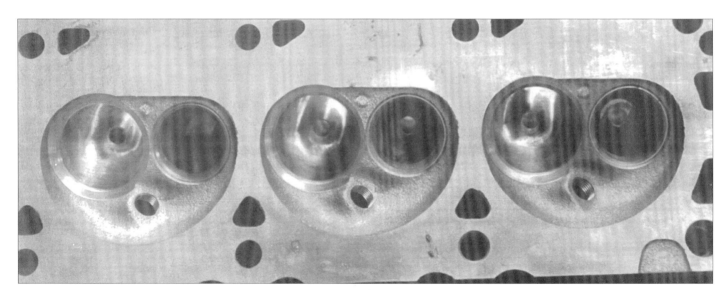

The most important area to pay attention to when porting a head is the "bowl" around the valve guide. It is very important to center the guide in the bowl with smooth, generous radiuses where possible. Shortening and recontouring the guide into a cone will improve transition through the area.

chamber is up and you are looking down into the bowl area below the valve seats. Tear off 1/2" strips of duct tape and tape several layers over the valve seats. This is to minimize the damage to the seats when you run the grinder over a valve seat. It happens.

Step 7

Depending on the type of grinder you are using, you probably want something to brace your arm to steady your hands. Set the fan off to your right about shoulder high. Aim the fan so the air passes right–to–left over the head and turn it on high. This will blow the steel slivers away as they are being ejected by the cutting burr and greatly reduce the chance of getting a sliver in your eyes. Before you start grinding, spray the porting burr with WD–40 (or dip in a wax paste when cutting aluminum). After every few minutes of constant grinding you should stop and spray the burr again. This will prevent metal from collecting in the burr's grooves, which would reduce its porting efficiency. Also, use the speed regulator to adjust the porting speed to a level you are comfortable with. Don't rush!

Step 8: Shorten Intake Guides

Before beginning the porting process, I like to shorten the intake guides about .250" to .375" (Fig. 3-3). If the guides have not already been shortened, use a long, straight, cylinder porting burr through the port inlet. Steady your hands and carefully cut the top of the guide down. Take your time and check your progress regularly so you don't overdo it. Make sure all the guides are the same length (as measured from the head surface). The exhaust guide will be worked down as the bowl below the valve is cleaned up. If you will be installing solid replacement guides, generally it is best to grind the stock guide away and blend it into the port

Head Porting
Centering Guides

1. Measure distance from edge of valve hole in guide to wall of port in all directions.
2. Carefully grind closest walls to match distance from wall that is greatest distance from guide. Take regular measurements to prevent over grinding.
3. Create a smooth radius on all walls to insure matching flow characteristics.

Fig. 3-2

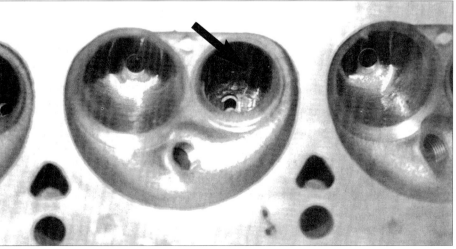

Hurrying to get the job done will generally turn your expensive racing head into a door stop. The exhaust port above had to be welded up after removing "just a little more." Take your time. You can always remove more—however, it's harder to put it back.

floor. Typically, the stock guide will split and crack when the solid guides are installed. Consequently, it is easier to remove them before than after.

Step 9: Recontour Intake Valve Guides

With a tapered porting burr, insert the porting tool into the port and turn it on. Carefully recontour the intake valve guides to a cone shape. Leave approximately a .100" wide rim at the end of the guide. Carefully blend the guide into the port floor and smooth the surrounding walls. Try to keep the port walls as straight as possible below the intake valve for the first inch. The key to improving airflow is to center the valve in the bowl. This means carefully grinding the walls so the bowl area has a constant radius around the guide. However, be careful. Some of these heads can be very thin due to casting shifts. Get as close as you can without getting into the water jacket. If you get into a water jacket you will probably have to junk the head. Welding a head is a real art and there are few who can do it

without screwing it up. If the head you are working on is an expensive high–performance head, send it to one of the top head shops for repair. Anytime you weld on a head, it will probably warp all the surfaces, including the guides and seats, so plan on a complete re–do.

Step 10: Smooth Side Walls

Carefully smooth the side walls at the bend below the valve, especially the sharp radius side. Again, you will be attempting to straighten the port and center the guides in the bowl without getting into the water jacket. This is a very restrictive area and must be massaged carefully. Don't overdo it though. If you cut too much the port volume will not be balanced and you will get a reduction in air velocity, reducing the overall porting efficiency. Stop at regular intervals and measure the port to determine how much more to cut. Generally it is best to do one wall at a time. This way you can take measurements that have a constant base (the opposite wall).

Step 11: Exhaust Bowl

The exhaust bowl must be widened slightly. Carefully shape the exhaust guide so it has small furrows on each side that follow a straight line to the exhaust port exit. Basically you will be increasing the port volume in this area as much as possible without getting into the water jacket. Grind the walls smooth and widen the exhaust port at the bend. Like the intake bowl, try to center the valve in the port bowl. Remember that the purpose of porting is to balance the flow volume at all points in the port. As discussed at the beginning of this section, porting modifies the length or width of the port at any given point. Take careful and regular measurements and calculate the area (length x width), and compare that to other areas of the port. Don't overdo it. In the exhaust port you will essentially be widening it as you move toward the port exit.

Step 12: Intake Port Inlets/Outlets

Change to a round-headed, straight-tapered burr and set the head so you can

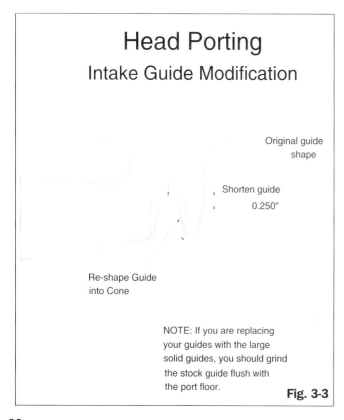

Head Porting
Intake Guide Modification

Original guide shape

Shorten guide 0.250"

Re-shape Guide into Cone

NOTE: If you are replacing your guides with the large solid guides, you should grind the stock guide flush with the port floor.

Fig. 3-3

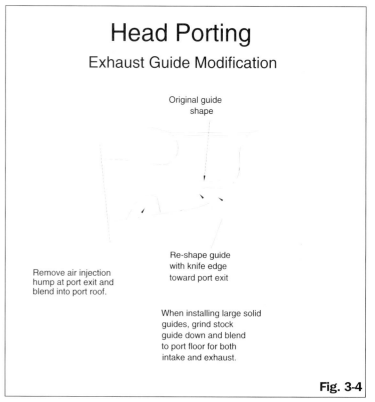

Head Porting
Exhaust Guide Modification

Original guide shape

Remove air injection hump at port exit and blend into port roof.

Re-shape guide with knife edge toward port exit

When installing large solid guides, grind stock guide down and blend to port floor for both intake and exhaust.

Fig. 3-4

access the intake port inlet at a comfortable angle. Slowly grind the intake ports out to 1/32" of the scribe marks, extending into the port approximately 1". Do one side of the ports at a time and do it to all the ports before moving to another side. Compare your work as you do each port, taking regular measurements for comparison. To the amateur porter, this will prevent overdoing any single port and will generate a more consistent port job. Be very careful around the pushrod holes. Casting shifts may limit porting here.

Step 13

Once you have ground the port outlets out to within 1/32" of the scribe marks, use the inside screw adjustable calipers (similar to dividers) and measure the width every 1/4" of each port where you have ground. Check the length and width. Carefully balance each port to each other by grinding any additional amounts necessary to achieve that relationship, while working your way back to the valve bowl. Basically you will be squaring the intake ports to increase their volume.

Step 14: Exhaust Port Inlets/Outlets

Follow Steps 12 and 13 for the exhaust ports with the following exceptions: When grinding the port outlet at the top, don't follow the corners of the gasket scribe marks. Instead, use a 3/8" radius on the upper corners to give the port exit the appearance of a "D" laying down (see Fig. 3-5). This will help the exhaust to flow better and provide some pulse reversion protection. As you port the exhaust toward the guide it is important to maintain the "D" shape as much as possible. Do not bother to port the exhaust port floor (surface closest to the combustion chamber) on a stock head. Just knock the burrs off and polish it. No real flow improvement can be realized by modifying this area.

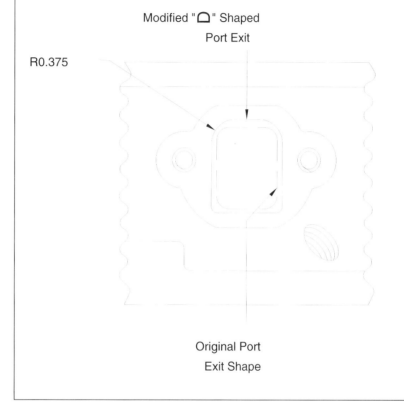

Head Porting
"D" Exhaust Port Exit
Stock Cast Iron Head

Modified "⌂" Shaped
Port Exit

R0.375

Original Port
Exit Shape

Fig. 3-5

Step 15: Air Injection Hump

Removing the air injection hump in the exhaust port is no fun at all. There is a lot of metal in some of these humps and there are eight of them to do. On the bright side, exhaust flow is improved dramatically on stock heads when these humps are removed, so it is worth the effort. Look at the basic contour of the port and try to follow that as you remove the humps. Don't grind so much that you end up with a small valley. This will significantly reduce the effectiveness of the port. The key is to end up with an exhaust port that is reasonably straight. As you grind the hump off, work the valve guide so you end up with a knife-edge taper to the sloped exhaust bowl, pointing to the exhaust port exit, that blends back into the bowl below the valve.

Don't waste your time trying to grind the port floor lower (side closest to block). This will not help exhaust flow. Work to straighten and smooth the short-side radius of the port from just below the valve to just outside the short floor radius. Be careful not to get into the water jacket. The biggest performance gain in the exhaust port will come from raising the upper port exit as much as possible and straightening the port to the exit. Patience is a real virtue when

The last phase in porting a head is matching the combustion chamber outline to the gasket and contouring for high swirl flow, especially around the spark plug outlet. Shown here is a 2.3L head getting a trick port job from the experts at Esslinger Engineering.

porting. Again, take regular measurements and adjust your grinding accordingly. Always remember you can take more out, but you can't put it back.

Step 16

After you have roughed in the ports in the previous steps, fit the rotary grinding stones and smooth out and blend the grinding you have done. The only tricky area is in the exhaust short-side radius where a back-tapered stone is necessary to properly blend the port floor. Again, take your time.

Step 17

Fit a pencil roll arbor to the grinder and install a sanding roll (100-grit). Carefully blend and polish the ports, taking the intake port inlet out to the scribe marks. The exhaust port outlet should be polished out to the vertical scribe marks, leaving a large smooth radius at the top corners. Don't bother putting a mirror-like finish on the intake ports. The small turbulence created by a sanded finish seems to maintain better fuel atomization. However, on the exhaust you want as close to a mirror-like finish as possible.

Step 18

Finish the intake port by using a 6"

strip of 1" wide 100-grit emery cloth on a split arbor to create a satin finish where the sanding marks are clearly visible.

Step 19: Combustion Chamber

Set the head with the combustion chamber up. Remove the tape on the valve seats. Insert an old intake and exhaust valve to protect the seats when

A good porting job can be done on the small-block Ford head with careful and consistent work. To squeeze every horsepower possible will require a visit to a flowbench like the SF601 SuperFlow™ flowbench shown here. These machines are invaluable if winning in the big leagues is your goal.

working on the combustion chamber. Use duct tape around the valve stem on the spring side to keep the valves from jacking up when the sanding roll strikes them. This will prevent any possibility of damaging the seats.

At each corner where you scribed the outer limits of the head gasket, carefully sand the chamber vertical wall to within .005" of the scribe line. You should sand an area approximately 3/4" long. Do not go past the natural design of the combustion chamber. This is done to unshroud the valves and improve the airflow cone around the valve head.

Work the sanding roll over the combustion chamber to smooth the surface. Do not remove any more metal than is necessary to achieve a smooth surface. Removing metal adds volume to the chamber and consequently reduces the compression ratio. Not a problem for a pressurized engine, but important to a normally aspirated one.

At the spark plug hole, carefully sand the hump just outside the hole on the combustion chamber wall, so you have a more open path for the combustion flame to travel. This will promote better flame propagation and burn efficiency. On the intake valve side of the spark plug hole there is also a hump that forms around the threads. Work this down to where you create a slight concave feature to the wall. This will enhance combustion swirl and improve fuel atomization.

Once you have completed the reworking and polishing, use the abrasive impregnated rubber discs and bullets to put a mirror-like finish on the chamber. If your porting kit does not have these, they can be purchased from C.C. Specialty, Mondello Performance and virtually any abrasive supply company. Polishing the combustion chamber is a real pain, but will significantly improve flame propagation and reduce the possibility of detonation by preventing the formation of hot spots. Like all aspects of porting, take your time.

Step 20: Oil Drain Holes

Flip the head over where the spring valley is exposed. Use a tapered rotary stone and carefully chamfer and blend the oil drain holes to improve oil return flow.

Step 21: Valve Job

If your heads have not had a competition valve job yet, do it now. Turn to page 32 in this chapter for guidance on how to properly cut the valves and seats. Instruct the person doing the valve job to leave the heads disassembled when he has completed the work. Be sure the valve seals have not been installed as they will probably be damaged when you complete the porting work.

Step 22

If the heads are assembled when they are returned from the valve grinder, disassemble them, being sure to keep all the pieces properly separated and

Extrude Hone™

The Extrude Hone process is a great addition to a well-ported set of heads. Yes, I said addition. The abrasive putty that is used by Extrude Hone sands all surfaces evenly. Consequently, the polishing process does not correct any port section deficiencies nor recontour inadequate port design. If it is your intention to have your heads polished with Extrude Hone after they have been ported, be sure to tell the person doing the porting. They will probably want to leave a little extra metal to allow for the sanding action of the Extrude Hone putty. For more information, contact: Extrude Hone, 8800 Somerset Blvd., Paramount, CA 90723. 310/531-2976.

organized to return to the same seats and springs. Reinsert a pair of old valves and tape the spring side to prevent the valve from jacking up when tapped by the sanding roll. Carefully blend the valve seat top cut made by the seat cutter into the combustion chamber (Fig. 3-6, p. 33). This probably seems like a real pain and waste of time. However, that small .005" or .010" lip will dramatically reduce the effective valve lift and airflow. That translates into lost horsepower. A 15% reduction in flow efficiency is not uncommon when the valves are shrouded this way. This should be done with a pencil sanding roll of 120- or 180-grit, followed by polishing the chamber with abrasive rubber discs or bullets. It is important to keep the combustion chamber as slick as possible. The closer you get to a mirror-like finish the better.

Step 23

Tape the valve seats with several layers of duct tape for protection. Attach the pencil sanding roll arbor to your grinder

and use a 100-grit sanding roll. Carefully blend and radius the bottom-cut edge the valve grinder made, just below the valves, into the port shape. On the intake port use the same method in Step 18 to finish the port wall. Pay particular attention to the area below the exhaust valve. Try to create a smooth radius from the seat into the port. Polish the exhaust port as close to a mirror-like finish as possible.

Step 24

At this point you have completed a mild port and polish job. The last thing to do is thoroughly wash the heads in a 6-gallon pickle bucket. Fill the bucket with hot water and one cup of Tide laundry detergent. Get a scrub brush and knock yourself out scrubbing the heads clean. Use mass quantities of hot water to rinse. (The best approach is to attach a garden hose to the drain outlet on your hot water heater.) You want to be able to eat off these heads when you are through.

After all the uglies have been removed, spray the heads down with a water displacing fluid. If you used hot water to rinse the heads, you will only need to spray the ports and mating surfaces to prevent rust.

Before you reassemble the heads, you should epoxy discs cut from brass screen (found at most hardware stores) over each of the drain holes on the top of the heads (valve spring side). This will slow down any broken valve pieces draining back to the oil pan and possibly prevent locking up an oil pump and lunching your engine.

VALVES

Valve selection, like everything in a high–performance engine, depends on your budget. Basically you can choose between stock, stainless or titanium valves. For a low-mileage engine running a stock camshaft, the stock valves will do just fine. However, when you go to a performance cam and the

Do not depend on the valves to all be the same size. Measure each one accurately. Grind all the valves so they are the same diameter. This will insure balanced flow between all the cylinders.

associated stiffer springs, the stock valves just don't fair well. The welded heads tend to separate from their stems, which can be most uncool. Run stainless valves. They will cost you a couple of hundred dollars, but if you want your engine to stay together, there can be no compromise here.

Titanium Valves—Unless you have large quantities of money, stay away from the titanium valves. It's true that they are the cat's meow. However, they require special equipment to grind the face. This significantly increases the cost of servicing the heads. Titanium valves are great stuff, but they are for the serious competition engine running in the 7500 rpm twilight zone. If you are running a stock computer on your EFI engine, with a 6250 rpm rev limit, titanium valves amount to overkill. Spend the bucks on something else.

Valve Faces & Seats

One of the most important points in making horsepower is the *valve job.* How the seats are cut and valves are faced can make a difference of 40 horsepower on a 500-horsepower engine. Although you may not be building a 500-horsepower engine, a 20-horsepower increase on a 300-horsepower engine is a significant difference.

The Figures accompanying this section provide graphic guidance on how to cut the seats and valves. These are the results of 30 years of my personal experience racing the small-block Ford. I do not claim to have definitive answers to the perfect valve job. Technology changes every race weekend. However, the information provided here will get you within 5% of the best there is. If you are a big-budget racer running a trick set of Roush or similar heads, you won't be concerned with the quality of the valve job anyway. However, for the average racer, have your machine shop follow the guidelines I have provided.

The relationship between the valve face and the seat is critical to optimum performance. I can not count the number of "trick" competition valve jobs I have seen that were not any better than a regular valve job. One of the biggest mistakes made by some machinists is thinking that as long as the seats and valves have the requisite three–angle cut, they are trick. This is simply not true.

If the shop doing your valve job does not have a sophisticated valve seat cutting machine, it is very important that the following procedures be followed to insure a proper valve job.

Most performance machine shops can do top-quality valve jobs with the standard Sioux valve seat grinders. However, for optimum results, stick with the machine shops that use state-of-the-art head machines such as the Head Shop machine shown here at Texas Turbo.

Step 1

Before cutting the seats, it is very important to set the valve stem–to–guide clearance correctly. If the guides are worn beyond tolerance, they should be replaced with solid guides. Close tolerances on stock street engines work wonders over 150,000 miles. However, tight clearances on racing engines spell disaster. On a normally aspirated engine, without nitrous, you will want to keep the clearance about .0018" to .0022". For those engines running nitrous or superchargers, run .002" to .003". This is particularly important when running stainless valves. If you are running unleaded gasoline in your engine, you should be aware that stainless valves will gall easily without sufficient clearance. It is best to run stainless valves a little loose.

Step 2

With a micrometer or vernier caliper, measure the exact diameter of the valve heads. Don't trust what it says on the box they came in—measure them all. The valves should be within .010" of each other. If necessary, square the edges of the valves so they are all exactly the same diameter.

Step 3

Cut a 45° face on all the valves. Based on the width of the valve seat you have chosen (see Fig. 3-7 for width, p. 34), cut a 35° undercut on the intake valve face to bring the 45° seat to exactly .010" wider than the chosen seat width for a drag racing engine or .020" on an endurance racing or street engine. Use good lighting and make sure the faces are all exactly the same width. It is very important that the cutting stone be re–faced between each cut to insure a flat and consistent cut. It may seem silly but it does make a difference. *Do not undercut the exhaust valves!* Leave the face width as it is. If the face seems excessively wide, replace the valve.

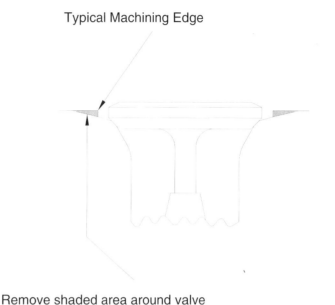

Valve Seat
Residual Machining Edges

Typical Machining Edge

Remove shaded area around valve
and blend into combustion chamber

Fig. 3-6

Step 4

Next, chamfer all the valves with a 25° top cut on the combustion chamber side. The width of this cut should extend toward the center of the valve to approximately a line, perpendicular to the combustion face of the valve, that intersects the inside edge of the finished 45° valve face (see Fig. 3-8, p. 35). When you are through, you should have an edge margin of approximately .030" on a drag racing engine and .040" to .060" on a road racing or street engine. For the road racing engine, the margin can be toward the smaller side if the races are 1 hour or less in length. This may require that you re–cut the 45° face to adjust the distances to achieve this margin. Obviously, the narrower the margin the less the valve can be re–faced

before it must be replaced. However, the width of that margin and the sharpness of the edges has a significant effect on flow. You and your budget be the judge.

Step 5

Cut a preliminary 15° top cut on all the valve seats to provide a clean top edge. It is very important that the depth of the seats from the head surface be within .005" of each other when the seats are finished. Sink the exhaust seat approximately .035" deeper than the intake seats (see Fig. 3-9, p. 36). This will help scavenging on engines using long overlap cams.

Step 6

Carefully cut the valve seats out to where they are .005" to .010" larger in

Competition
Valve Machining Widths

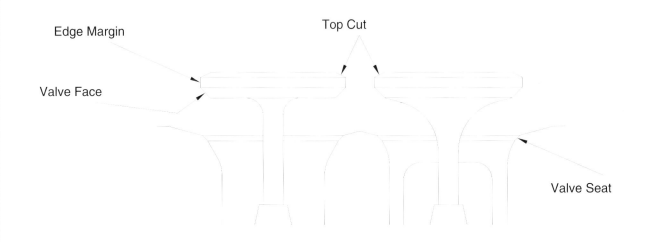

Edge Margin

Top Cut

Valve Face

Valve Seat

Intake	Valve Face	Edge Margin	Valve Seat
Performance Street	.100	.065	.060
Drag Racing	.060	.030	.030
Road Racing	.075	.045	.035
Endurance Racing	.100	.050	.060

Exhaust	Valve Face	Edge Margin	Valve Seat
Performance Street	.110	.070	.075
Drag Racing	.075	.035	.035
Road Racing	.085	.045	.045
Endurance Racing	.110	.060	.075

Fig. 3-7

Competition
Valve Angles

Intake

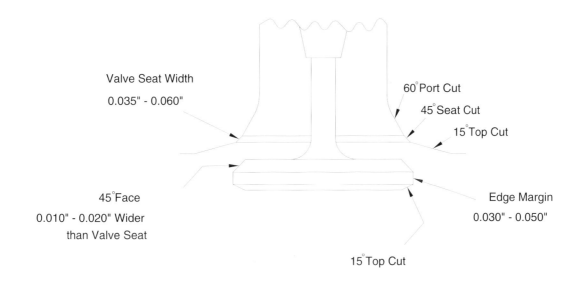

Valve Seat Width
0.035" - 0.060"

60° Port Cut

45° Seat Cut

15° Top Cut

45° Face
0.010" - 0.020" Wider
than Valve Seat

Edge Margin
0.030" - 0.050"

15° Top Cut

Exhaust

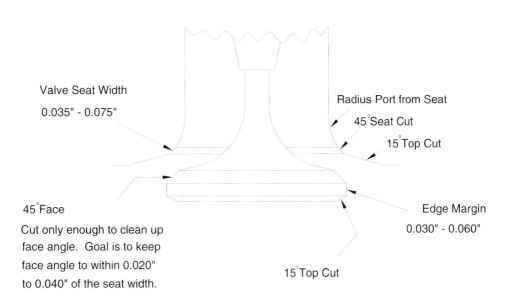

Valve Seat Width
0.035" - 0.075"

Radius Port from Seat

45° Seat Cut

15° Top Cut

45° Face
Cut only enough to clean up
face angle. Goal is to keep
face angle to within 0.020"
to 0.040" of the seat width.

Edge Margin
0.030" - 0.060"

15° Top Cut

Fig. 3-8

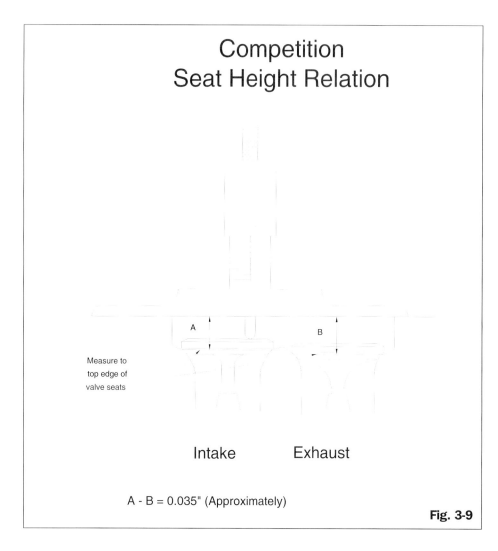

Competition
Seat Height Relation

A

B

Measure to
top edge of
valve seats

Intake   Exhaust

A - B = 0.035" (Approximately)

Fig. 3-9

so do not mix them up. Examine the face of the valve in good lighting and measure the margin on each side of the contact area of the seat with a micrometer. That margin should be .005" on a drag race engine or .010" on an endurance or street engine. If the margin is too narrow simply cut the valve face ever so little and check it again. This is a real pain and is quite time consuming. However, the results are well worth it. Generally, you can expect to spend a full day or more just doing a correct valve job.

Step 9

If your heads are not fitted with a spring locator or seat cup, it is imperative that you have them machined to utilize them. A considerable amount of heat and energy are expended if the springs are not aligned and secured in position. The life of the valve spring is reduced without these. If you are turning your engine to the upper limits of the rpm band (more than 6500 rpm) without spring locators or seat cups, you improve your chances of sucking a valve. This modification is not expensive and the spring cups or locators are sold by Manley, Moroso, Ford SVO, Crane and most cam manufacturers.

Step 10

Based on your needs and budget, if you

diameter, on the combustion chamber edge, than the valve head diameter. This is very important. When you lap the valves, you will end up with about a .010" margin on each side of the valve face beyond the width of the valve seat. This will insure the valve and seat edges match exactly, after the seats hammer in, for optimum flow.

Step 7

Use a 60° stone for the bottom cut to narrow the valve seats to the desired width as selected from Fig. 3-7, p. 34.

Step 8

After getting the valves back from the machinists, you can lap them in yourself. Swab the valve face of each valve with machinist layout dye. Smear a thin coat of 3M auto paint compounding paste on the valve seats. After the machinist dye

has dried on the valves, insert each valve in a seat and rotate left and right while applying gentle pressure against the head of the valve. A valve *lapping stick* would be best. Once you insert a valve in a seat, it becomes unique to that seat,

Any head that is expected to turn more than 6000 rpm should have spring locators or seats. At higher rpm the springs dance around and can cause premature failure if not properly located.

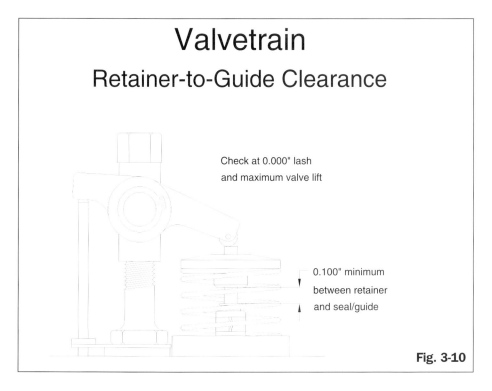

Valvetrain
Retainer-to-Guide Clearance

Check at 0.000" lash
and maximum valve lift

0.100" minimum
between retainer
and seal/guide

Fig. 3-10

are going to utilize screw–in rocker studs, they should be machined for them now.

Step 11

The last thing is to machine the valve guides for positive sealing valve seals. I prefer the white nylon seals sold by Perfect Circle and Ford SVO. However, any quality positive sealing seal will do, especially the positive sealing pieces used on the later 5.0 engines.

A competition engine thrives on the quality of the valvetrain. The heads should be removed after every race, examined for fatigue, and the valve seats and faces freshened up. There is no substitute for the airflow that accompanies a quality valve job. Keep the seat and valve face edges clean and sharp for optimum flow. On a street car, the valve job on a high–performance engine must last many thousands of miles. However, as the seats beat out and the edge of the valves round off, flow diminishes and horsepower slips away. Keep the valvetrain in top shape.

One of the best improvements that can be made to your head assembly is having the combustion chamber and valve heads (combustion chamber face) ceramic-coated. This coating process will reduce the amount of energy that is transferred to the valves and water in the form of heat, and therefore apply more to the piston. The result is a more powerful combustion with higher btu's and more horsepower. There is also the additional benefit of increased valve life and a cooler running engine.

CYLINDER HEAD ASSEMBLY

The best porting and valve jobs won't mean much if the heads are not properly assembled. This means valve guide-to-retainer clearance and valve spring coil separation clearance. If you follow Murphy's advice and assemble your heads without checking these things, you'll probably find yourself doing it later when you have to rebuild a blown engine.

Retainer-to-Guide Clearance

The first step in assembling a head is to check the retainer–to–guide clearance. In a particularly stupid period in my life, I got lazy and assumed a set of trick heads were machined for sufficient clearance

for the cam I was running. Unfortunately, this was not so. I found myself changing rocker studs several times on the side of the road while wearing a $1,500 suit in 100° weather. Always check, no matter who builds the heads!

Calculate Valve Lift—Before you address this, you must first calculate the maximum theoretical valve lift your camshaft and rocker arm will generate. This is done to determine the distance the retainer will move downward at maximum lift. Add to this number .125" to define the minimum clearance needed. The formula is simple and is as follows:

$$Rc = (Ll \times Rr) + 0.125"$$
where:
Rc = retainer clearance
Ll = cam lobe lift
Rr = rocker arm ratio

For example, let's say we're using a single-pattern camshaft with a lobe lift of .320" and SVO Motorsport rocker arms with a ratio of 1.72. When we add the minimum clearance below the retainer (0.125") at maximum valve lift (.320" x 1.72 = .550") we determine that a minimum clearance of .675" is required for safe valve operation.

Make the calculations for the camshaft you have chosen and write them down on a copy of the Engine Data Sheet located in the Appendix for future reference.

Stand the heads on one end and insert all the valves in their proper guides. Tap the heads of the valves with a rubber or leather mallet. Install the retainers and keepers without the springs. Smear a little bearing grease on the valve grooves and keepers to hold them in place. With a vernier caliper or spring gauge and micrometer, measure the distance between the bottom edge of the retainer and the top of the valve guide (see Fig. 3-10). You should pull the retainer tightly to seat the keepers and the valves before taking this measurement. Write down

Valvetrain
Coil Bind Clearance

Check at 0.000" lash
and maximum valve lift

0.010" minimum
between coils

Fig. 3-11

While you are installing the rocker arms, it is imperative to check the retainer-to-guide and coil bind clearances. With the pushrod and rocker arm installed at .000" valve clearance, rotate the engine until maximum valve lift is achieved. At this point you should have at least .100" clearance between the retainer and seal and at least .010" between the spring coils (see Fig. 3-10 and Fig. 3-11).

the results for each separate valve. If any valve has less than the minimum required clearance, return the heads to the machine shop and have the guide cut down the exact amount that is necessary to provide the minimum clearance. Do not machine any more than is necessary. The length of the guide is important for valve stability, especially when the guides have been shortened on the port side. *Note:* If a guide has to be shortened, make certain there is sufficient machined relief remaining for the valve seal to seat properly.

It is very important to keep the measurement data in case you want to change camshafts. This data will help you determine the maximum lift your heads can endure before major modifications (longer valve stems, special retainers, new heads, etc.) are in order.

Valve Springs

Coil Bind—The next area that must be addressed on a fresh set of heads, or one with new camshaft, valve springs, or rocker ratio, is the *coil bind* limit of the springs. To avoid having your valve springs self–destruct, you must have a minimum of .010" clearance between the coils at maximum valve lift. If you have followed the advice of the cam's manufacturer, the springs recommended for their camshaft should have sufficient clearance between the coils. However, the smart engine builder will always check for himself.

There are two methods that should be used to check for sufficient coil clearance. The first is by doing the math and the second is by checking it on the engine. Doing the math first could save you the time you might have to spend removing and disassembling the heads after you discover the clearance is wrong.

Much like the retainer–to–guide clearance procedure, you will need to measure the distance from the bottom of the retainer, at the outer spring perch, to the valve spring seat. If you are using spring seat cups, they must be in place for this measurement. It is best to take these measurements with an inner spring installed. Take measurements at each valve and record your findings. If there is more than a .020" deviation on any one valve, check the valve seat depth and correct as necessary. If the valve seat depths are correct, have the spring seats machined to balance them.

Check the spring data to determine the manufacturer's recommended installed height. That is the installed compressed length of the valve spring when the valve is closed. Subtract from the installed height number the manufacturer's coil–bind length to determine the maximum theoretical lift the spring can endure. Read the spring specification card carefully. Determine whether or not the coil–bind length includes the requisite .010" coil separation clearance. If it does not specify, call the spring manufacturer and find out. If the coil–bind length does not include the required coil separation clearance, you must subtract from the maximum theoretical lift the spring can endure an amount equal to the number of coils multiplied by .010". This will provide the maximum safe lift the spring can handle.

Armed with the spring lift limits, you must determine: (1) if the springs are sufficient for the maximum theoretical lift at the valve and; (2) if the distance between the bottom of the retainer and the recommended installed height of the spring provide sufficient lift capability. For the first step, simply compare the maximum theoretical valve lift to the maximum safe lift the valve springs can handle. If the valve lift exceeds the safe lift capability of the springs, you've got a problem. Obviously the springs will coil bind at maximum lift and break things, so new springs will be needed.

The second item you must test requires careful calculations. You must subtract the coil–bind length (including the

Valve springs are typically referred to by the number of springs involved, dual or triple springs in high-performance engines. Generally speaking, the dual springs will provide higher seat pressure and are well suited for a blower motor turning 6200 rpm on a stock computer. High rpm operations will require a triple spring (the one on the left) for sufficient pressure to close the valve as the inertial mass of the valve increases in the red zone of your tach.

required coil separation clearance if not included in the specs), from the measured distance from the retainer–to–spring seat (including spring cups if used, measured at the outside spring perch). This is the maximum lift your head can withstand without coil bind using the selected springs.

Let's look at a simple example to better understand this. We will use a camshaft with a lobe lift of .380" and a rocker arm with a 1.72 ratio. Using the formula from the retainer–to–guide clearance section, we see the maximum theoretical valve lift to be .654" (.380" x 1.72 = .654"). We look at our spring specification card and it indicates the spring has a recommended installed height of 1.900" with coil bind at 1.200". We also note that the card specifically states that coil–bind does not include any

coil separation clearance. Given this information, we determine the maximum safe lift the spring can handle to be as follows:

$$Msl = Mih - (Cb + Cn \times .010")$$
$$= 1.900" - (1.200" + 7 \times .010")$$
$$= .630"$$

where:

Msl = Spring Maximum Safe Lift
Mih = Manufacturer's Installed Height
Cb = Coil Bind
Cn = Number of Spring Coils
Mvl = Maximum Theoretical Valve Lift

In this example, when we compare the maximum theoretical valve lift with the

Choosing the correct valve spring for your application should be left up to the cam manufacturer's recommendation. However, mistakes can and will happen. This photo shows the result of using a spring that was designed for 7200 rpm instead of the 7800 rpm the engine was operated at.

calculated safe lift capability of the proposed valve spring we find we have a problem. We need a spring that can handle .654" lift, yet our example spring can only handle .630". Obviously this is most uncool. A new spring with more lift capability must be purchased, or a camshaft with less lift installed, or a rocker arm with a smaller ratio must be used.

To continue testing, let's assume we have a new spring that has an installed height of 1.900", coil bind at 1.100" and a calculated maximum safe lift capability of .730". These new springs meet the needs of our example camshaft, providing .076" additional clearance (.730" – .654" = .076").

The next step requires testing the capability of the springs, when installed on our example heads, to handle the valve lift. Returning to the heads with the valves, spring cups and retainers installed, we find the smallest measured distance between the bottom side of the retainers (measured at the outer spring perch) and the spring seat to be 1.855". Obviously, the first thing we notice is that

this height is less than the manufacturer's recommended installed height. This reduces the safe lift capability the spring can handle. To determine the safe valve lift capability of the springs when installed on our example heads we make the following calculations:

$$Vsl = Rms - Mvl$$
$$= 1.855" - (1.900" - .730")$$
$$= .685"$$

where:

Vsl = Valve Safe Lift Capability
Rms = Measured Retainer–to–Seat Clearance
Mvl = Maximum theoretical valve lift
Cb = Coil Bind or (Mih - Mvl)

When we install the example springs, there is a safe valve lift capability (Vsl) of .685". Since our example cam only needs .654", we have additional clearance of .031". Now we can safely assemble the valves and springs knowing

the springs should work. Again, I caution: You still have to check the springs on the engine at zero valve lash and maximum valve lift. *Note:* Before you assemble the valves, seals and springs, compress the springs to coil bind, twice, on a drill press or in a vise. For some reason, this seems to reduce the tension loss the springs inevitably have after they are run in.

Spring Pressure—The specification card on the valve springs will stipulate the valve spring pressure the springs should have at an installed height and a maximum theoretical lift. Any time you deviate from the manufacturer's recommended installed height you will modify the spring seat pressure. Obviously if you shortened the installed height, as was the case in the preceding example, the seat pressure and open pressure will increase. Although the amount can be mathematically calculated, it is best to have the springs tested individually. High-quality valve springs will generally test out within a few percentages of one another; however, it is best to check.

It is very important to follow the cam manufacturer's recommendation for spring pressure. They know the limits of their cams and what is necessary to make them live. It is important to remember that every camshaft has recommended spring pressures based on the average valve weight for the engine it was ground for. Therefore, if you are installing a set of Trick Flow heads with a 2.20" intake valve, and the cam kit you purchased was designed for a 5.0 engine running stock heads, you probably won't have sufficient spring pressure to close the heavier valves in these heads at the upper rpm range of the cam (ignoring the fact that installed heights are significantly different between the two heads). When ordering a cam, make sure the cam grinder knows exactly what heads and valves you will be using, as well as the rocker ratio.

Another important point to recognize is that as the rocker ratio increases, the valve float limit moves downward. Basically you can count on a 500 to 1000 rpm loss in safe rpm capability beyond what the valve springs were designed to meet, for every 1/10 increase in rocker ratio. The higher the rocker ratio, the more spring pressure you need.

There is a limit to the spring pressure that can be used on any head. First, stock valves have the heads welded to the stems and will generally separate at high rpm when subjected to high spring seat pressures. If you run the stock valves with seat pressures above 120 lbs., you are probably going to experience valve failure. Second, every camshaft has limits to the spring pressures it can endure before the lobes will deteriorate. This is particularly true of the cast flat-tappet mechanical cams. Spring seat pressures over 130 lbs. will significantly reduce their lives. A typical flat-tappet mechanical cam (solid lifters) will go flat within 7,000 miles running seat pressures of 135 lbs. Unfortunately, spring pressure equates to rpm capability. This "Catch-22" means selecting the spring pressure carefully and understanding the limits of the cam. The cam manufacturer's recommendations are best.

A third problem arises when using hydraulic lifters such as the roller cams installed in the 1985 and later 5.0 engines. These hydraulic lifters will collapse if subjected to spring seat pressures over 145 lbs. Due to the weight of these roller lifters, a considerable amount of spring pressure is necessary to close them once the rpm limit moves past 6000 rpm. Generally it will take 150 lbs. of seat pressure just to return the lifter, pushrod, rocker arm and valve to the closed position on a 5.0 engine turning 6500 rpm. This is why you don't see roller hydraulic camshafts designed for the 5.0 that have power curves much above 6000 rpm.

Rocker Studs & Girdles

The stock 5.0 heads use either a stamped-steel rail to hold the rocker fulcrums in position, or they have machined grooves to align the fulcrums. Either way the bolt that secures them is a puny 5/16" size. This setup works pretty well as long as the rpm stays low and the valve spring pressure is also low. Unfortunately this does not coincide with the normal approach to hot rodding. If you want valvetrain reliability, have your heads machined for the 7/16" screw-in studs. Forget the 3/8" studs. If you are going to spend the money, get the larger studs. The cost of roller rocker arms are the same for either size.

For turning your engine above 7500 rpm you should use a stud girdle or a set of the shaft-mounted roller rockers marketed by several of the cam and rocker arm manufacturers. The valve spring pressures that are necessary to turn an engine above 7500 rpm generate tremendous stress on the studs. Without some sort of girdle or shaft mount, the rocker arms can not maintain the correct geometry. The probability of valvetrain failure goes up exponentially as the rpm passes 7500.

The only way to go when using rocker studs is the 7/16" pieces. Do not waste your money on the 3/8" studs. Roller rocker arms cost the same whether you buy them for a 3/8" or 7/16" stud, so go with the bigger piece.

Spring pressure is also a killer on the rollers in a roller lifter. High seat pressures, which also translate into high open pressures, will beat the rollers out on a street engine within 5,000 to 8,000 miles. This is particularly acute in the mechanical roller (solid) lifter that occasionally gets run a little loose. If you have a roller go bad, and you do not catch it, you will ruin a camshaft and maybe an engine block as well.

Probably the most important point to understand about valve spring pressures, is the amount of horsepower that is consumed operating the valvetrain. On a typical engine developing 450 horsepower, the engine will have consumed nearly 250 horsepower to get that 450 horsepower to the flywheel. The most significant portion of that horsepower consumption is in the valvetrain. If you have ever tried to turn a high performance engine over with your hands, you can appreciate the effort it takes to rotate it. Obviously if you have increased the valve spring pressure you have also increased the horsepower that will be consumed to open the valves. This is of course another "Catch-22." You need spring pressure to turn rpm, but you consume more horsepower as the spring pressure increases. Again, the amateur engine builder will listen carefully to the recommendations of the cam grinder. It's hard to beat their experience.

For those racers running a supercharger or turbocharger, you will need to increase your intake valve seat pressure by 200 to 300% of the maximum amount of boost you will be running. This will compensate for the pressure in the intake track that will tend to hold the valve off the seat. If you are running a 2.19" intake valve it will probably have an exposed area inside the port of about 3 square inches. The pressure that is trying to push the intake valve off the seat can be determined by multiplying the exposed area times the boost. Using the 2.19" valve as an example in an engine running 12 psi of boost, we would find a pressure of approximately 38 lbs. trying to lift the valve.

This was determined with the formula:

$[(pi \times D^2) /4] \times psi$, where D = valve head diameter.
$[(3.14159 \times 2.19 \times 2.19) /4] \times 12 = 38$ lbs.

Try to use springs that increase the seat pressure without significantly increasing the open pressure. You just want to keep the valves on the seats and not waste horsepower unnecessarily on the heavier springs. *Note:* Always completely back off the rocker arm nuts and release the pressure on the valve springs on a racing engine after each race weekend. This will prevent the springs from "taking a set" and losing their tension.

If you are building a 7000+ rpm engine, it is important to include modifications to the oiling system to prevent valve spring failure. Most racing valve springs will overheat above 7400 rpm without adequate oil to cool them. Valve spring failures at or above this level are almost a certainty if operated for

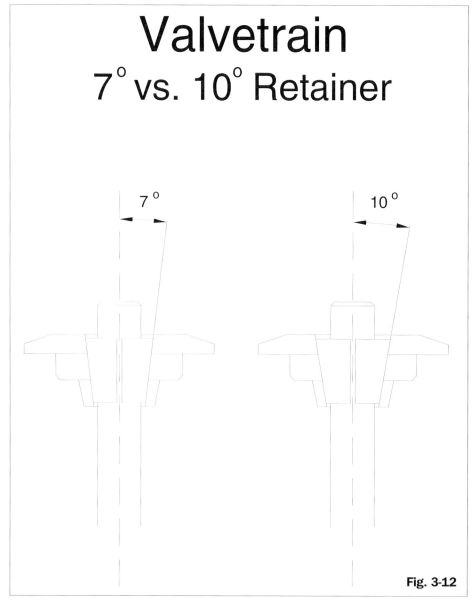

Valvetrain
7° vs. 10° Retainer

7°

10°

Fig. 3-12

The degrees indicated by these retainers refer to the angle of the retainer seat from the centerline of the valve.

If you have replaced your valves, keepers or retainers, check the fit. Your valve should fit in the retainer like the one on the right. If your valve sinks into the retainer like the one on the left, you must go to a larger keeper or new retainers. The keepers on the left have significantly less contact area in the retainer and may pull through at high rpm or with high spring pressures.

any length of time in this range. The only cure is to epoxy 1.250" tall tubes in the drainback holes in the heads to maintain an oil bath for the springs or provide direct oil spray on the springs. Most NASCAR teams figured this out a long time ago and have either used the short tubes or, as is more common today, built special valve covers with oil spray bars inside that feed directly off the engine's oiling system. If the short tube is the route you choose, be sure to install the positive sealing valve seals. This will prevent the standing oil from being sucked by the valve stems and spoiling the incoming air charge.

Retainers & Keepers

The retainers and keepers you use should be from the same manufacturer as the valve springs. This will save some potential hassles that often occur on spring I.D. fit. You will also have the advantage of knowing the retainers have been tested on your head combination, which could reduce the possibility of

additional machining costs. It is necessary for the amateur engine builder to realize the importance of matching components in the valvetrain. In no other part of the engine is this so important.

Retainers—Presently, there are two designs of high–performance retainers on the market, 7° and 10° (see Fig. 3-12).

Pictured here is an assortment of valve spring shims. When installing these it is important to place them at the base of the spring with the "this side up" showing.

The degrees indicated are in reference to the angle of the retainer seat from the centerline of the valves. Generally the 7° design is used when the engine is to be operated at high rpm for extended periods. The 7° design provides for a very tight lock on the valve that insures it will not release as the valve moves about from the influence of the harmonics that develop at high rpm. Some engine builders prefer the 10° design as they claim the valve has less tendency to pull through the retainer when subject to extreme valve spring pressures. Also, the 10° retainers are generally offered with .100" offset for additional installed spring height. However, for the typical 5.0 engine running a hydraulic roller cam, stick with the 7° retainers.

Retainers are generally offered in chrome-moly steel, aluminum, titanium, and beryllium. With weight being a factor in determining the spring pressure necessary to close the valves, the lightweight alloy retainers are the choice to make, assuming you have the budget.

The chrome-moly steel retainers will work just fine on engines turning less than 6500 rpm. Beyond 6500 rpm a lightweight alloy retainer should be used. Stay away from the aluminum retainers. They do not hold up well. Generally they will shed small slivers of aluminum as the springs rotate. Those small slivers can jam an oil pump or trash bearings. Also, valves with high spring pressures tend to pull through the aluminum retainers.

If your budget permits, go with the titanium retainers. They are light and very strong. If your last name has any relation to Getty, you'll want to skip the titanium stuff and go directly to the exotic beryllium retainers. They are incredibly strong and will outlive you or any engine you build. However, you can buy a low-mileage car for what they cost.

Keepers—Choosing keepers is much more simple: buy the machined and hardened types that are high-grade steel. The stamped cheap ones should never have been manufactured. They're junk and have no place in a high–performance engine shop, much less in any engine.

Assembling Valves & Springs

When assembling the valves and springs, it is very important to make sure everything is sterile. One small speck of metal or sand can trash a fine engine, so be sure everything is clean, including all the parts, the workbench and the tools you will be using.

Smear a light coating of anti–seize compound and engine oil on the valve stem before inserting them into the valve guides. Install the valve seals, making sure they are completely seated on the guides. Take considerable care when installing the seals. If you see a small strip of nylon peel off the seal as it passes over the valve keeper groove, trash it. That little sliver generally comes from the sealing rim of the seal. This means the seal is compromised and will leak, so replace it.

Trial-fit all the keepers in the retainers. Make sure they all seat properly. This is very important to insure all the retainers and keepers are of the same design, 7° or 10°. This is one of Murphy's favorite areas to screw up, so always check.

Shims—When installing the springs, it is very important to observe the placement of the spring shims that are typically necessary to correct the installed height. Although it is common practice, do not use shims to correct an inadequate valve spring. You are asking for trouble. Generally, a spring will perform better when it is not operated

Before installing the valve springs, each valve must be measured to determine the shim thickness necessary to correct the installed height of each spring. The photo shows a measurement of approximately 1.890". If an installed height of 1.860" is necessary to achieve the correct valve seat pressure, a .030" spring shim will be required.

The Fel-Pro graphite head gaskets have eliminated the need for head studs on normally aspirated engines. If nitrous oxide, a blower or turbocharging is in the game plan then you can save yourself a lot of grief by installing a set of ARP studs. The cost of replacing a set of those expensive head gaskets will easily pay for the studs.

close to coil bind. If your springs require more than .040" to correct installed height, you should go for a longer spring.

Valve spring shims come in thicknesses of .010", .020" and .040", and are installed with the serrated face against the head. Do not install these with the serrated face up against the valve spring. Installing the shims wrong side up will cause damage to the shim and it will probably break. Broken pieces always find their way to the oil pump.

After you have installed all the springs, rap the ends of the valves with a leather or hard rubber mallet. This is important to set the keepers in the retainers. Take a long look at the assembled valves and springs. Look for anything that doesn't appear exactly right. Springs not properly seated on the retainers, valve seals that may have shifted, and keepers

that don't seem to be seating correctly are things to watch out for.

Attaching Cylinder Heads

In my opinion, the Fel–Pro *Fel–Graphic* head gaskets are the best currently available. These gaskets are tough and will withstand significant abuse before blowing, especially on pressurized engines. Note that these gaskets are indexed to fit with a specific end facing the front of the engine. Look for the "FRONT" indicator and install accordingly. If you install one of these backwards, the water passages will be blocked and the engine will run hot. A cracked head will generally result.

Before you attach the heads, thoroughly clean the head and block mating surfaces with lacquer thinner and clean cotton cloths (cloth diapers that

have been washed work great). Before installing and torquing the bolts, squirt a small amount of light oil on the threads and the bearing surface of the heads. Never use synthetic oil or an anti-seize compound. I once mistakenly coated a new set of high-grade head bolts with synthetic oil before torquing them. At the 60 lbs-ft. setting the bolts began to stretch, destroying them. The synthetic stuff is just too slick and will generate torque readings that are inconsistent with published settings. Standard 30w motor oil will do just fine. Torque the heads to 70 ft-lbs. in steps of 35, 50, 60, then 70 ft-lbs. Use the torque sequence shown in Fig. 3-13, p. 47. Re–torque the inside row of head bolts (next to the intake manifold) to 80 ft-lbs., beginning with the center bolt and working outward (starting with the closest front bolt then the closest rear) until all five bolts are re–torqued.

This will compensate for the pull made by the intake manifold. I used to re–torque these bolts only 5 additional ft-lbs. However, a study that was done by Fel–Pro a couple of years ago proved that 10 ft-lbs. was the ideal amount. In conjunction with this head torquing sequence, it is important to torque the intake manifold bolts to 24 ft-lbs.

Always remember to re–torque the heads and intake, using the sequence in Fig. 3-13, after the engine has been warmed to operating temperature. Of course, let it cool to ambient temperature before torquing. I have heard statements about it not being necessary to re–torque when using the new Fel–Graphic gaskets. However, I'd rather be sure than sorry.

Watch the head bolts as you torque.

Any bolt that feels spongy must be replaced. When you re–torque the head after warm–up, any bolt that requires excessive re–torquing is probably suspect and should be replaced. Head bolts are cheap and blown head gaskets are a pain, so don't overlook this, especially when you are in a hurry.

Studs—Most 5.0 high-performance engines running on the street use stock head bolts. On non–pressurized engines they are adequate. But if you have upgraded the compression or installed a blower or turbo, you should replace your head bolts with studs. Yes, they can be a real pain when removing the heads with the engine in the car. However, the small-block Ford just doesn't have enough bolts around the cylinders for sufficient

clamping force. This is further complicated by the fact that bolts tend to distort the block surface considerably more than studs. Obviously a distorted block surface promotes head gasket failure. Put up with the hassles of the studs and improve the life of your engine.

Recently, Fel-Pro introduced a new head gasket for the 5.0 H.O. engine that is designed to be O-ringed. This is the latest technology and will prevent gasket failure on high-boost supercharged and turbocharged engines as well as nitrous applications. This trick setup is great, but the gaskets are expensive and O-ringing the engine will eat a significant hole in your high-performance budget. Unless you are going for a mega-horsepower setup, skip this approach. ■

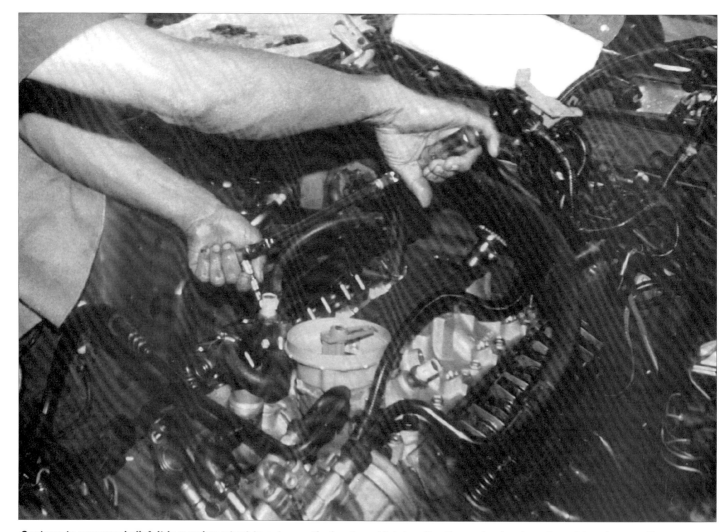

Contrary to common belief, it is very important to re-torque the heads and intake after the engine has been brought up to operating temperature and allowed to cool overnight. The metal in these thin-walled 5.0 engines expands and contracts considerably, especially on a new engine. This changes the torque settings. Do not forget this step.

Head & Intake
Torque Procedure

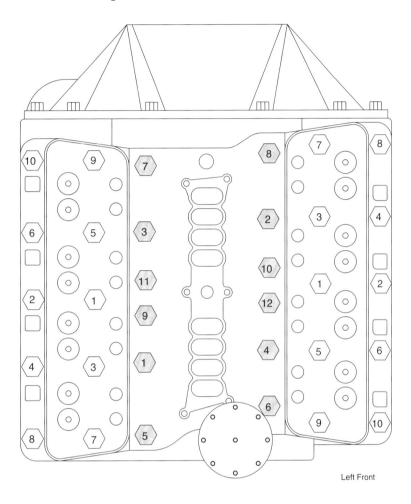

Left Front

A. Tighten head bolts in indicated order in four steps:
   1. 35 ft-lbs.
   2. 50 ft-lbs.
   3. 60 ft-lbs.
   4. 70 ft-lbs.

B. Re-torque inside row of head bolts (next to intake
   manifold) to 80 ft-lbs., in the following order:
   1, 3, 5, 7, 9

C. Torque intake manifold bolts (the shaded bolts above) in the order indicated
   in three steps:
   1. 15 ft-lbs.
   2. 20 ft-lbs.
   3. 24 ft-lbs. (absolutely do not exceed 24 ft-lbs.)

D. Start engine and allow fluids to reach operating
   temperatures.

E. Allow engine to cool overnight or until engine block
   is cold to the touch.

F. Re-torque heads and intake as indicated in Steps A
   thru C.

Fig. 3-13

CAMSHAFTS & VALVETRAIN

4

I n this chapter we will cover the camshaft, lifters, pushrods, rocker arms and cam drive mechanism. This will include a discussion on selection of the correct camshaft and how to properly install it. The installation section will also deal with the correct way to adjust valves.

SELECTION

Selecting the correct camshaft for your particular application is critical to extracting the maximum level of performance from the modifications made to your engine. Every high–performance car nut loves the sound of a "cammed" engine. That

"lumpity–lump" sound produces visions of tire–shredding horsepower. Unfortunately, camshaft selection is where the biggest mistake is generally made by the amateur engine builder. Most racers live by the slogan that "Too much is just right." In camshaft reality, "too much is too much." Unless you are an experienced engine builder, follow the recommendations of the cam grinder you have chosen. Call their tech line and tell them exactly what you are running in your engine. The camshaft they recommend will provide the best compromise for your particular engine combination and application.

The stock heads on the small-block Ford have very restrictive exhaust ports, even when ported. Generally a camshaft with 10° to 15° more exhaust duration will provide better cylinder scavenging on stock heads. This is particularly true if they are unported. A good balance between the intake and exhaust flow requires a relationship so that the exhaust has a flow of about 80% to 85% of the intake flow on a normally aspirated engine. If the heads do not have this relationship, then a dual-pattern cam, with more exhaust duration, is necessary to properly scavenge the cylinders. Most of the replacement roller camshafts on the market for the 5.0 are single-pattern cams with matching intake and exhaust lobes. This is no doubt due to the proliferation of high-flow replacement heads.

If you are intent on making a selection

Correct camshaft selection is critical for optimum performance. Long duration camshafts, with wide fat lobes such as this Crane Cams bumpstick, sound intoxicating but require 11:1 or higher compression, race gas, and rpm operations that are beyond the stock computer's redline. Stick with a cam that will operate within the parameters of your ignition and engine.

Camshaft
Dual vs. Single Pattern

Dual-Pattern Cam
Intake and Exhaust Lobes
are different

Single-Pattern Cam
Intake and Exhaust Lobes
are identical

Dual-Pattern cams are
ground using two different
lobe patterns. They are
commonly used in engines
where the flow relationship
between the intake and
exhaust ports is not well
balanced.

Ford heads have very
restrictive exhaust ports
and generally benefit from
a dual pattern cam with 10°
to 15° more exhaust duration
than intake.

Single-Pattern cams are
ground using the same
lobe pattern. They are
used in engines with a
well balanced flow between
the intake and and exhaust
ports.

Most aftermarket Ford heads
have excellent flow balance
and generally do not require
a dual pattern cam.

Fig. 4-1

without the guidance of one of the cam grinder's technicians, you should understand some very basic rules concerning lift, duration, lobe separation angle and the type of camshaft used.

Lift

If your heads are stock iron heads, you are wasting your money purchasing a camshaft with more than .500" lift. There is no appreciable airflow in these heads above .500" lift. Even when ported, these heads still will not flow above .550" lift. Installing a camshaft with lift exceeding these levels means you are eating horsepower (heavier valve springs) and unnecessarily wearing valvetrain components. The only exception is when running a supercharger.

Duration

When selecting the duration of your cam, it is important to realize that as duration increases, so does the need for compression. The longer the valves are open, the less time there is for the cylinder to build pressure on the compression stroke. If your engine is a stock 5.0 with 9:1 compression, keep the duration under 225° at .050" lift on a

Emissions

Nothing in an engine creates more headaches for emissions control than a performance camshaft. Valve overlap and lobe separation angle are very critical in defining how environmentally clean a cam is. Some 5.0 engine combinations can be enhanced significantly with a camshaft while improving the exhaust emissions at the same time. Unfortunately, we generally find the big horsepower numbers come when we ignore the emissions output at lower engine speeds. For the limited amount of time a race car's engine spends operating at speeds outside its most efficient range, the emissions output is negligible. However, put that same engine combination in traffic on a daily basis and the story changes.

It is the responsibility of all car enthusiasts to build the cleanest-burning high–performance street engines possible. Every major cam grinder is developing a selection of emissions-legal camshafts that provide significant power improvements. However, if hot rodders continue to ignore this responsibility, the voting public (a majority of them non-car people) will turn against us and hot high–performance street cars will be relegated to a museum. Unless your car is a trailered race car or a vehicle designed for off-highway use only, stick with the camshafts that have EPA certification.

roller hydraulic cam.

The longer the duration the higher the powerband. If your car is a street car you'll need more gear to keep the engine in the operational range for the cam's power curve. Fortunately the overdrive 5th gear found in the manual transmission cars provides a small measure of help for the lost fuel economy that accompanies a gear change. However, if your car is running the factory hydraulic roller lifters, or the stock computer, long duration camshafts are useless. The rpm limit of the heavy roller lifters, as well as the 6250 rpm redline in the stock computer, prohibit the use of long duration valve openings.

When running a supercharger or turbocharger, duration numbers become more critical. Since the intake system is pressurized, there is no delay in airflow cone formation around the intake valve. Consequently, the instant the valve moves from the seat there is airflow. Excessive duration can be detrimental on a pressurized engine, especially on the exhaust with a turbo application. Most small displacement engines running turbochargers do not like gross exhaust durations (measured from .000" lift) of more than 265° to 270°.

Camshafts & Vacuum

It is important for you to recognize the effect camshaft duration has on engine vacuum. This is especially important when the car is equipped with power-assisted brakes. Long-duration camshafts typically have very poor low-speed vacuum. Lack of vacuum at low engine speeds means you probably will not have power assist for your brakes when your foot is off the accelerator. Since most people stop without their foot on the gas, this can be pretty disconcerting, especially when the car in front of you happens to be a state trooper. These guys really hate to be rear–ended. You can generally expect to have vacuum problems when the camshaft's duration approaches 240° at .050" lift. This is not a hard and fast rule. Large overlaps and tight lobe center angles also affect this.

If your car suffers from this problem, install a vacuum reservoir. These things are inexpensive and can be purchased through most high–performance parts retailers. The best price is typically through one of the mail–order suppliers, most notably Summit Racing Equipment (P.O. Box 909, Akron, OH 44309. Order Line: 216/630-2200. Tech Line: 216/630-0240). They have a slick little canister with all the valves for a reasonable price.

A close-up of a serious Crane Cams high-boost turbocharger roller camshaft for the 5.0. Designed for 30-lbs. of boost and 1100 hp, this cam sports .579" lift and a 115-degree lobe separation angle.

Superchargers require camshafts that provide wide lobe separations to minimize valve overlap crossflow. Generally the stock roller camshaft will work better in a supercharger application than a racing cam that is designed for a normally aspirated engine. (Photo courtesy Steeda Autosports)

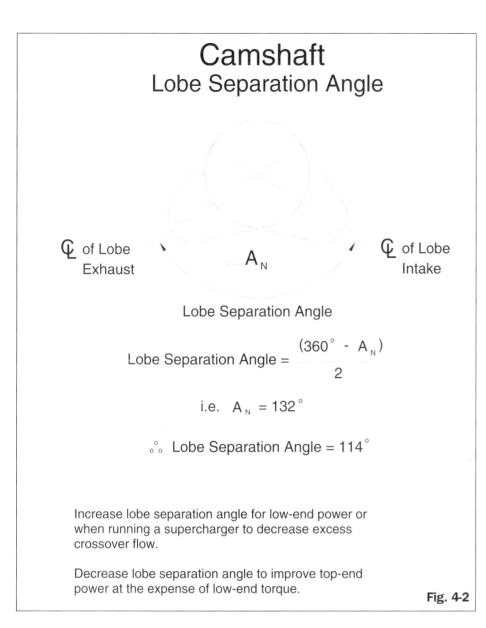

Camshaft
Lobe Separation Angle

$\mathbb{C}$ of Lobe Exhaust A_N $\mathbb{C}$ of Lobe Intake

Lobe Separation Angle

$$\text{Lobe Separation Angle} = \frac{(360° - A_N)}{2}$$

$$\text{i.e.} \quad A_N = 132°$$

$$\therefore \text{Lobe Separation Angle} = 114°$$

Increase lobe separation angle for low-end power or when running a supercharger to decrease excess crossover flow.

Decrease lobe separation angle to improve top-end power at the expense of low-end torque.

Fig. 4-2

Lobe Separation Angle

The lobe separation angle will have a dramatic effect on where the power is produced. This characteristic of a camshaft is second only to duration in importance. Lobe separation angle is the angle that is formed between the geometric centers of the intake and the exhaust lobes. Generally, closing up the angle moves the power curve upward and improves mid–range torque. When you open the angle, you get the opposite effect. Most high–performance cams are ground with a 106° to 112° lobe separation angle.

Camshafts designed for low-compression engines with emissions control will generally have lobe separation angles of 114° to 116°. Emissions cams with wider lobe separation angles reduce the scavenging effect and consequently leave some quantity of spent gases in the combustion chamber. The re–burning of this spent mixture improves emissions and gives the added benefit of increased low–end torque. The wider lobe separation angle provides greater time for the cylinder to build pressure and sort of "artificially" increases the compression ratio. All of these wonderful things are, of course, at the expense of top–end power.

Blown Engines—Supercharged or turbocharged engines generally require wider lobe separation angles than normally aspirated engines. With a pressurized intake system, the need for the crossflow pulling effect associated with lobe overlap is significantly reduced. Turbo systems are far more sensitive to cam design than a supercharger. Since the exhaust gases are utilized to drive the compressor on the turbocharger, tight lobe center angles will tend to build very high, damaging exhaust temperatures. Shorter duration and higher lift cams, with slightly wider lobe angles, are generally more effective, especially for the street.

Excessive overlap on a supercharged engine will generally move the powerband up significantly. On supercharged engines using a camshaft with a narrow lobe separation angle, the power will generally tend to come on suddenly in a very narrow rpm range. This may be great for drag racing, but it's the pits for road racing, autocross or the street.

Aftermarket Choices

Given the basic variables associated with cam selection, it should be clear that you need to consult the experts before selecting a cam. However, if your approach is modifying the stock roller cammed 5.0 short block to run with the stock computer, there are several excellent replacement cams on the market. Crane seems to have the edge in street cams that have emissions certification. Crane also grinds Ford's SVO cams. Lunati, Crower, Ultradyne and Comp Cams also have good replacement cams that will work with stock Ford hydraulic roller lifters.

Roller Cams

One of the things that has significantly contributed to the success of the 5.0 engine is the roller cam. Roller cams generally provide the same power as a flat-tappet cam sporting 10° more duration, but they do it with a better torque curve. Unless you are going for increased rpm, stay with the Ford

To avoid the potential breakage of a distributor gear, always check the distributor gear-to-block clearance. The minimum clearance should be .040".

Under severe racing conditions, the driven gear roll pin in the stock distributor can work loose. The stock pin is too small and must be replaced with the next larger roll pin. When drilling for a larger pin, be sure to secure the gear and shaft so there is no movement. This is necessary to insure correct alignment and prevent wallowing the holes out.

hydraulic rollers. You can actually get close to 400 honest horsepower on a normally aspirated EFI 5.0 roller engine with several of the top replacement roller cams. Add a B–trim Vortech supercharger and 500 horsepower is not out of the question.

Crane's Roller Conversion Kit—
If you have a non–roller block but want the performance and convenience of the Ford hydraulic roller lifter, Crane Cams offers a conversion kit (PN 44306–1). This kit uses the spider spring plate from the 5.0 H.O. engine that holds the roller lifter guides in position as well as the Ford hydraulic roller lifters. Included in the kit are two studs that fit into the oil drain holes in the lifter galley to secure the spider plate. Unfortunately, this setup requires a unique small-base-circle cam. However, there are several to choose from that essentially match the performance of the 5.0 roller replacement cams. (You will still be saddled with the rpm limit associated with the heavy hydraulic roller lifter.) I have tested this kit in a 351W and found it to be excellent. This particular engine easily made 500 horsepower using the conversion kit.

CAMSHAFT INSTALLATION

Once you have decided on a cam, the installation process should proceed in a

specific order. First the distributor gear clearance must be set and then the cam thrust clearance checked. Next, the cam should be indexed. After this, the retainer–to–guide, pushrod and coil–bind clearances must be checked. Finally, the rocker arm geometry must be tested and corrected if necessary.

Distributor Clearance

Before installing the camshaft, it is very important to drop the distributor into its hole and check the clearance between the bottom of the distributor gear and the block. The distributor gear is pulled down due to the natural torque that occurs between the camshaft drive gear and the driven gear on the distributor. If there is little or no clearance, the gear can bind against the block and break. Obviously a broken distributor gear means you're going to have to park it.

Use a long-blade feeler gauge and insert it through the front cam bearing hole to check the clearance. Bolt the distributor housing down and press the shaft firmly down when checking the clearance. There should be at least .040" clearance. If the clearance is too tight,

determine the actual clearance (find the thickest feeler gauge that will fit between the gear and the block). Drive the roll pin out and remove the gear. Either machine the additional required clearance or use a sander to remove the excess metal. When using a sander, be sure to constantly rotate the gear to insure a reasonably flat surface. Do not

If you have upgraded your oil pump drive to one of the aftermarket or Ford Motorsport heavy-duty oil pump driveshafts, often it will be necessary to cut 1/2" off the end of your EFI distributor shaft to accommodate the longer HD shaft. This is a comparison of the EFI shaft on the left and the shorter, older style on the right.

Installing a flat-tappet camshaft means correct break-in and proper pre-lubrication. The black anti-scuffing grease sold at most speed shops or supplied with a new cam must be generously smeared on all the lobes. This is very important.

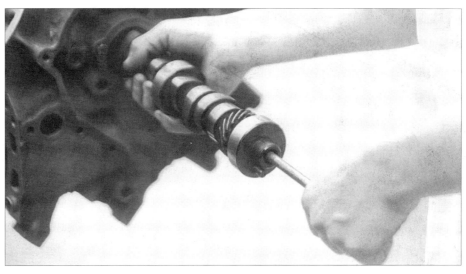

There is only one way to install a cam without damaging the bearings—screw a long, 3/8" NC bolt into the end of the cam to use as a handle. Insert the cam slowly, keeping it in a level plane, using the long bolt as a lever to guide the cam.

overheat the gear (turn the sanding surface blue) when sanding. You can ruin the temper and cause the gear to fail. Take your time. *Note:* If you have not drilled the spring pin that secures the distributor gear out to the next larger size, do it before you check the clearance. Parts have a way of shifting in the home shop when holes are drilled.

HD Oil Pump Driveshaft—If you have replaced your oil pump driveshaft with one of the heavy-duty pieces that has a thicker body, you may experience a

problem when installing your distributor. Some replacement heavy-duty oil pump driveshafts are designed to work on the older distributors that have a shorter shaft below the distributor gear. The distributor with the longer shaft will not seat completely in the block when attempting to mate with this type of new shaft. To utilize the heavy-duty oil pump driveshaft, you must cut .500" off the end of the distributor shaft below the gear. No big deal. This shaft can be cut with an ordinary hacksaw and dressed

with a file. No special machining is necessary.

Installing the Cam

To install the cam into the block, attach a long 3/8–18 bolt into the cam gear bolt hole. This will serve as a handle for guiding the cam into the block. Use the long bolt and you'll prevent possible damage to a bearing from a cam lobe as you slip the cam into the block. Be sure to bottom the bolt in the cam for a tight fit.

Flat-Tappet Cam—If you are installing a flat-tappet cam, smear the lobes with a generous coating of black moly cam lobe grease. This is an anti–scuffing lubricant that will allow the cam to break in without galling a lobe. Do not install a new flat-tappet cam without it. Furthermore, do not put the black grease on the bearing surfaces. Before you slip the cam into the block, pour a 50/50 mixture of high–performance 30w non–detergent oil and GM's EOS (Engine Oil Supplement) over the lobes and bearing surfaces. Do not run synthetic oil or any of the engine oil additives with the Teflon coating processes (Slick 50, etc.) in an engine with a new flat-tappet cam. You must run a 30w non–detergent oil for the first 500 miles to allow the cam to break in

To install a camshaft with the engine in the car, the radiator must be removed and the A/C condenser must be lifted and rotated out of the way. It is not necessary to disconnect the condenser, as there is sufficient play in the spring-lock coupling to allow for the rotation.

53

properly. The slick synthetic oils and additives will not permit the new cam and lifters to seat to one another and a cam failure is sure to occur. The only additive that should be added to the engine's oil, when breaking in a new flat-tappet cam, is the oil supplement specifically provided by the cam grinder. If you do not have the correct additive, use GM's EOS, PN 1052367. (Yes, I know it belongs to those "other guys," but at least they do not manufacture it.)

Roller Cams—Roller cams are made from steel billet, so a generous coating of fresh engine oil is all that is required. Since there is no seating process with the lifters on a roller cam, synthetic oil can be used.

With oil dripping from the camshaft, slide it slowly into the block. Maintain a constant and level attitude with the cam to avoid dinging any of the bearings. If the block is still in the car, you will have to remove the radiator and rotate the A/C condenser up and to the right side of the car. It is not necessary to disconnect the condenser. There is sufficient play in the couplings to allow it to rotate sufficiently to install the cam.

Galling or Binding—Once the cam is in the block, slip the driven cam gear on the cam and spin it. The cam should turn freely without binding. If it binds, remove the cam and check it for straightness. Cams do warp. If the cam is straight, then you probably have a cam bearing problem. Unfortunately this problem is particularly acute on small-block Ford V8s when new cam bearings have been installed. The factory fits oversize bearings in all new blocks and bores them to the correct size. This avoids any problems with casting core shifts that could scrape a new block. However, if you rebuild your engine and have the cam bearings replaced, it is standard procedure to simply drive the old bearings out and drive in the new ones without checking the align bore. It is only when you go to install a new

After you have checked the rotation of the cam for binding in the bearings, it is important to check the end play. Use a dial indicator or feeler gauge to determine the in and out travel. This should be between .005" and .008". If it is too tight, sand the thrust plate using 240-grit paper on a hard flat surface. If it is too loose, you must sand the cam gear-to-cam mating surface of the gear. Take your time.

camshaft that you discover things are not cool. A good friend discovered this on his freshly rebuilt Boss 302, right after he fired it up and it seized two cam bearings. If you are planning an engine rebuild for your 5.0 block, have the machine shop check the camshaft align bore, after the old bearings have been removed and before the new bearings have been installed. If things are not straight, have the machinist install oversize bearings and align bore them to size. Do not kid yourself about this. If the bores are not straight in the block you will either seize a bearing and destroy a cam and block or you will have no oil pressure. Either way, the engine has to come apart.

Thrust Plate—With the cam in the block, install the thrust plate. If you are installing a new cam gear and chain set, be sure to use the new thrust plate if one comes with the kit. Bolt the cam gear in place and check the camshaft end play between the cam driven gear and the thrust plate. Never assume it is right. A dial indicator is best for checking the clearance but a feeler gauge will work.

Use a screwdriver to pry the cam gear back and forth to get an accurate measurement. You must have .005" to .008" clearance. If the clearance is too tight, machine the mating surface of the cam gear. For the friction reduction nuts, Danny Bee Racing Products manufactures a very slick roller bearing camshaft thrust plate that replaces the stock piece.

TIMING CHAINS, GEARS & BELTS

The camshaft in the stock 5.0 H.O. engine is driven by a double–roller chain and gearset. These have been the standard for high–performance engines for a long time. Unfortunately they are junk after about 1000 miles. The life of a cam chain is directly affected by the weight of the valvetrain and the valve springs used. Fit stiff valve springs and the chain will stretch immediately. This will cause the cam timing to constantly vary from advance to retard as the chain whips in an "S" fashion through the rpm band. Obviously this whipping destroys the efficiency of the engine and has a

Precise cam timing is critical to optimium performance. For accurate cam timing control, the Danny Bee Racing Products belt-drive kit is the slick setup. This kit is simple to install, provides 20 degrees of adjustability and will eliminate the scrambled cam timing that is associated with a chain drive. (Photo courtesy Danny Bee Racing Products)

Step 1: After you have checked the end play, mount a dial indicator on the number one piston, and rotate the crankshaft back and forth until you have an approximate location for TDC. Adjust the degree wheel and pointer to TDC and set the dial indicator to .000". Next, rotate the crankshaft counter-clockwise until the dial indicator reads approximately .100", then rotate clockwise until the dial indicator reads .050". Note the exact number of degrees before TDC indicated on the degree wheel.

significant effect on the horsepower and torque output.

If you are serious about performance, particularly if you are road racing, do not waste your money on a chain and gear set. The only ones that will hold up for any length of time are expensive. Given the fact that you will have to replace the expensive chain and gear set often, you are miles ahead by using a Jesel belt drive or any one of the gear drive sets (Pete Jackson, Milodon, Summers Bros., etc.) currently available. Ford SVO markets a trick belt drive that runs inside the engine. It provides excellent cam timing control without the noise of the gear drive sets. Danny Bee Racing Products also offers a very trick belt drive that runs outside the engine. This is a very slick setup that allows for quick timing changes. However, the gear drives are the best approach, especially for the endurance or road racing engine. If your current budget permits, go with the Ford belt drive (PN M6268–U302 or heavy-duty M6268–U351) or the Danny Bee kit for your hot street or drag car and stick with the gear drives for road racing.

Degreeing the Cam

Degreeing the camshaft is generally

The standard in small-block Ford cam drives for many decades has been the Pete Jackson dual idler gear set. This setup has been the favorite with roundy-rounders and road racers. Absolute reliability and perfect cam timing control are the hallmarks of this cam drive. However, it is a bit noisy.

Step 2: Continue to rotate the crankshaft clockwise, past TDC, until the dial indicator reads .050". Note the exact number of degrees past TDC indicated on the degree wheel. Add the degrees from this reading to the amount noted before TDC and divide the sum by 2. The result is the exact number of degrees that should be read before and after TDC at .050". With the dial indicator on the piston reading .050", adjust the degree wheel or pointer to read the result.

Step 3: Rotate the crankshaft to TDC on the #1 piston. Securely mount a dial indicator to read the vertical travel of the intake lifter on the #1 cylinder. Preload the dial indicator and adjust it to read .000".

Step 4: After you have checked the camshaft specification card to determine where the intake is supposed to open and close and at what lift it is to be measured (typically .020" or .050"), calculate the lobe center angle if it is not stated on the card (Fig. 4-4). Rotate the crankshaft until the dial indicator reads the specified measurement lift.

not done by an amateur engine builder. Most assume things are right and just install the cam as it comes out of the box. But you should always check the cam index. Small machining errors in the cam drive gears or pulleys, combined with a small error in the cam grinding process, can result in a significant variation in the specified cam timing.

To degree your cam you will need a degree wheel, wire for a pointer (coat hangers or 1/8" gas welding rod), a dial indicator with stand, and pencil and paper. Although I demonstrate the process with the engine on a stand, it can be done while in the car. Rotate the engine to approximately top dead center on cylinder number 5 (left front). Secure the degree wheel to the crankshaft snout with the harmonic dampener bolt. Attach a section of wire and fashion a pointer that aligns with the 0° mark on the degree wheel.

If the head is off, use the dial indicator to find exact top dead center (TDC) of the piston stroke. Pre–load the dial indicator against the center of the piston dome about .150" and set the indicator to zero. Slowly rotate the piston about 20° to either side of the highest point read on the indicator (TDC). Take a reading on the degree wheel, on both sides of the maximum reading on the dial indicator,

at exactly the same distance down in the bore. Split the difference between the two readings and adjust the degree wheel for the new zero position. For example, at .020" lift BTDC, the degree wheel reads 17° and at .020" lift ATDC, it reads 13°. Add the two degree readings together and divide by 2, or 15°. The center is 15° from each reading and requires the degree wheel be rotated clockwise 2° to correct the center. Recheck your alignment and adjust until the degree wheel reads the same degrees

before and after TDC at the same depth reading on the dial indicator. If the heads are installed, use a positive stopping device in the spark plug hole and split the difference, just like with the dial indicator, to determine TDC.

Insert an intake and exhaust lifter on the number 5 cam lobes (or whichever cylinder you chose to test). Secure the dial indicator so it is sturdy and will not move as the engine is rotated. Mount the indicator in such a fashion so that the plunger is in direct line with the vector of

Step 5: With the dial indicator showing the measurement lift (.050" for the cam being tested) note the exact (within 1/4 of a degree) reading on the degree wheel. Compare this to the opening point specified on the cam card. A 1/4 of a degree sounds ludicrous, however, meticulous accuracy wins races.

Camshaft
Cam Timing

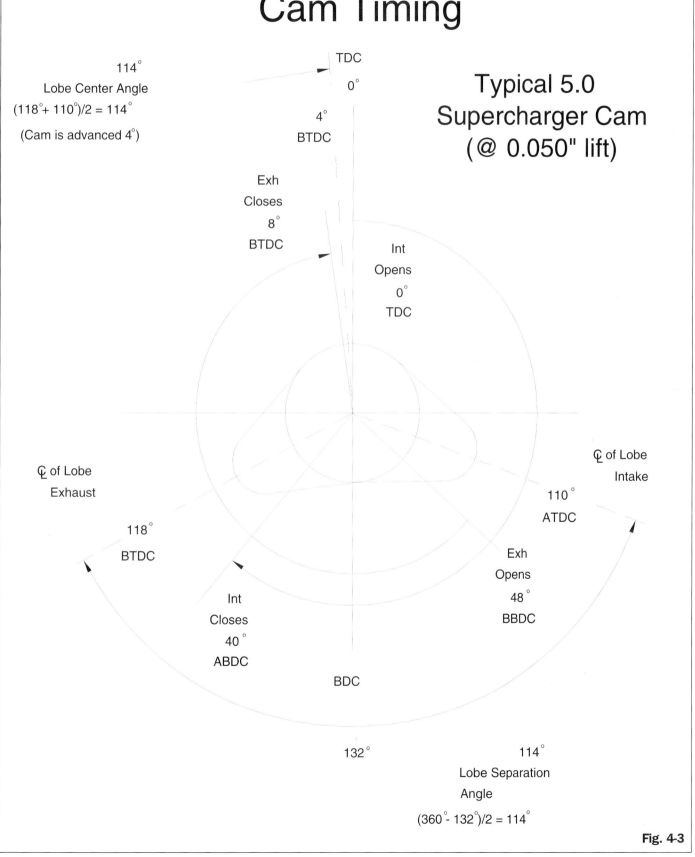

114°
Lobe Center Angle
(118° + 110°)/2 = 114°

(Cam is advanced 4°)

TDC
0°

4°
BTDC

Exh
Closes
8°
BTDC

Int
Opens
0°
TDC

Typical 5.0
Supercharger Cam
(@ 0.050" lift)

℄ of Lobe
Exhaust

118°
BTDC

Int
Closes
40°
ABDC

℄ of Lobe
Intake

110°
ATDC

Exh
Opens
48°
BBDC

BDC

132°

114°
Lobe Separation
Angle
(360° - 132°)/2 = 114°

Fig. 4-3

Camshaft
Lobe Center Angle

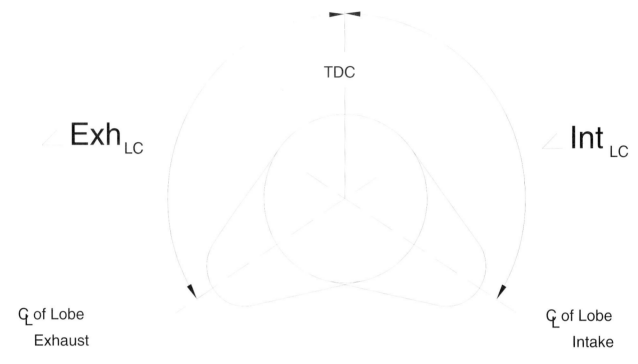

TDC

Exh$_{LC}$

Int$_{LC}$

C$_L$ of Lobe
Exhaust

C$_L$ of Lobe
Intake

$$\text{Lobe Center Angle} = \frac{(\text{Exh}_{LC} + \text{Int}_{LC})}{2}$$

$$\text{i.e.} \quad \text{Exh}_{LC} = 114^\circ$$
$$\text{Int}_{LC} = 110^\circ$$

$$\therefore \text{Lobe Center Angle} = 112^\circ$$
$$(\text{Cam is advanced } 2^\circ)$$

Lobe center angles that fall after TDC are said to
be retarded. This type of cam timing will generally
improve high rpm torque and horsepower.

Lobe center angles that fall before TDC are said to
be advanced. This type of cam timing will generally
increase low-end torque and horsepower.

Fig. 4-4

Step 6: Continue to rotate the crankshaft, counting the rotations on the dial, until the lobe reaches its maximum lift. Note the lift and check it against the cam card. (If it is more than a few thousands off, be sure the stroke of the dial indicator is exactly vertical. Now go back to Step 3.) Now rotate the crankshaft (counting backwards on the dial indicator rotations) until the dial indicator reads .050" lift again.

Step 7: Note the exact degree reading on the degree wheel. Compare this to the closing point specified on the card. If the readings taken in Steps 4 & 5 do not match the specifications on the cam card (or the same number of degrees each side of opening and closing) calculate the lobe center angle as provided in Fig. 4-4 and compare it to the lobe center angle per the cam specification card. The angles should be identical. If the angle is different, the number of degrees before or after will define the cam's advance or retard. Change the crankshaft gear to correct the advance or retard and recheck.

the lifter travel. This is important to prevent distortion of the readings if checking cam phasing and lift. Rotate the crankshaft until the lifter being tested is on the heel of the cam, pre–load it approximately .100" and set the indicator to zero.

Slowly rotate the crankshaft clockwise until the dial indicator reads .050" lift. Note the degree indicated on the degree wheel and write it down. Continue rotating the crankshaft to the maximum lobe lift point. Note the location of this point and write it down. Rotate the crankshaft until you have reached the point where the lobe is at .050" from the heel. Note the reading on the degree wheel and write it down. Repeat the process testing the other lifter. Split the difference between the opening and closing readings on each lobe to find the lobe centerline. The calculated centerline should coincide with the measured centerline within a couple of degrees. If it does not, try again.

Examine the cam card carefully to determine the centerline of the lobe as specified (Fig. 4-4). Just split the opening

and closing numbers and you'll have it. Compare the centerline as specified to the one you measured. If the measured centerline is different than the cam card specifies, advance or retard it to correct the centerline by changing the slot on the crank gear. If the crank gear does not have multiple slots for adjusting cam

timing, you will need to replace it or use offset cam bushings to correct the timing.

Playing with Timing — Retarding and advancing a cam can be used to soften the bottom end or produce more low–end. However, unless you are an experienced engine builder, stick with the timing specified by the cam grinder, at

After you have completed degreeing the cam, rotate the engine to TDC on the degree wheel. Remove the degree wheel, slip the harmonic dampener on and fabricate a pointer or modify the factory pointer so that it reads correctly at 0 degrees.

Consistent rocker arm ratios are very important to optimizing engine performance. **Stock rocker arms vary significantly and must be replaced. The Competition Cams "Magnum" series rockers shown are an inexpensive semi-roller rocker arm with precise and constant rocker ratios.**

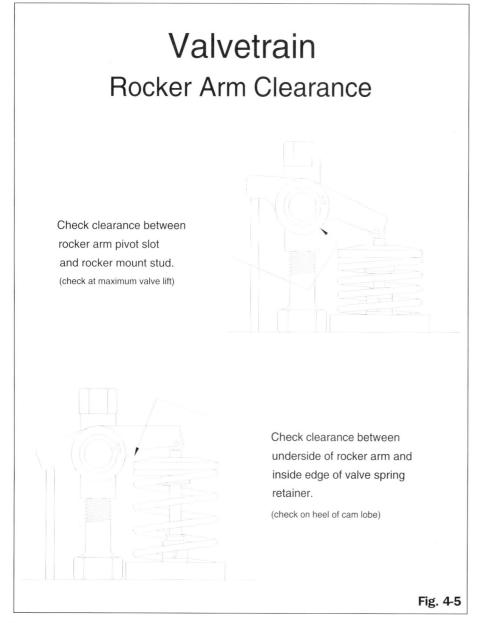

Valvetrain
Rocker Arm Clearance

Check clearance between rocker arm pivot slot and rocker mount stud.

(check at maximum valve lift)

Check clearance between underside of rocker arm and inside edge of valve spring retainer.

(check on heel of cam lobe)

Fig. 4-5

least for the initial setting. As you develop experience with your engine you can play with the cam timing to move the powerband around.

When modifying the cam timing on a 5.0 engine, you must make a change of at least 4° for there to be a significant difference in performance. Do not go more than 6°. If you find your engine needs more than a 6° change, replace the cam. It is also very important to understand that small changes in cam timing can have a significant effect on the piston–to–valve clearance. Unless you have a couple of feet under each valve head, check the clearance when advancing or retarding your cam. It may save the engine.

A serious engine builder pursuing optimum engine output will always check the cam timing on each cam lobe. Cam grinding machines are not always perfectly adjusted and sometimes the lobes are out of phase. Checking the lobes can also show if the lifter bores are not correctly aligned. If you are going for mega–horsepower, check them all.

Checking Clearances

After you have degreed the cam, you should re–check the coil bind clearances and the retainer–to–guide clearances with the valvetrain fully assembled. Just rotate the crankshaft until the valve is at its highest lift point. Run a .010" feeler gauge between each spring coil. If the gauge won't go, you've got a problem. Same goes for the retainer–to–guide clearance. If you can't fit at least a .100" wire gauge between the top of the valve seal and the bottom of the retainer, fix it. These clearances were explained in greater detail in Chapter 3, p. 37-40.

Rocker Arm—It is also important to check the clearances around the bodies of the rocker arms. The areas of concern are between the bottom of the rocker arm and the base of the rocker stud and between the rocker arm and the valve retainer (see Fig. 4-5). This is particularly

Proper rocker arm geometry can improve torque as well as extend the life of the valvetrain. Find the center of the valve lift and correct the geometry per the text by selecting pushrods or lash caps that bring the angle to the optimum point.

True roller rocker arms are the best way to go if your budget permits. Always remember to consult with your cam grinder before upgrading to a higher than standard rocker ratio, such as the 1.72 SVO rockers shown. Ask your cam grinder if the cam and springs you are using are compatible with the higher ratio. This could save you the expense of a blown engine from rocker ratio-induced valve spring surge.

important when running roller rocker arms. There should be a minimum of .100" between the rocker arm and the rocker stud base, as well as the clearance to the valve retainer. If you have inadequate clearance between the rocker arm and the base of the rocker stud, it will be necessary to machine the rocker stud boss to increase the clearance. Additional clearance can be gained between the rocker arm and the retainer by carefully grinding a long smooth radius on the underside of the rocker arm with a pencil sanding roll. Take off only what is needed. Unless there is interference with the rocker arm operation, you should wait until you have set the rocker geometry to correct any clearance problems.

Piston to Valve—When you have upgraded to a high-lift camshaft, it is important to check the piston–to–valve

clearance. The stock EFI short block (except the '86) has considerable valve relief clearance on the pistons. However, if you are running larger valves, heads with wider valve spacing, or higher compression pistons, it is imperative that the clearance be checked. Tapping a valve with a piston because you did not check the clearance is just plain stupid, not to mention expensive. If your short block is a stock '86 5.0 H.O. you have a problem. The '86 engine does not have valve reliefs and requires machining for anything larger than the stock camshaft.

Checking the clearance is simple and only requires some molding clay and a razor blade. Remove both heads and place a .250" layer of molding clay on top of the valve reliefs on a piston in each cylinder bank. Reinstall the heads using the same type of head gasket that the engine will be run with, and torque them

following the torquing sequence on p. 47. Adjust the valves for .000" clearance. Rotate the engine 720 degrees to insure complete cycling of the cam. (Generally the only area where there is a potential for valve-to-piston contact is between the 20° to either side of TDC.) Remove the heads. Carefully lift the compressed clay and cut through the thinnest part with a new razor blade. Use a vernier caliper to measure the thickness of the clay in the valve relief area. There must be a minimum of .100" on the exhaust and .080" on the intake. If you are running aluminum rods, increase the minimum clearances by .030".

Flycutting—If your engine does not have the minimum clearances, you will have to change to a cam with less lobe lift, go to a rocker arm with a smaller ratio, or flycut the pistons. As less lobe lift will probably mean less power (which no true hot rodder wants) then flycutting has to be considered. Generally you have to disassemble the engine to have the pistons flycut for the additional valve clearances. However, Manley and Moroso sell a flycutter that

Valvetrain
Rocker Arm Geometry

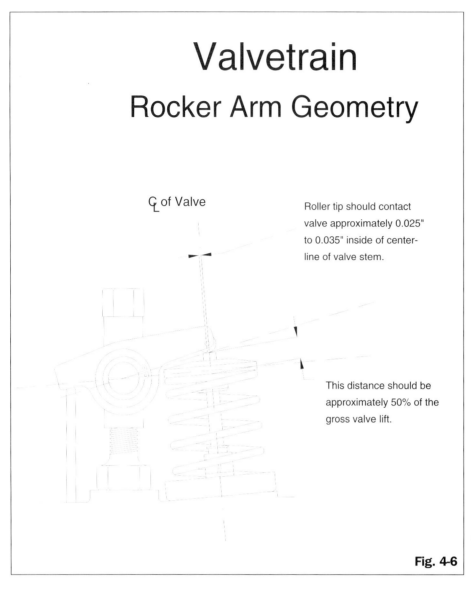

C̸ of Valve

Roller tip should contact valve approximately 0.025" to 0.035" inside of center-line of valve stem.

This distance should be approximately 50% of the gross valve lift.

Fig. 4-6

fits through the valve guides that can cut the reliefs without disassembling the engine. Considerable care must be taken when using these cutters. A little clay around the edges of the piston can prevent the aluminum shavings from getting where they should not. But, the real problem is the damage that can be done to the valve guides if there is any radial loading on the cutter stem as it is rotated by the drill. It's a slick way to get perfect valve relief clearance. However, like all modifications to an engine, take your time and be careful.

Pushrods

The stock pushrods on the 5.0 H.O. engine are better than average. However, for high–performance purposes they should be replaced with hardened pieces. The stock units will flex too much when using a performance cam and valve springs. If you are using heads that have pushrod guide plates, you must upgrade to the chrome-moly hardened pushrods. Regular pushrods are not hardened along the sides and will wear immediately from the guide plates. This will put small slivers of steel in the oiling system. Even if the pushrods do not wear, the heat from the rubbing will destroy them and they will break or bend. Pushrods are cheap so do not skimp here.

The standard diameter chrome-moly pushrods will work just fine for the 5.0 engine running a hydraulic roller cam. There will be some flex, but generally not enough to warrant upgrading to the

expensive Kevlar or large diameter pieces. Most NASCAR engines use the standard diameter pushrods. If they can turn 7500+ rpm for several hours, your small-block Ford should be okay with them. Generally, these exotic pushrods are utilized in engines running high spring pressures or turning high rpm.

ROCKER ARM GEOMETRY

The last phase of installing a camshaft is checking and correcting the rocker arm geometry. This is one of the most important points to address in squeezing out every bit of horsepower your cam can produce. This is where the experienced engine builders spend considerable time making things right.

There are two schools of thought on how a rocker arm should be aligned. Virtually everything you read says the tip of the rocker must be centered on the valve axis at 50% of the valve lift. Typically you are instructed to set the tip toward the outer edge of the valve with the rocker arm tip and pushrod pivot in the same level plane. This allows the rocker tip to move across the valve tip toward the inside as the rocker lever shortens, thereby maintaining constant contact with the valve tip. This is great for the masses, especially the GM sled drivers. However, there is a second school of thought that I believe provides a couple of advantages over the previous method.

The rate that horsepower builds in an engine is directly proportional to the valve acceleration rate, or the speed at which the valves open. If you look at the rocker arm from a level side angle, you can clearly see the rocker ratio diminishing in relation to the valve tip axis as the rocker arm rotates. With the rocker ratio on a constantly diminishing curve, the valve acceleration rate is also constantly slowing down. If you change the rocker tip–to–pushrod pivot relationship so that the pushrod pivot is below the valve tip of the rocker arm, the rocker ratio goes through a period of increasing ratio when the valve initially opens. As the valve approaches maximum lift, the acceleration rate slows and reduces the inertia shock the valve and spring go through when changing direction. This arrangement opens the valve faster and keeps it at higher lifts longer while maximizing the de-acceleration rates of the cam lobe to improve valve life. This gives a slight improvement in horsepower while reducing the stress on the valves and springs. Good stuff.

The best setup for the rocker arm is to have the pushrod pivot slightly below the rocker arm tip, with the rocker arm tip inside the centerline of the valve axis (toward the rocker stud), depending on what rocker ratio you use and the design of the rocker arm. The higher the ratio the more you move from the centerline toward the rocker stud. The real key is aligning the pushrod pivot height so that the tip of the rocker arm covers the least distance across the tip of the valve. This means the rocker arm tip will be on the same plane as the center of the rocker arm fulcrum at 50% valve lift. This relationship will provide the optimum utilization of your cam, while also keeping the rocker tip closer to the valve axis. Keeping the rocker tip closer to the valve axis will reduce the valve guide elongation that seems to go along with high performance cams.

Setting up your rocker geometry would be simple if rocker arms were built with the pushrod pivot and the rocker tip in the same plane, or basically a straight lever. The approximate distance that the pushrod pivot had to be below the valve tip could be calculated simply by halving the theoretical valve lift and dividing the result by the rocker ratio.

For example, let's look at an engine using a 1.6 ratio rocker arm in combination with a camshaft that produces a theoretical valve lift of .600".

Assuming the rocker arm is a straight lever, the ideal pushrod pivot location would be found by dividing .600" by 2 (the mid-point of valve lift), then dividing the result by the rocker ratio, or (.600"/2)/1.6 = .187" (3/16"). However, things are never that simple.

Rocker arms are manufactured with many different designs. Generally a well-designed rocker arm will have the pushrod pivot below the plane of the rocker tip to compensate for the diminishing rocker ratio at the valve tip end as the lever is rotated to the fixed valve axis. Essentially, placing the pushrod pivot below the rocker tip creates an increasing lever ratio on the pushrod end to compensate for the decreasing ratio on the valve tip, and thereby maintaining a more constant overall rocker ratio. More engineering feldagarb. Fear not, there is hope for those who insist on knowing the math. Simply add the calculated distance from the formula to the distance the pushrod pivot is below the horizontal plane of the rocker tip and the rocker fulcrum. Well, it's actually easier than it sounds.

Roller rocker arms are a must upgrade to the stock 5.0 engine for consistent valve lift. Do not make the mistake this racer did and install rocker arms that are designed to operate with a guide plate on a head that is designed to use the rail alignment rocker. Without the guide plate, the rocker arm dances on the pushrod and valve until the pushrod breaks or the retainer is pushed from the valve. Very ugly results.

For example, let's assume that we measured the rocker arm from the previous paragraph and found the pushrod pivot to be .100" below the rocker tip, when the tip and fulcrum are in the same plane. We would add the .100" to the previously calculated number of .187" to determine our best rocker angle. This means the pushrod pivot should be .287" below the rocker tip, for optimum utilization of the rocker arm ratio.

The unfortunate thing about setting rocker arm geometry is that it generally entails custom length pushrods, dressing the valve stem tips, lash caps, or changing brands of rocker arms. Different brands of rocker arms have different pushrod-to-tip relationships and may be worth trying. However, custom length pushrods are easily obtained and the price is considerably cheaper than the rocker arms. Just remember when ordering pushrods that the length you specify should be approximately .025" longer to compensate for the oil holes drilled in the ends of the pushrod. A pushrod manufacturer will typically make them to your length before the holes are drilled, consequently the need for the additional length. To make things easier, Crane Cams offers an adjustable length pushrod that can be sent back to them to get an exact fit.

Selecting Rocker Arms

The selection of rocker arms will be dictated by the type of camshaft and heads. The choices vary from using the stock rocker arms (total brain failure mode), the Competition Cams "Magnum" roller tip rocker arms, the pedestal-type full roller rockers, conventional full roller rocker arms, and the shaft-mounted roller rocker arm. Obviously the shaft-mounted full roller rocker arms represent the upper extreme in strength and reliability. The conventional full roller rockers are the standard in high–performance engines and are generally the way to go for the average racer. If your budget does not permit this, then at least go for the Comp Cams "Magnum" pieces.

Stock Rockers—The stock stamped-steel rocker arms on the 5.0 H.O. are adequate, at best, in a stock lo–po 5.0 engine. Although they are designed as a 1.6 ratio arm, they seldom actually are. I have tested the stock rocker arms and have found them to vary in ratio from 1.45 to 1.66. Now this will really screw up your cam timing and valve lift. Additionally, the stock stamped rockers will flex considerably when subject to high spring rates and high rpm. Probably the biggest limitation of the stock rockers is the length of the rocker slot. Generally, the stock rockers will not take more than about .280" to .290" lobe lift before things start breaking. The rocker slot is just too short to handle the additional lift. You can modify it with a Dremel, but you still have a sow's ear. For any high–performance engine, the stock rocker arms should be one of the first things to go. Just replacing them with a set of the precision cast Comp Cams "Magnum Roller Rockers" can improve the seat–of–the–pants feel of your car.

Roller Rockers—Regardless of how you feel about the rocker arm issue, it would be wise to go with the full roller rocker arms. This will permit upgrading to more radical cams without having to spend money on new rockers at the same time. The difference between the cost of full roller rocker arms and the Comp Cams Magnum rockers is not much and should be seriously considered.

Full roller rocker arms are sold in the conventional rocker stud mounted style, requiring a pushrod guide to keep them centered on the valves. However, if your heads have not been machined for standard rocker studs, Ford SVO and Crane Cams offer a full roller rocker arm that comes with a replacement pedestal

that fits the standard slot on the Mustang head. The Ford units are designed for hydraulic cams only. They require the use of shims under the pedestals to adjust the lifter plunger depth. The shims come in two sizes and are packaged as a kit. The Ford SVO rocker arms are great on the 5.0 engine utilizing the stock hydraulic rollers and the price is reasonable. The Crane Cams rockers have adjustable pushrod seats to set the correct valve clearances. They are more expensive than the Ford pieces but do allow the use of a mechanical lifter camshaft.

Using Higher Ratios—There are several different rocker ratios available for the 5.0 engine. Upgrading your stock 1.6 ratio rocker arms to a higher ratio will increase the valve lift and acceleration rates on your camshaft with a noticeable seat–of–the–pants improvement. However, there are two things to keep in mind when making this change. First, valve guide elongation will increase and reduce the life of the valve guides. Anyone who believes otherwise has their head buried in the sand or someplace more personal. The fact is, the higher the ratio, the greater the rocker tip movement across the valve tip and consequently

increased side thrust on the valve stem. This translates into stress-induced wear on the guide. Any time you increase the valve lift this happens.

The second and most important item to understand is what happens as a result of the change in valve acceleration rates that occurs when using a higher rocker ratio. Increasing the rocker ratio on the stock 5.0 roller cam is not critical. However, making changes to the rocker ratio on racing cams, especially as they get more radical, can cause valve spring failure and lower the valve float rpm limit. Every cam grinder designs their high–performance cams based on a specific rocker arm ratio, typically the factory ratio. For the 5.0 engine, the standard design ratio used is 1.6. The acceleration and de–acceleration ramps of the cam's lobes are designed to work in harmony with valve spring harmonics based on that standard rocker ratio. When the ratio is increased, the harmonics of the valve spring change, which can induce a surging, where multiple harmonics begin to act against one another. These harmonics may manifest themselves by locking the valve in position and dramatically increasing the effort necessary to move the valve. If

When using non-adjustable pedestal-mounted roller rocker arms, you will need to shim the base of the pedestal to achieve the correct lifter preload. Shown here is a Ford Motorsport rocker being fitted with a shim from the Motorsport shim kit (M6529-A302).

severe enough, the surging can cause catastrophic spring failure or even hold the valve open for that up close and personal interview with the piston. Either way, things are not good.

Using higher ratio rocker arms can be great stuff on a stock or mildly cammed engine. However, always consult the cam grinder before making this change. I cannot emphasize this enough. It is far better to select a camshaft that has the additional lift designed in it than using a higher rocker ratio to achieve the same end. *Note:* On some of the aftermarket roller rocker arms that are designed to be used on the stock heads, the rocker geometry will often times not work out right. Never assume they are a "bolt on" replacement.

One last time: Replace the rocker arms on your 5.0 engine. The considerable flex and inconsistent ratio characteristic of the factory pieces hurt the performance of your stock engine.

Precision rocker arms are a must to achieve the maximum output of your engine. Do not compromise here.

VALVE ADJUSTMENT

Once all the bits and pieces have been assembled and all the clearances set, the valves must be adjusted. Follow the cam grinder's recommendations for the initial valve clearance settings. When setting the valves, don't follow the usual approach provided in the Motor or Chilton manuals. The optimum way to adjust the valves is to set the intake valve just as the exhaust valve starts to open. Set the exhaust valve just as the intake closes. Using this method will insure the valve is always on the heel of the cam and thereby eliminate one more variable in tuning your engine consistently.

Valve Lash

Fine tuning the engine with the valve clearances (mechanical cams) is one of the tricks top tuners use to dial in their engines to changing track conditions. Tightening the valve lash increases the effective duration of the cam and in turn softens the low-end torque. Increasing the valve lash will improve the low end at the slight expense of upper rpm power.

Small changes in valve lash have a significant effect on cam timing. Typically, for every .001" change in valve lash clearance, the cam duration changes 3°. Most performance mechanical cams can be tightened up .012" to 014" without problems. However, .004" is pretty much the limit beyond the manufacturer's recommended lash setting. A loose setting places the lifter beyond the acceleration ramps and will cause excessive shock loading to the valve head. The excessive shock loading transmits throughout the valvetrain, hammering the rocker arms, pushrods, and especially the cam and lifters. Loose valve settings that are run too long will adversely affect the durability of the camshaft and lifters. Roller lifters are particularly allergic to loose valve settings. Generally if you have to run the camshaft with an excessively loose or tight setting, you need to try another bumpstick.

Lifter Pre-Load—When using a hydraulic lifter camshaft, it is very important not to over-adjust the lifter pre-load. Pre-loading the lifter pushes the hydraulic piston down into the lifter. As the engine revs and reaches the upper rpm range, the momentary slack that develops in the valvetrain, as the lobe passes its centerline, is taken up by the piston in the lifter. However, at high rpm there is not sufficient time for the lifter to bleed down the additional oil before it must react to another valve opening cycle. Consequently, the hydraulic lifter essentially becomes a solid lifter. Excessive pre-load will mean the piston can travel considerably as it takes up the valvetrain slack, resulting in the valve being held open. Proper adjustment of

Valve Adjustment Procedure

1. Set No. 1 cylinder at BDC.
2. Rotate crankshaft until intake valve just closes.
3. Adjust exhaust valve.
4. Rotate crankshaft until exhaust just starts to open.
5. Adjust intake valve.
6. Move to next cylinder in firing order and start sequence over.

the pre–load is critical to high rpm performance. The amateur engine builder should follow the cam grinder's recommendations. Typically this will require you to adjust the rocker arm, while spinning the pushrod between your fingers, until the pushrod starts to drag. At that point you turn the adjustment in 1/8 to 1/2 turn increments. This should pre–load the lifter approximately .005" to .020". The optimum setting will be determined by your engine's personality and can only be found by testing.

CAMSHAFT BREAK-IN

Installing a new roller camshaft does not require any special break–in procedure. The flat-tappet camshaft is, however, another matter. Since the flat-tappet cam requires the camshaft and the lifter wear a fit much like the rings and cylinder, a very specific procedure must be adhered to. The life of a flat-tappet cam is decided in the first few minutes after the engine is started. Failure to follow the correct break–in procedure will guarantee a camshaft failure. This process is so critical that even when followed correctly, a new cam will sometimes fail during the break–in process.

Those camshafts that are being run with multiple valve springs should be broken in only with the outer spring installed on the valves or a very lightweight spring, say 70 lbs. Spring seat pressures beyond 110 lbs. generally equate to open pressures well into the 300 to 400 lbs. range. High spring pressures create tremendous stress on the cam lobe and lifter face. That stress equates to high heat friction that can break down the temper of the cam or lifter and cause galling. The end result is a useless camshaft and possibly a damaged engine block. I know it is a real pain to have to change the valve springs, but make the effort and save a camshaft's life.

As previously mentioned, do not use synthetic oil to break in a flat-tappet camshaft. It is just too slick for the cam lobe and lifter to wear in. Use a quality racing 30w non–detergent oil.

To provide the best opportunity for a new flat-tappet camshaft to survive, follow these procedures:

Step 1

Pre–lube the engine by spinning the oil pump drive before installing the distributor. A simple speed wrench can generate 60 psi oil pressure so nothing fancy is needed to get the job done. Be sure to spin the oil drive until oil is seen at the rocker arms. Remember when spinning the oil pump that the Ford distributor turns counterclockwise.

Step 2

Before you ever engage the starter, double check all of the components necessary to fire the engine immediately and run continuously for 25 minutes. This includes all electrical, oil, fuel and cooling components and lines. It is very important that everything is right so the engine fires immediately. Camshafts are lubricated from the oil that slings from the crankshaft. Without that oil, excessive cranking can ruin a new camshaft.

Step 3

Once you are satisfied everything is right, fire the engine. Do not let the idle speed fall below 2000 rpm or go beyond 2500 rpm for the next 25 minutes. This is necessary to provide mass quantities of oil to the camshaft. Do not rap the throttle a couple of times to hear that sweet engine sound. There will be plenty of time for that later. Not only will you take a chance on ruining the cam, but if you followed the correct procedure and fitted lightweight valve springs for the break–in, you may float the valves and tap a piston. It happens.

After the break–in, re–check all valve clearances. If you have a valve that requires considerable tightening, you may have a problem with that lobe. Run it for another 15 or 20 minutes and check it again. If it has loosened again, the lobe is probably going flat and the cam is junk.

Do not forget to re–install the inner valves or correct springs if you used lightweight springs. Change the oil to a quality synthetic lubricant, Red Line, Valvoline, Mobil 1, etc. It would probably be a good idea to re–torque the heads after they have cooled, especially if they are aluminum. ∎

If you are breaking in a flat-tappet cam, you must liberally coat it with black moly cam grease. Once the engine fires off, do not allow the idle to fall below 2000 rpm nor go above more than 2500 rpm for the first 25 to 30 minutes. To improve the chances for a successful cam break-in, especially one with fat lobes like this Competition Cams piece shown, run only the outer valve spring on applications with dual or triple springs. (Photo courtesy Competition Cams)

INTAKE & FUEL INJECTION SYSTEMS

5

The intake system on the mass air-equipped electronic fuel-injection 5.0 H.O. engines is state of the art. With the Ford EEC-IV computer managing fuel ratios, the system provides remarkable flexibility, producing high horsepower output with streetability and emissions control. What I would have given for this setup in 1971 at the SCCA runoffs. This may come as a shock, but we owe it all to the environmentalists. Without the constant demand for better fuel economy and cleaner emissions, the Ford EEC-IV would probably not have made it to the passenger car market for some time to come.

Increasing the performance of 5.0 computer engines requires careful and balanced modifications to achieve optimum performance. Proper selection of components, injectors, manifolds and mass air sensors must be balanced with an understanding of fuel flow needs. Simply adding bigger and better pieces without the correct component changes will result in an engine with mediocre performance and poor fuel economy. The Ford EEC-IV computer can correct for some pretty large discrepancies in the

Edelbrock put their reputation on the line with the introduction of their 5.0 intake. As always, they produced an outstanding intake manifold. Sold as a complete upper and lower package, this intake makes a significant improvement in horsepower and torque.

67

fuel system that a carburetor can not handle. However, a stock, properly set up computer can turn your small block into a 500 horsepower Camaro buster.

Unlike carbureted engines, any modifications to the fuel system must be coordinated with the capability and limitations of the Ford ECU computer. A successful Mustang racer will recognize the importance of understanding exactly how the ECU system works. This computer-managed engine system is the most sophisticated ever offered on a production car. During the course of a few milliseconds, the ECU examines the barometric pressure, the inlet air temperature, the engine water temperature, the throttle position, engine timing, engine speed, the intake air volume and the oxygen content in the exhaust, then adjusts the fuel pressure, injector opening pulse, and timing to maintain the optimum settings for the engine operating conditions and speed. Absolutely amazing!

The modifications in this chapter are geared to the EFI 5.0 H.O. engines. The carbureted 5.0 H.O. engine installed in the GT Mustang prior to 1986 is basically just like the legions of other Holley equipped cars. There are volumes of excellent books written on modifying and tuning this type of engine combination and so they will not be addressed in this book.

EEC-IV LIMITATIONS

Although modifying or replacing the EEC-IV computer will be discussed in greater detail in Chapter 7, a brief discussion of its limitations is necessary here before you can proceed with modifying the intake and fuel delivery systems. The pre-mass airflow "speed/density" systems do not handle cam changes very well and typically have idle problems when modifications go much beyond mild. This is a real bummer. However, the only way you can make significant horsepower in your

5.0 with this setup is to go to a separate fuel management system, like the Digital Fuel Injection control, or convert your wiring and computer to a post-'88 factory mass air harness from a salvage car, or upgrade your system with the SVO Motorsport Mass Airflow conversion kit (M9000–A51 manual trans, M9000–B50 automatic trans).

Rpm Limit—Probably the most common complaint on the Ford EFI system is the 6250 rpm redline built into the EEC-IV computer. Don't believe your tach, 6250 is it. This redline was set to keep warranty costs down. Although the hydraulic roller cam is one of the characteristics that makes the EFI engine so desirable, the hydraulic lifters are heavy. Heavy valvetrain pieces mean lower rpm valve float and so the redline limit. Changing this limitation requires either replacing your computer with a racing unit or piggy–backing one of the many systems on the market such as the SVO Motorsport EEC–IV EFI Extender (M12650–A50), Crane Cams Interceptor II, or the Progressive Performance computer control. Again, see Chapter 7 for more details on these systems.

Horsepower Limit—On stock mass airflow systems, horsepower is limited to approximately 330 without upgrading the mass airflow meter. The stock mass airflow meter is calibrated to run 19 lbs-hr. injectors. Since fuel flow equates to horsepower, without the fuel you can not make the horsepower. There are several mass airflow meters on the market that can handle larger injectors. Basically your budget determines the quality of what you get.

One of the wonderful capabilities of this computer managed system is its ability to adjust timing and fuel flow based on the engine's operating condition. However, that same capability can be a real nuisance when your engine temperature exceeds 230°. When this happens, the ECU goes into a low–performance mode and limits timing

advance. This can be very frustrating when it occurs in the middle of a race. Obviously, controlling engine temperature is very important. Maintaining a cool operating temperature is generally not a problem for the drag racer who cools his engine down between each run. Substitution of a 5,500K ohm resistor or potentiometer for the ECT (Engine Coolant Temperature) sensor can also be used to fool the ECU. However, to the road racer, a balanced cooling system that can maintain a constant temperature under all conditions is a must.

MODIFYING THE EFI SYSTEM

The electronic fuel injection system found on the 5.0 engine comes in four different systems. The first system was the low fuel pressure CFI (Central Fuel Injection) throttle body injection found on A.O.D.–equipped '84 and '85 GT Mustangs. It came with two 52 lbs-hr. injectors and used a 38 lph fuel pump located in the tank for fuel delivery. Other than snappy low-speed throttle response and great fuel economy, this system has nothing to offer for high–performance.

The second system is found on the 1986 GT Mustang and was the predecessor to the current system. Fuel management is based on the "speed/density" system. Unfortunately this system has an intake with tiny ports that are unsuitable for high–performance modification. The kindest thing to do is give it to a Camaro owner and replace it with a high–performance manifold or an '87 or newer factory intake.

Beginning in 1987 Ford re–cast the intake and enlarged the ports. This manifold is now standard issue on the 5.0 H.O. engine fitted to the Mustang. It has remained basically unchanged since its introduction. This third intake system, also speed/density managed, was used on the 1987 & 49-state 1988 Mustangs. It is a great system but the speed/density fuel

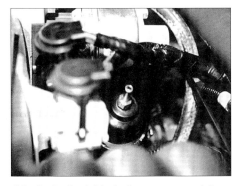

A typical adjustable fuel pressure regulator for the 5.0 engine generally requires the vacuum hose nipple be turned inward to increase pressure. Always make adjustments with the vacuum line disconnected and plugged.

Correct fuel pressure is critical for optimum performance with the EFI engine. One of the finest regulators on the market is the billet aluminum unit from Mallory. Very tough and reliable.

management lacks the flexibility to handle major modifications, such as a performance camshaft.

The best mass-produced system, and the one currently sold on the 5.0 H.O. equipped Mustangs (other than the Cobra), is the Mass Airflow meter equipped EFI system found on the 1988 California Mustangs and all 1989 or newer Mustangs. The 1993 Cobra intake is similar to the GT–40 intake but is made of cast aluminum. The Cobra intake is also the best of the factory-installed intakes, assuming you do not count the Saleen Mustang's intake as a factory system.

Fuel Pressure

Regulating fuel pressure is a key ingredient to developing horsepower in an EFI engine. Unlike a carbureted engine that depends on the pressure differential in the carburetor's venturi to draw fuel into the air stream, the EFI engine must have a constant supply of fuel at a high pressure level. The 5.0 H.O. engine typically has fuel pressure fixed at 38 to 39 psi from the factory. Since the factory fuel pressure regulator can not be adjusted, you must install an adjustable fuel regulator. This is not an option. Proper fuel pressure is critical to performance on an EFI engine.

There are numerous companies that sell an adjustable fuel pressure regulator,

including the one by Kenne-Bell which is installed in the sidebar on p. 70. If you have a Ford dealership nearby, an adjustable regulator can be purchased under the Motorcraft part number E0SY–9C968–A. This is an excellent regulator that has a rear exit for the vacuum line. Fuel pressure is easily adjusted by inserting an Allen wrench into the top of the regulator and rotating it to the desired pressure.

Determining Fuel Pressure—The ideal fuel pressure will differ for each engine combination and personality.

Generally, you can start with a fuel pressure of approximately 41 psi, at idle, for most engines using the 19 or 24 lbs-hr. injectors (with the fuel pressure regulator vacuum line disconnected and plugged, for setting purposes only). Under racing conditions, that pressure may have to be set much higher. This is not set in stone. There are just too many variables to project where the pressure should be set. The size of the injectors, the camshaft, compression and whether or not the intake is pressurized, not to mention the barometric pressure and

For quick reference and ease of fuel pressure adjustment, install one of the liquid-filled fuel pressure gauges in place of the Schrader valve.

INSTALLING KENNE-BELL'S ADJUSTABLE FUEL REGULATOR

by Mark Houlahan

photography by Chuck James

This article is reprinted with the permission of *Super Ford* magazine.

One of the keys to building horsepower is to pack more air into the engine. However, if air intake is increased, fuel delivery must be increased as well. Seeing how Ford fits the 5.0 Mustang with fuel lines the diameter of coffee stirrers and a pump better suited to squirting window-wash solution when it comes to building power, it's highly advisable to modify the fuel system right away. Then you can take advantage of your modifications to their fullest extent, and with less worry of detonation.

Fuel delivery can be increased three ways; with increased fuel pressure, increased injector size or both. All require more fuel volume, so an aftermarket fuel pump is your first step. The extra volume the pump delivers must be controlled, however. This can be done by leaving the stock injectors and fuel pressure in place, which means the "big" fuel pump will perform the important task of keeping the fuel system supplied during momentary spikes of large fuel consumption—something the stock pump doesn't do. Or, an adjustable fuel pressure regulator can be fitted. Then the fuel pressure can be increased, so more fuel is available for building more power. Of course, when you're really making power, you use both increased fuel pressure and injector size.

It is smart to remember injector size should be kept to a minimum, though. Larger injectors certainly help build more power, but idle quality, around-town driveability, emissions and fuel economy all rapidly deteriorate when the injectors get too big. However, you can fool a 24-lbs-hr. injector into acting like a 38 lbs-hr. injector with the aid of an adjustable regulator and still maintain a clean idle and good low-speed drivability. Simply sticking 38-lbs-hr. injectors in your car could help on the top end, but it will barely idle. Using 24-lbs-hr. injectors with a regulator will allow you to drive around with near stock emissions, and when you nail it, you'll get the full regulated pressure to simulate the 38 pounders.

Luckily, adjustable fuel pressure regulators are easy enough to install, as shown in the accompanying photos. After installing the regulator on the car, you need to adjust it. Use the methods outlined in the text to determine the proper injector size and fuel requirements of your engine.

Source:
Kenne-Bell
10743 Bell Court
Rancho Cucamonga, CA 91730
(909) 941-6646

1. This is the billet adjustable fuel pressure regulator available from Kenne-Bell Performance. Nice touches are provision for a fuel gauge or nitrous fuel feed line. While adjustable regulators should require no service, this one is fully rebuildable.

2. Because accessing the fuel regulator involves lifting off the upper intake manifold, the first step is to remove all hoses and linkage from the upper intake. This includes the throttle and AOD TV cables, the three vacuum lines at the rear of the intake, purge solenoid hose behind the distributor, and all electrical wiring plugs such as the EVP and TP sensors. If you are unsure of the location of these items, consult your Ford shop manual for detailed descriptions and removal procedures.

3. After the 5.0 upper intake cover has been removed, the two center intake bolts can be removed.

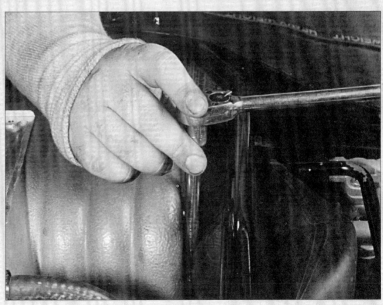

4. At this point, removal of the two front and two rear bolts are all that's necessary to free the upper intake from the lower. If your upper intake has never been removed before, there may be a bracket from the left rear upper intake bolt to the left rear lower intake bolt. This bracket must be removed first and it can be discarded.

continued on next page

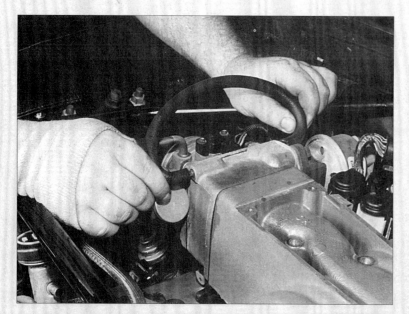

5. Just before removing the upper intake assembly, cover the two EGR cooler ports with a length of hose or two rubber caps to prevent coolant spillage. The two coolant hoses can be mated together with a short length of fuel or brake line to prevent coolant spillage as well.

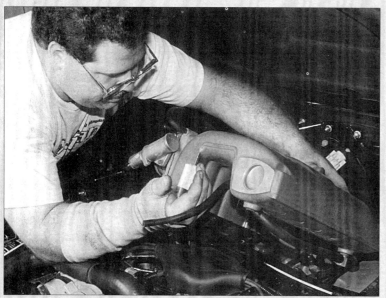

6. Now the upper intake can be lifted off. While our Kenny Brown strut brace did not interfere with removal, your brace may not be so cooperative and may have to be removed first. As soon as the intake has been removed, cover the lower intake openings with duct tape or clean shop rags to prevent foreign objects from entering the engine. Fumble a nut down the intake manifold and you'll be removing the lower intake to find it—assuming you notice the nut went down there in the first place...

7. With the upper intake removed the stock, non-adjustable fuel pressure regulator is plainly visible. Remove the three small allen head screws to remove the regulator from the fuel rail. If you wish, the fuel rail can be disconnected with spring lock coupling removal tools, available from your Ford dealer, and unbolted from the lower intake for transfer to a work bench to have the regulator removed.

8. The Kenne-Bell billet regulator uses the factory regulator's gasket, O-ring, and allen screws for installation. When fitting the new regulator make sure it is completely seated to the fuel rail and that all three allen screws are tight. The fuel pump will run with the upper intake removed, just cycle the ignition key off and on a few times, but do not try to start the car! Without a throttle, the engine would instantly head for whatever redline it could reach. Check for fuel leaks at the regulator and any other area you may have disturbed. If the fuel rail was removed, check the injectors and quick-disconnect fittings. Reinstall the upper intake and all of its related hoses and wiring. Also, momentarily disconnect the battery to clear the computer's memory.

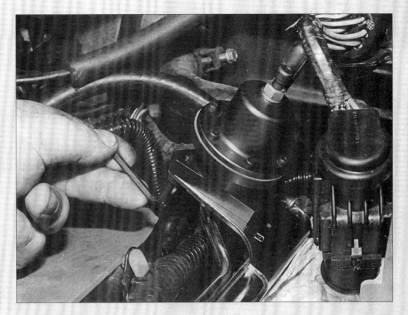

9. Install a temporary fuel pressure gauge and start the engine. To adjust the fuel pressure simply loosen the adjusting bolt's lock nut and adjust the fuel pressure as required. For quick tuning, set the fuel pressure to stock specs (38-40 psi) and then experiment from there. Each engine package will require different amounts of fuel.

10. After the fuel pressure has been set, a deep 7/16-in. socket will fit over the adjusting bolt and can tighten the lock nut without disturbing the adjustment you just made.

One of the simplest ways to improve performance on your 5.0 engine is to install a larger throttle body and EGR plate. The best buy on the market is the Ford Motorsport 65mm unit shown here (M9926-A302). This SVO component has been used on engines producing over 600 horsepower. (Photo courtesy Ford Motorsport/SVO)

High-boost engines generally require a big hole to get enough air into the induction system. BBK has been making oversize throttle bodies and matching EGR plates for some time. Their 75mm unit is one of the most popular on the market for mega-horsepower engines.

temperature, are just a few of the factors that must be considered.

Normally Aspirated Engines— When racing a normally aspirated engine, especially drag racing, it is often necessary to push the fuel pressure to 60 psi or more. Such high levels of pressure can cause problems when the injectors are not sized right, especially at lower engine speeds. Running high fuel pressures to provide sufficient fuel flow on an engine equipped with injectors that are too small will generally cause low-speed engine problems. With a short injector pulse-width, you can expect over-rich conditions or poor off–idle performance. There is a balance that must be maintained between the fuel pressure, fuel flow and injector size in order to achieve optimum performance. This will be covered in the injector section of this chapter.

Supercharged Engines—For those engines running a turbo or supercharger, there has always been a problem

regulating the fuel pressure under boost conditions. Typically you will have the fuel pressure set at idle around the 35 to 40 psi range to maintain low-speed driveability and more importantly, to insure sufficient fuel supply in the critical transition to boost period. Under boost, the fuel pressure that is necessary at idle is multiplied to provide sufficient fuel for the denser air mixture, as well as to override the increased pressure in the intake track. However, as the fuel pressure multiplies (especially on high-boost systems), an over-rich condition often develops. This is fairly common on supercharged engines running larger injectors and the auxiliary fuel management unit that is typically supplied with the kits. Maintaining that delicate balance between the fuel demands at low boost, low engine speed and W.O.T. maximum boost operation can be difficult at best.

However, Vortech Engineering (5351 Bonsai Ave., Ste. 1115, Moorpark, CA

93021. 805/529-9330) now has a kit that includes a new diaphragm plate for the fuel management unit and a small pressure release valve. The pressure release valve screws into the top of the fuel management unit at the vacuum line connection. At the end of the pressure release valve is a small knob that can be manually adjusted to release some of the boost pressure during W.O.T. boost levels. By reducing the boost signal at the fuel management unit, the fuel pressure is reduced. This allows you to fine tune the fuel pressure for the top end.

Throttle Body

The next step to upgrading your fuel-injection system is to replace the stock throttle body and EGR spacer for a larger unit. The factory unit has a 60mm throat (except '86 which was 58mm). The options available that will fit the factory intake vary from 65mm to 90mm. The 65mm unit works fairly well up to the 400 horsepower range and close to 500 horsepower on a turbo or supercharged engine. Beyond this level, the stock block can not handle the horsepower that a larger throttle body can make, so anything larger is a waste. Engines running high boost (10 to 12 psi) can benefit from 75mm throttle bodies when equipped with the Pro–M mass airflow meter. Because a blown engine (which forces compressed air into the intake) is not dependent on vacuum to generate airflow, the larger throat provides less restriction to airflow.

There are custom throttle bodies that are larger than the 90mm units. However, it takes an adult engine and sometimes a custom manifold to utilize anything larger than a 65mm piece, much less a 90mm unit. Since airflow velocity is significantly faster with multiple smaller-bore throttle bodies, most mega–horsepower systems use this approach. Trick Flow Specialties sells an upper intake that fits the 5.0 truck lower intake, which utilizes multiple throttle bodies. This setup requires a pretty radical engine to utilize this much airflow capability. As an example, Brian Wolfe's 9-second Pro 5.0 drag Mustang utilizes a custom-fabricated, twin 85mm system running two 80mm mass airflow meters. It generates around 800 horsepower.

Speed/density-equipped cars are limited to the 65mm units. Without more valve timing than the stock cam, anything larger than the 65mm unit will generally hurt performance. Those cars equipped with mass airflow meters can utilize the larger throttle bodies; however, the low-end throttle response may not be as snappy. On the stock engine, the SVO Motorsport 65mm unit (M9926–A302 & spacer M9474–A50) is the best buy on the market and it is definitely the way to go. BBK sells a 70mm unit that works very well on a well-tuned stock or modified engine. However, the only place you can use the big-throated throttle bodies, 75mm and larger, are on engines built to run high boost, high horsepower nitrous kits, or flat-out racing like the Nevada Silver State Classic. Since the thrust of this book is bolt–on performance for the stock block, stick with the 65mm to 75mm sizes.

TPS—The throttle body utilizes a Throttle Position Sensor (TPS) to relay to the ECU computer the exact opening position of the throttle butterfly. The TPS is a low-voltage potentiometer, where the pre–load is adjusted to determine how rich the fuel mixture will be at low speeds (as voltage increases, the air–to–fuel ratio goes down or enriches the mixture). The factory TPS

is non-adjustable and must be replaced with an adjustable unit from the SVO Mustang or modified so that it is adjustable. The proper adjustment of the TPS is vital to optimizing the fuel mixture at low speeds, especially when the engine has been modified. If the TPS is not adjusted correctly, the engine can develop an off–idle hesitation.

Adjusting TPS—Adjusting the TPS is no big deal. You will need a volt meter that can read low voltages accurately (less than 10 volts at maximum arc), and a safety pin. Just pierce the green wire coming from the TPS with the safety pin and hook the "+" lead from the volt meter to it. Ground the "–" lead from the volt meter to the throttle body. Loosen the two screws securing the TPS and turn the ignition switch to the "run" position. Carefully rotate the TPS until the desired voltage reading is achieved (usually between .98v to 1.5v), then tighten the screws. Sometimes you'll have to loosen the screws and try again, as the TPS voltage will often shift when it is tightened down.

Modifying Stock TPS—The stock TPS can be modified to be adjustable. Use a Dremel with a 1/8" grinding burr and elongate the screw slots approximately 3/16". Try to follow the

Before removing any fuel system component, you will need the correct spring-loc coupler disconnectors. It is virtually impossible to disconnect the fuel lines without them.

The first real high-performance manifold for the 5.0 engine was this modified truck intake from Trick Flow Specialists. With twin 50mm throttle plates, this thing could flow some air.

The most popular manifold on the market today is the GT-40 unit from Ford Motorsport (M9424-A51 upper and M9461-A50 lower). This manifold is the standard that all others are measured against. It is relatively inexpensive and capable of flowing air for engines producing over 600 horsepower. (Photo courtesy Ford Motorsport/SVO)

natural arc of a circle, the radius being the distance the screws are from the middle of the TPS, when elongating the slots.

The exact voltage you adjust your TPS will require experimentation. Fuel pressure, injector size, camshaft overlap and virtually every other engine modification has considerable effect on this setting. It is best to start out with a setting of .998 volts, then experiment. Small adjustments go a long way, so test

in small increments, generally .05 volts. Remember to re–adjust the setting every time you make a significant engine modification.

EGR Coolant Lines

Do not disconnect the coolant lines to the EGR spacer. A couple of years ago, a good friend read a Ford-related magazine article that recommended this, and took it as gospel. No matter how much I tried to explain the reasoning

behind not bypassing the coolant lines, he just could not be convinced. Finally, I had to resort to technology and use a pyrometer to demonstrate the difference in the temperature of the plate with and without the coolant lines attached. The coolant, although hot, is significantly cooler than the exhaust gas that is circulated around the spacer plate for the EGR valve.

Intake Manifold

Replacing and/or porting the intake manifolds should be next on your list. At this time you could publish a complete catalog just on the intake manifolds that are available for the 5.0 engine. What to choose? For my money, there are only three intakes to use on the stock-block 5.0 engine: the SVO Motorsport GT–40, the Edelbrock or the Saleen/5.0 truck lower setup. All are well designed and provide major improvements in performance over the stock pieces, with a slight edge in horsepower to the Saleen intake. They will also handle the demands of a highly modified engine up to approximately 500 horsepower. Beyond this level, a custom intake, or a large port, box plenum (when using a centrifugal supercharger or turbocharger system), will probably be necessary to get sufficient airflow to produce mega–horsepower.

Looking from the side, you can see the straight runners in the Edelbrock base manifold that provide increased torque and horsepower ratings. In this photo, Edelbrock has cut the rear cover off to view the large runners incorporated in this manifold.

The "Breadbox" intakes hit the scene in 1987 when Cartech developed an intake to work in conjunction with their turbo kits. These intakes are designed to work in a pressured induction system (supercharged or turbocharged) at high rpm and generally will not improve the performance of a normally aspirated engine that runs under 6000 rpm.

Aftermarket Intakes—There are other excellent intakes on the market and they generally fall into two significant categories. One group consists of those that are fabricated with runners much like the factory intake (i.e. Performance Resource.). The other group is made up of those that are a box-type plenum that bolts to a 5.0 H.O., 5.0 truck lower, or the GT–40 lower intake (i.e. CarTech, Texas Turbo, Hartman Enterprises, etc.). These two types of manifolds are distinguished primarily by the length of their port runners. The length of the port runner defines the optimum range that the intake pulse will perform. Intake pulse length is a function of engine speed. As the rpm increases, the pulse becomes shorter. Consequently, a shorter runner will be required to optimize the reversion effect that helps to drive the air mixture into the combustion chamber. Long runner manifolds can be expected to generate higher torque figures. The box plenum variety will generally produce horsepower at a higher level.

There is a third group that consists almost exclusively of the Trick Flow multi–throttle body upper intake that fits the 5.0 truck lower intake. However, as noted previously, this system requires a pretty serious engine.

Every manufacturer claims their intake flows as good as the GT–40. Sort of reminds you of the Mercedes commercial where they discuss the constant comparisons to the Mercedes–Benz, then ask the question "Why not get the real thing?" Unless you are running over 475 horsepower and a pressurized intake, where a large plenum generally provides better flow capability, stay with the GT–40, Edelbrock or Saleen intakes.

Porting Stock Intakes—There are shops that port the stock intakes. This provides a significant improvement over the unported pieces. The Extrude Hone process is also used to open up the stock intakes. This process is great and makes the stock intake substantially better.

Now this is a serious intake. Custom-built by Bennett Racing for Joe Rivera, this intake has a unique upper plenum that is welded to the lower intake. Large fuel rails and a 75mm throttle body are necessary to operate the 70 lbs-hr. injectors that will be used with this setup.

A noticeable gain in mid to upper rpm performance can be achieved by matching the intake ports to the heads. Before you fire up the grinder, swab the port exits with layout dye and carefully scribe the limits to be removed.

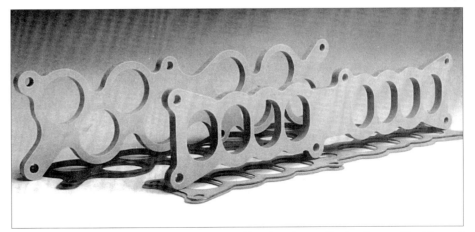

BBK's phenolic spacers insulate the upper manifold from heat, allowing for a colder (denser) incoming air charge, which translates into added power. BBK has them for stock, GT-40 or Edelbrock manifolds. (Photo courtesy BBK Performance)

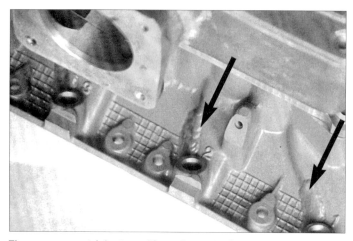

There are many tricks to making a few extra horsepower. Adding material to ports and runners so they can be recontoured can yield noticeable gains. These kinds of modifications should only be done by those with access to a flowbench and a lot of porting experience.

Where possible, always clean up the intake runners and blend any sharp radiuses, as shown on this Cartech "Breadbox" upper plenum.

However, for a little more money, you can buy a GT–40 intake.

Spacer — Regardless of which intake you choose, you should install a phenolic spacer between the upper and lower intake manifolds. (Ford Motorsport M9486–A52 for GT–40, and M9486–A51 for stock manifolds. BBK also has a good one.) This will significantly reduce the heat transferred to the upper plenum. The result is a cooler and more dense air mixture that enters the combustion chamber. Remember, the denser the air, the more oxygen available to handle

increased fuel flow.

Torquing — It is very important to properly torque the intake manifold to the correct torque settings. Over-torquing an intake will pull the heads up and contribute to head gasket failure. Always torque the intake manifold to 24 ft-lbs., following the factory torque sequence (p. 47), and not one pound more.

Port Matching — If your budget does not permit the replacement of your intake, it is very important to at least port-match the lower intake to the heads. This process is also applicable to any

intake fitted to your engine. The process is not difficult and will make a noticeable improvement in performance.

Step 1

Screw four 3-1/2 x 5/16"–18 bolts, with the heads cut off, at the corners of the heads as guides for the lower intake manifold. Use a gasket adhesive (Ford D7AZ–19B508–AA) and glue the intake gaskets to the heads.

Step 2

Scrape any residue off the gasket surface of the intake and clean thoroughly with lacquer thinner. Use a flat sanding block, or a 6" section of 2" x 4" lumber, and lightly sand the head mating surfaces of the intake with 240-grit wet/dry sandpaper. Re–clean the sanded surfaces with lacquer thinner.

Step 3

Smear the exposed surface of the intake gaskets with Prussian Blue layout paste. Slowly lower the intake over the four guide studs and torque to factory specifications.

Step 4

Let sit for 15 minutes, then remove the manifold. Let the Prussian Blue dry completely.

I hate to state the obvious, but take the time to scrape all gasket residue and scale that has formed on the heads and intake mating surfaces. It does not take much to create a leak that can rob horsepower and allow oil to be sucked into the incoming air charge.

Step 5

Use a rotary grinder fitted with a porting burr designed to cut aluminum, and grind the intake port outlets to within 1/16" of the intake port demarcations made by the Prussian Blue. If your engine will be using a supercharger or turbocharger, cut the port exits to within 1/32" of the demarcations. Blend the new port openings at least 2" into the ports.

Step 6

Replace the porting burr with an arbor with a sanding roll of 100 grit. Polish the port openings on the normally aspirated intake to within 1/16" of the Prussian Blue demarcations. This will provide a small measure of reversion pulse control. For those intakes that will be used on engines running a supercharger or turbocharger, polish the port right to the demarcation lines. Reversion pulses are secondary to unobstructed airflow, in the pressurized intake.

Injectors

The amount of horsepower an engine produces is determined by the volume of air that finds its way into the combustion chamber, be it drawn by vacuum or

Adding higher flowing heads, intake manifold and throttle bodies will mean more fuel. The stock 19 lb-hr. fuel injectors just don't cut it. SVO offers these 24 lbs-hr. injectors to be used with the above types of modifications. (Photo courtesy BBK Performance)

forced by a supercharger. However, once the air has entered the engine, it must have a combustible fuel added to it, in specific quantities, in order to create a mixture that will burn rapidly under pressure. The relationship that exists between the air volume and the fuel, or air–to–fuel ratio, is critical to performance. In fact, fuel flow is the most important thing in a high performance engine. Without precise fuel ratio control, the engine's output will be unpredictable and erratic.

In the 5.0 H.O. EFI engine, the fuel ratio is managed by the ECU by regulating the pulse width of the fuel injectors. The pulse width is the length of time the ECU electrically grounds the injector, thereby activating the solenoid that opens the fuel valve in the injector. (Injectors have 12 volts D.C. applied to them at all times after the ignition is turned on.) Injectors used in the 5.0 H.O. engine are activated by the ECU once every other engine revolution in sequence with the firing order, or as each cylinder requires it. This is a very sophisticated fuel management system.

Although the ECU can provide very precise fuel management, it can only inject fuel into the airflow at the maximum flow capability of the injector. Better heads, free flowing exhaust, larger throttle bodies and bigger mass airflow meters all induce more air into the engine and demand more fuel to maintain the correct air–to–fuel ratios. That ratio, typically around 13:1 on a normally aspirated racing engine, can not be maintained if the flow capacity of the injector, rated in pounds of fuel per hour, is too small. Essentially, if the injector is too small, the engine will lean out under W.O.T. operations and begin to detonate, which is most uncool.

Sizing your injectors and fuel delivery system is dependent on the bsfc, as measured on a dyno or calculated with good-old fashioned mathematics.

Flow-Balancing Fuel Injectors

The do-it-yourself hot rodder can test and balance his own injectors using a simple system. You will need five feet of 3/8" fuel line, 2 Ideal 4203 clamps, a graduated measuring cup (found at photo supply stores), 15 feet of 14 gauge wire, four small electrical alligator clips (Radio Shack), a SPST (single pole, single throw) switch, masking tape and a stopwatch or clock/watch with a second hand. Do this test only when the engine is completely cold to prevent a fire hazard should the hose become dislodged. Also observe the usual precautions when dealing with a flammable liquid.

1. Remove the Schrader valve on your high pressure fuel line (right front of the engine).

2. Install a pipe fitting and nipple that will accept a five foot section of 3/8" fuel line.

3. Fit the fuel line to the nipple and secure with an Ideal 4203 clamp. Drape the hose over the right fender.

4. Cut a section of the wire long enough to run from the positive side of the battery or solenoid to the end of the five foot fuel hose. Fit alligator clips to both ends. Cut the wire about six inches from one end and install the SPST switch in series.

5. Attach alligator clips to the ends of the remaining wire and ground one end to the car.

6. Attach a strip of masking tape to each of the injectors to be tested and number them. Remove the O-rings on the fuel log end.

7. Fit an injector into the end of the hose and secure with the remaining clamp.

8. Attach the alligator clips to the two connector spades on the injector, one from the short grounded wire and the other to the long wire with the switch near.

9. Turn the ignition switch to the run position and check for fuel leaks. Correct as necessary.

10. Drape the injector into the graduated measuring cup.

11. With the switch in the "off" position, attach the other end of the wire to the positive battery terminal or solenoid.

12. Turn the ignition switch to the run position. DO NOT START THE ENGINE.

13. Hold the injector in the measuring cup and turn the switch on for exactly one minute. Note the exact amount of fuel that was sprayed into the cup.

14. Repeat the test for each injector. If the results are too close, extend the test time to 3 minutes. When you have completed the tests, turn the ignition off to disconnect the pump. Remove the nipple from the fuel line and re-install the Schrader valve.

15. Compare the results. Try to use injectors that have flow rates that are close to one another. If you have an injector that is more than 3% from the others, replace it. Obviously a deviation of less than 1% is best.

It is important to note that injectors are rated based on their flow volume over a given time span at a specific pressure. Increasing the fuel pressure beyond the designed rate can increase the flow of the injector. However, the pressure required to increase the flow rate (typically double the percentage of flow increase) can adversely affect the operations of the injector. The surging pulses that develop in the fuel log as the injectors cycle magnifies as the fuel pressure increases. This surging can create tremendous turbulence in the fuel flow, and can also create a low pressure state at the injector when the harmonics of the surging gets in sync with the injector opening cycle. Lean conditions and detonation follow.

Pulse Width—Probably the most common problem associated with elevated fuel pressure on an inadequate injector, is the shortened pulse width at low engine speeds. In an effort to maintain the correct air–to–fuel ratio at low engine speeds, the ECU will shorten the pulse width to compensate for the high pressure. When the pulse width becomes very short, there is not enough time for a proper fuel spray cone to develop and poor fuel atomization is the result. Poor fuel atomization means poor low-speed response and maybe even fouled spark plugs. It doesn't take a genius to see the importance of properly sizing the injectors for the intended application.

Sizing Injectors—Calculating the fuel demands of your engine and determining the proper injectors can be very complicated. However, it is possible to use some simplified formulas to determine your basic needs that will get within a tunable range. Before bailing off into the math, you must have a pretty good idea what your horsepower goal is. This is where the racer must be clear about what his expectations are. Living under the delusion that your stock 5.0 engine will make 350 horsepower by simply putting enough fuel in it, via

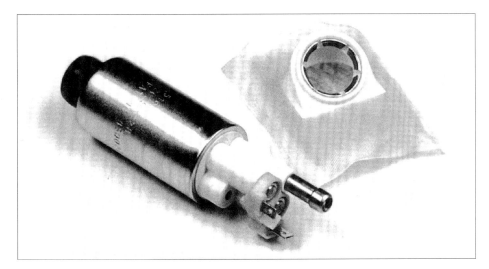

The Ford Motorsport 110 lph fuel pump is adequate for mild bolt-on improvements, such as headers, exhaust kits, and larger throttle bodies.

larger injectors, is ludicrous. You need progressively more radical racing pieces to make it work, so be realistic about your projections.

The simplified approach to calculating the injectors needed for your engine requires that you know the expected horsepower and the fuel efficiency of your engine. These numbers can then be fitted into a formula to determine the injector size you will need. Based on the discussion in the previous paragraph you probably have an honest figure for the expected horsepower of your modified 5.0 engine, say 1,150. Okay, maybe 350 horsepower just to keep the math simple.

The second ingredient, the fuel efficiency of your engine, is expressed in terms of brake specific fuel consumption, or bsfc. Since bsfc is dependent on the horsepower output of the engine and the amount of fuel used to make that horsepower over a one hour period, it can be defined as:

bsfc = lbs. fuel per hour/horsepower

If you had access to a dyno to determine the bsfc of your engine, injector sizing would have already been taken care of. However, since the dyno is for big bucks racers, we'll make an assumption about the efficiency of your engine. Racing engines will have bsfc

numbers from an extremely lean and efficient rate of .45, to a rate of .55 that is more commonly found on supercharged engines (bsfc is typically higher on a supercharged engine to provide an additional margin against detonation). To make the 350 horsepower, your engine will probably need to have at least a .50 bsfc rate. This rate is reasonable to use as a baseline for most high–performance engines. Given these assumptions the required fuel injector can be calculated as follows:

HP = Horsepower
Nc = Number of Cylinders
Injector = (HP x bsfc)/Nc

Example Injector   = (350 x .50)/8
                    = 21.88
                    or
                    22 lbs-hr.

Based on our projection of 350 horsepower and a bsfc of .50 lbs fuel per horsepower per hour, we determine the injectors we need must operate at a rate of at least 22 lbs-hr. However, since injectors are rated at 100% flow capacity, expressed as 100% of their duty cycle, we will need to adjust the number for the percentage of time the injector must be shut down to avoid damage. Running an injector at a flow rate greater than 85% of

its duty cycle will significantly reduce the life of the injector. In practice the injector should not be run at a rate greater than 80% of its duty cycle in a continuous mode, i.e. road racing. Using 80% duty cycle as the standard, we can modify the injector sizing formula to determine our injector needs as follows:

HP = Horsepower
Nc = Number of Cylinders
Dc = Safe Injector Duty Cycle
Injector = [(HP x bsfc)/Nc]/Dc

Example
Injector: = [(350 x .50)/8]/.80
             = 27.34
             or
Injector Needed: 28 lbs-hr.

Now we can take this formula, apply a few basic mathematical axioms, and modify it to easily determine the maximum horsepower capability of any injector.

HP = (Nc x Injector x Dc)/ bsfc

Example Injector (stock): 19 lbs-hr. injector (yellow or tan)
HP   = (8 x 19 x .8)/.50
HP   = 243.2 hp

This example shows the safe extended use range for the stock 5.0 H.O. injector. In practice, most injectors can be pushed to operate at 100% of their duty cycle when used for short bursts, like drag racing. With a well-built and tuned engine operating with an efficient bsfc of .46, the stock 19 lbs-hr. injectors can produce 330 horsepower. However, this will require the injectors be in optimum condition and flow balanced. They will also require regular replacement.

Flow Balancing—One of the old tricks for squeezing the last ounce of horsepower from a fuel-injected engine is putting together a set of injectors that have the same fuel flow curves. This

For more serious horsepower packages producing up to 350, you'll need to upgrade the in-tank pump with a Ford Motorsport 155 lph unit. A newer 190 lph pump can service up to 475 hp.

process, commonly advertised as *flow balancing,* entails taking a bucket full of injectors rated at the same flow rate and testing them until a group of eight (V8 engine) is found that flow within 1% or less of each other. This is done to insure the cylinders will all receive equal amounts of fuel.

The ECU reads the oxygen content in the exhaust gas three times per second, via the oxygen sensors, and adjusts the pulse width of the injectors to maintain the correct air–to–fuel ratio. Unfortunately, the pulse width is an average necessary to correct the ratio and is the same for all injectors. Consequently, if you have an injector that flows only 95% of the capacity of the other injectors, that cylinder will run leaner and probably produce less horsepower. This becomes particularly important on engines that are being run with low bsfc rates. Leaning out a cylinder that is already running lean means detonation, followed shortly by a blown head gasket, holed piston, or possibly a trashed engine. Having an injector or injectors that flow considerably more than the others will also rob your engine of its maximum capability. The average pulse width necessary to maintain a correct air–to–fuel ratio will mean some

cylinders are running rich while others are running lean.

Using injectors that have balanced fuel flow curves will improve the performance of even a stock engine. However, as horsepower increases, the need for balanced injectors becomes more critical. If you intend to produce over 300 horsepower, you should use injectors that have been balanced. If your goal is over 400 horsepower, then you really have no choice—balanced injectors are a must.

FUEL DELIVERY SYSTEM

Next to overcamming an engine, improper fuel pump and fuel line sizing is the most common mistake made by amateur engine builders. Countless engine misfires and failures have been blamed on carburetion and ignitions, when actually they were caused by a lack of fuel volume. You already know the relationship of horsepower to fuel flow from the discussion on injectors. However, if the volume that is delivered to the injectors is below the flow requirements, the ECU will attempt to increase the injector pulse width to provide the needed fuel. This may not be a problem on an engine with injectors that are operating well below their maximum duty cycle. But, when the

Fuel pressure increases proportionally with the boost to compensate for the increased resistance to fuel flow from the injectors. As fuel pressure increases the flow rate of the in-tank pumps takes a dive, requiring an auxiliary pump. Shown here is the industry standard Bosch 15764 pump mounted just under the fuel filter on the author's 400 hp 2.3L SVO.

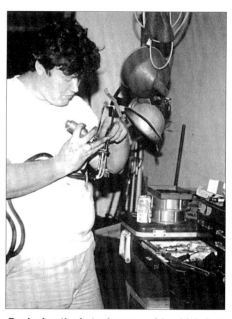

Replacing the in-tank pump with a high-flow Motorsport unit means dropping the tank and removing the factory pump from the fuel pickup. Chris, the friendly giant, is seen here trying to remember why he is doing this at 4:00 in the morning.

injectors are operating at or near 100% duty cycle, the additional fuel needs cannot possibly be met. The results are reduced horsepower output, lean condition misfires and possibly a blown engine.

Fuel Pump

The first item of business when setting up your fuel delivery system is determining the maximum fuel volume your engine will need. This is a simple matter of applying the bsfc rate to the engine horsepower and converting it to gallons or liters per hour. To insure adequate fuel volume under all conditions, you will also need to add a little to cover any tuning changes (fuel pressure elevation) that may occur, typically 30%. You will need to know the liters–per–hour (lph) rate for the in–tank Ford Motorsport fuel pumps and gallons–per–hour (gph) rate for most auxiliary fuel pumps sold in America. Once you know the gallon or liter volume requirements, you can select the correct fuel pump. The formula is as follows:

Fvg = fuel volume, expressed in gallons per hour

Fvl = fuel volume, expressed in liters per hour.

$$Fvg = HP \times bsfc \times .1613 \times 1.3$$
$$Fvl = HP \times bsfc \times .6094 \times 1.3$$

Example — If we take the 350 horsepower engine used as an example in the previous section on injectors, we can determine the fuel volume requirements as follows:

$$
\begin{aligned}
Fvg &= HP \times bsfc \times .1613 \times 1.3 \\
&= 350 \times .50 \times .1613 \times 1.3 \\
&= 36.70 \text{ gph}
\end{aligned}
$$

or

$$
\begin{aligned}
Fvl &= HP \times bsfc \times .6094 \times 1.3 \\
&= 350 \times .50 \times .6094 \times 1.3 \\
&= 138.64 \text{ lph}
\end{aligned}
$$

Based on the calculations above, it is pretty obvious that the standard high–volume 110 liters per hour Ford Motorsport fuel pump (M9407–A50) will be inadequate for this application. Things are further complicated by the fact that the flow rates of all fuel pumps are rated at a specific pressure. The Ford Motorsport 110 lph pump is rated at 38 psi. Increase the fuel pressure to compensate for inadequate injectors or boost conditions, and the flow volume from the pump takes a dive. Always check the flow verses volume limitations of the fuel pump you are considering before you buy. Make sure the fuel pressure you expect to run falls within the fuel flow curve of the proposed pump. If you are running a supercharged or turbo application, use a 200% margin to insure adequate fuel volume. Typically a Ford Motorsport 155 lph in–tank pump and an auxiliary external pump (NOS/Bosch PN 15764) are required to meet the demands of a 5.0 engine running 10 psi of boost. Engines that are more radical will generally require two pumps, mounted in parallel.

When mounting the auxiliary fuel pump(s), it is very important to mount it as close as possible to the fuel pickup. Fuel pumps are far better at pushing fuel than they are at sucking it. On the Mustang, the auxiliary fuel pump will generally be mounted under the car on the flat area, located on the front right corner of the wheelwell, just behind the rear axle. This will put it as close as possible to the fuel pickup. Also, it is a must that the pump be mounted in rubber. Failure to do this will significantly shorten the life of the pump. If your pump did not come with a rubber mount, the rubber shock mounts for the factory airbox on the EFI Mustang make pretty good mounts.

If you are running the in–tank pump only, be sure your battery is charged to the correct level. The factory in–tank pumps require a minimum of 13.2 volts to function at rated flow capacity. A small reduction in voltage will significantly and adversely affect the output of these pumps. This problem can be particularly acute on cars running underdrive pulleys at night. The current draw of halogen lights will require a minimum of 2000 rpm just to stay even.

Fuel Lines

In order to get the fuel to the injectors,

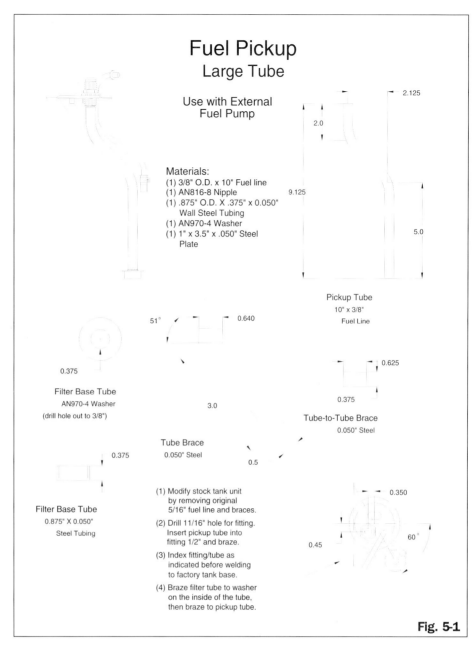

Fuel Pickup
Large Tube

Use with External Fuel Pump

Materials:
(1) 3/8" O.D. x 10" Fuel line
(1) AN816-8 Nipple
(1) .875" O.D. X .375" x 0.050" Wall Steel Tubing
(1) AN970-4 Washer
(1) 1" x 3.5" x .050" Steel Plate

2.125
2.0
9.125
5.0

Pickup Tube
10" x 3/8"
Fuel Line

51°   0.640

0.375

Filter Base Tube
AN970-4 Washer
(drill hole out to 3/8")

0.625
0.375

Tube-to-Tube Brace
0.050" Steel

3.0

Tube Brace
0.050" Steel
0.5

0.375

Filter Base Tube
0.875" X 0.050"
Steel Tubing

(1) Modify stock tank unit by removing original 5/16" fuel line and braces.
(2) Drill 11/16" hole for fitting. Insert pickup tube into fitting 1/2" and braze.
(3) Index fitting/tube as indicated before welding to factory tank base.
(4) Braze filter tube to washer on the inside of the tube, then braze to pickup tube.

0.350
60°
0.45

Fig. 5-1

Fuel Sump

f your car is only run at the drag strip, runs sub-12's and is still using the stock fuel tank, you will probably need to fabricate a rear sump for your fuel tank. Instead of hooking the fuel pickup to the standard in-tank hardware, the fuel lines attach to the fittings in the sump. A fuel pickup sump is necessary to ensure fuel is available to the pickup during the high "g" conditions at launch. Sudden acceleration off the line will drive the fuel to the rear of the tank. If the fuel level is less than 1/2 tank, there is the possibility that the fuel pickup will be uncovered at launch.

An excellent fuel sump pickup is sold by Competition Engineering (PN 4040). Installation of one of these pickups will require the tank be drained and removed. A hole will have to be cut at the bottom rear of the tank for the sump. Then you'll have to take the tank to a radiator shop that welds fuel tanks and have the sump welded in position.

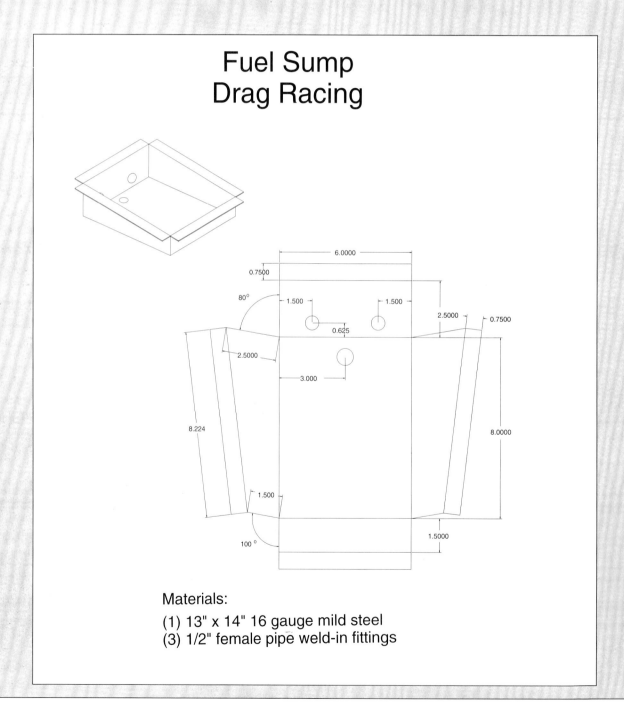

Fuel Sump
Drag Racing

Materials:
(1) 13" x 14" 16 gauge mild steel
(3) 1/2" female pipe weld-in fittings

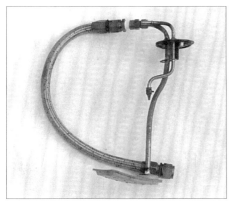

When horsepower moves beyond the 450 hp level, the in-tank fuel pumps will not allow sufficient fuel to be drawn through to feed the injectors. The solution is to fabricate a new pickup per the accompanying drawing that will replace the factory pump and lines.

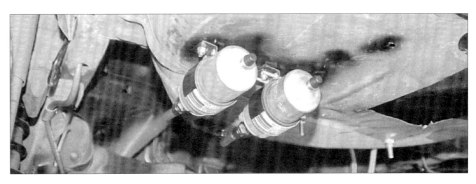

For mega-horsepower drag cars, dual, parallel running Bosch 15764 pumps are necessary to prevent top-end fuel starvation and engine-killing detonation.

the delivery system must include fuel lines that have adequate inside diameter to meet the required flow rates. The stock 5.0 Mustangs have 5/16" outside diameter (O.D.) fuel lines. With a wall thickness of approximately .060", these lines have an inside diameter (I.D.) of about .192". This is a pretty small hole to push enough fuel for your racing engine. The stock fuel lines are generally adequate for fuel flow needs of up to approximately 150 lph. Beyond this flow requirement, the pressure drop that occurs in the small diameter line, when sudden demands are made for fuel, will typically cause a momentary lean condition. At the speeds the injectors are opening and closing, "momentary" may mean a holed piston.

To avoid fuel volume problems, you should upgrade your fuel lines to a 3/8"

inside diameter (AN8) high pressure line for applications expected to generate up to 450 horsepower. Engines generating more than 450 horsepower, especially when operated at continuous high rpm (road racing, Nevada Silver State Classic), will require you to switch to at least a 5/8" line (AN10) from the tank to the pump(s), a 5/8" line from the pump(s) to the filter, a 1/2" line (AN8) from the filter to the fuel log splitter, and a 3/8" (AN6) return line. Mega–horsepower applications will generally require an increase in size of all the lines by an additional step.

One of the problems with the EFI engine's fuel delivery system has always been the fuel distribution in the fuel log on a modified engine. High fuel flow injectors will often cause a problem with those cylinders that are farthest from the fuel delivery line, cylinders 7 & 8.

Under W.O.T. (wide open throttle) conditions, the demands of the injectors closest to the fuel delivery line can cause enough of a pressure drop that cylinders on the fringe will run lean. You already know what the relationship between lean and detonation means. To rectify this problem, it is very important to feed the fuel to the rear of the fuel log.

Installation Tips—Run your new and larger fuel delivery line to the rear of the engine to a "Y" design splitter block. Use only the machined billet aluminum type splitter blocks sold by Aeroquip, Russell or Earl's. The block should have a 1/2" pipe thread inlet and two 3/8" pipe thread outlets. Use a Dremel to polish the sharp edges from the interior machining. "AN" type should be used exclusively to connect your fuel lines to the fuel block, budget permitting. Connect the lines from the "Y" fuel

For road racing or sub-12-second quarter-mile E.T.s, most sanctioning bodies require the stock fuel tank to be replaced with a safety fuel cell.

For the Mustang that is geared for straight-line acceleration, the Racer Components fuel cell with the built-in rear sump is the hot setup. This fuel cell will provide considerable peace of mind and comes with the requisite dual pickups for a mega-motor car.

AN FITTINGS

There is considerable confusion about what the "AN" number means for designating the size of hoses or fittings. ("AN" is the old Army–Navy numbering system originally used for military hardware.) The "dash number," the number that immediately follows the part designator, determines the inside diameter of the hose or fitting. For example, AN815–6 is a male union for 3/8" flared tubing. The "815" is the part number and the "–6" is the "dash number" size identifier. To convert the size identifier to inches, simply divide the dash number by 16. The inside diameter of aviation hoses and fittings, as designated by the dash number, are expressed in 16ths of an inch.

AN flare fittings use a 37° seat angle and are not interchangeable with standard automotive/hardware type flare fittings. The automotive/hardware type flare fittings have a 45° seat angle. Do not flare tubing that will be connected with aviation "AN" type fittings with a standard automotive flaring tool. Most metals "work harden" as they are bent, especially steel or aluminum tubing. The 45° seat angle of conventional tubing flaring tools will either crack when tightened in the aviation 37° seat angle or will crack shortly thereafter. You may not detect the crack when you install the tubing or a crack will occur at the worst possible time. Sometimes the 45° flared tubing, particularly steel tubing, will not seat correctly on the 37° seat and a leak develops. Either way, the result could cause a high pressure fuel leak on a hot engine. Not only is the ensuing fire hazardous to your health, but your favorite race car becomes toast.

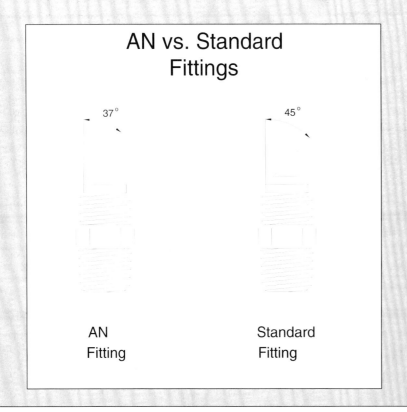

AN vs. Standard Fittings

37°   45°

AN Fitting   Standard Fitting

block to the two ends of the injector fuel log at the rear of the engine with a compression coupling. For the more industrious, the larger 351W truck fuel log can be adapted. The key to this setup is providing optimum fuel volume to both ends of the injector's fuel log.

For those engines running beyond the 450 horsepower threshold, you'll probably want to consider stepping up to a high volume fuel log. Beyond 450 horsepower, the demands of giant injectors can exceed the storage capacity of the stock fuel log and a lean condition can occur. If you have access to the tools, you can fabricate a larger fuel log without a great deal of difficulty. However, they are readily available from several vendors at a reasonable price.

When selecting replacement fuel lines, be sure to use a continuous (one piece) line. Everywhere there is a coupling, the fuel has to deal with changes in the diameter and direction associated with a coupling. The aircraft-type stainless-steel braided high pressure hoses sold by Aeroquip, Earl's and Russell are definitely the way to go.

To reduce heat absorption in the fuel system, cover the fuel lines under the hood and all areas of the fuel line that pass closely to a heat source with Aeroquip "Firesleeve." This red hose slips over the fuel lines (and spark plug wires too) providing an insulator against the heat. If your budget does not have room for this stuff, slip a loose fitting neoprene fuel or heater hose over the fuel line. Loose fitting is important. The real insulator is the air gap between the cover and the fuel line so do not go for a tight fit.

When installing new fuel lines under the car, be sure to route them to the outside of the subframe and subframe connector, if installed. Note that some race sanctioning bodies require the lines to be routed to the inside of the frame rails. Check before you install them. Use aviation Adel clamps (MS21919) every

12" to secure flexible lines and every 18" on metal lines. Routing the lines in this fashion will reduce the exposure to drivetrain heat and provide some measure of protection to the lines in the event of a catastrophic clutch, transmission, or driveshaft failure. This precaution could also prevent a fire.

It is very important to use aviation type tubular line fittings to connect the lines to the fuel tank pickup, pump(s), filter and fuel logs. These fittings are designed to maintain a constant inside diameter and have smooth bends to provide low resistance to liquid flow. The typical 3/8" inverted–flare brass elbow, purchased at your local hardware or auto parts store, will have an inside diameter of only 1/4" and a very sharp right angle turn that has been drilled from both ends. Compare that to an AN type connector (aviation), with an internal diameter that closely matches the I.D. of the hose and a long generous bend, and you'll understand. Large fuel lines are pretty useless if the fittings used to connect them have small inside diameters or sharp bends. See the sidebar on p. 86 for more information.

Fuel Filter

Increased fuel flow requirements mandate that the fuel filter be upgraded. If you have ever changed your fuel filter, you have seen the tiny 1/4" inlets and outlets. Obviously, there will be significant flow restriction at this size. When upgrading your fuel filter, you should look for a filter that has large inlets and outlets, typically 1/2" pipe thread or an AN8 flare fitting. The filter must be designed to operate at high pressure levels, generally 100 psi for safety.

Recommendations—There are numerous high-quality fuel filters on the market that will filter the fuel. However, it is very important to make sure the filter can handle the flow at the projected fuel pressure. This is critical. Just because a

If you are running one of the small drag-race fuel cells that fits through a hole in the spare tire well, NHRA and IHRA will require a metal bulkhead between you and the tank. An acceptable solution is shown here on David Pederson's beautifully built 10-second Mustang.

filter is advertised to flow 100 gph (gallons per hour) does not mean it will flow 100 gph at 60 psi. One of the popular Fram filters advertises it will flow 90 gph. However, if you read the fine print that flow rating is at .5 psi of pressure. Check before you buy.

Do not use cheap inline plastic filters. They just will not provide sufficient flow volume. In addition, they typically lack the ability to filter the very fine particles necessary to avoid damaging or clogging your injectors. Fram and Mallory offer filters that can trap very small particles (10 microns) and have replacement filter elements. Accel has a stainless steel, throwaway, inline filter, with 3/8" female inverted–flare fittings, that can trap particles as small as 5 microns. The slickest filters are the inline, machined billet aluminum pieces offered by Bo Laws and Russell. These things can withstand tremendous pressure with very high fuel flow rates. Regardless of what your budget will permit, you must run a filter. Injectors don't cotton to trash in the fuel.

MASS AIRFLOW METERS

Mass airflow meters provide

information to the ECU on the amount of air flowing into the engine. The Ford-built, Bosch-type meter measures the change in voltage drop in a heated wire that is affected by the velocity of the incoming air stream. This gadget is the cat's meow for making horsepower in an EFI engine. When the throttle is jammed to the floor, the ECU ignores the usual signals and relies on the signals from the mass airflow meter to adjust fuel and timing requirements.

The stock 5.0 H.O. mass airflow meter has a 55mm throat and is therefore very restrictive. The stock unit can be bored out to approximately 60mm and will provide a small improvement in performance on a stock engine. However, no significant improvement to horsepower can be made without upgrading the mass airflow meter to a larger unit.

Aftermarket Meters

There are numerous manufacturers of larger replacement mass airflow meters. All claim to have the best unit on the market. In reality, they all seem to work pretty well. The real key to performance improvement lies in the throat diameter. For a stock engine, the bored-out stock

On an EFI engine, an upgrade or installation of a large mass air meter is essential for developing real horsepower. The 55mm stock mass air meter is just too restrictive to allow significant horsepower improvements. The Auto Specialties 75mm billet aluminum mass air meter is a real bargain. It uses the stock mass air electrics and requires no modification to the computer to run properly.

Recognized as the standard, the Professional Flow Technologies Pro-M meters come in 77mm or 81mm throat diameters. These are calibrated for specific injector sizes, consequently if you change to a larger or smaller injector than originally calibrated for, you must send the meter back to Pro-M for resetting.

meter seems to provide the best performance. Obviously Ford did their homework when they designed the original unit. The 70mm unit found on the '93 Cobra is calibrated for the 24 lbs./hr. injectors and should provide a significant improvement in performance.

Testing the numerous larger meters on the market (Auto Specialties 75mm, C & L 73mm, and Pro–M 77 & 81mm) has demonstrated a general rule–of–thumb: the greater the throat diameter, the better the modified engine will run. To that end, the only meters on the market worth considering (cost no object) are the Professional Flow Technologies Pro–M meters. The Pro–M comes in two sizes, 77mm and 81mm. The 77mm meter is the industry standard and comes calibrated for 19, 24 or 30 lbs-hr. injectors. However, Professional Flow Technologies will re–calibrate your meter for any injector size you wish to run.

For the mega–horsepower engines, the Pro–M 81mm meter is the trick unit. This meter is designed to run a minimum injector size of 40 lbs-hr. and can be calibrated for the giant 70 lbs-hr. injectors commonly found on 9-second cars.

AIR TEMPERATURE

Maintaining a cool, dense airflow to the engine will significantly improve performance. The underhood air temperatures can be extremely high, especially on turbo and supercharged engines. It is not uncommon to see underhood temperatures in a Mustang around 200° under racing conditions. Heated air contains less oxygen by volume than cool air and consequently cannot use as much fuel per cubic inch. This translates into less BTU for each combustion incident and of course, less horsepower. No doubt you have experienced the difference in the performance of your car on a cool day.

Air Filters

Modified intake systems that use air

It's hard to beat the factory for a correctly balanced fuel system. The new Ford Motorsport 70mm Mass Air Induction Kit (M9000-C52) with computer, 24 lbs-hr. injectors and 70mm mass airflow meter will significantly improve the performance of your 5.0 engine.

filters attached directly to the mass airflow meter will draw air from the hot underhood area. This setup is commonly seen on Pro–M mass airflow-equipped cars sporting a cone-shaped K & N filter. That giant Pro–M hanging out from an engine meter is an awesome sight. However, sucking hot air defeats some of the benefits of this setup, and can contribute to detonation. Even though it looks really cool mounted under the hood, the best approach is to use the under fender mounts and keep it out of the hot air.

If you are running a cone-shaped air filter attached directly to your mass airflow meter and are intent on keeping the mass airflow meter mounted in that position, at least fabricate an airbox to cover and seal the air filter so it draws air from under the fender. That cooler air can mean a 10 horsepower advantage on the top end.

Always run a quality air filter, with K&N being the best choice. Not because of the usual need to keep dirt out of the mass airflow meter and engine, but because a well-designed air filter will also straighten the airflow. A straighter airflow has less turbulence. Turbulence can cause the mass airflow meter to improperly interpret the air volume and therefore affect optimum performance. This is particularly acute on engines using a stock airbox.

This very clean and fast '89 LX belonging to Paul Jannes typifies the well-balanced approach to performance. A GT-40 intake with 24 lbs-hr. injectors, drawing through a Professional Flow Technologies 77mm Pro-M and K&N filter, make this pony scream.

Ram Air Kits

Keeping the air cool can also be enhanced by adding one of the several ram air kits that are available for the Mustang. Street car kits for the LX model Mustangs typically fit under the front valance and route cool air to the airbox or directly to the mass airflow meter filter. Texas Turbo offers a slick, molded ABS plastic ram air kit for the GT Mustang that fits in the right fog light hole. This kit comes with the molded plastic ram cone for the fog light hole, a hose, and a tight-fitting molded plastic plenum that replaces the air silencer. I have tested this particular kit at Texas World Speedway at speeds in excess of 150 mph and found it to significantly improve top end horsepower.

For the drag race crowd, there is also a ram air kit that replaces the right headlight. It's an excellent kit, easy to install. It can also be easily removed for the drive home from the track.

AFTERMARKET EFI SYSTEMS

For those individuals with deep pockets, the ultimate ride can be built using one of the Haltech or Accel/DFI fuel management systems. Ken Duttweiler incorporated an Accel/DFI system on the 748 horsepower engine used to propel the CAR CRAFT COBRA 200 project Mustang Cobra to over 200 mph. This system worked flawlessly, while feeding the demands of this monster at 18 lbs. of Vortech boost. If speed and power are what you want, one of these trick stand–alone fuel systems (and a SVO block, crankshaft and rods) is the hot ticket. ∎

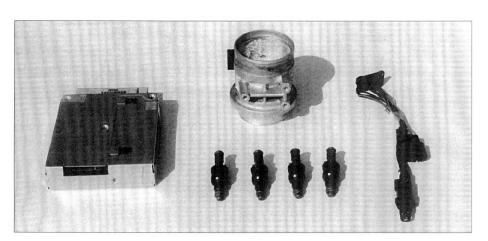

If you are an SVO Mustang driver, this is the kit you have been waiting for. Esslinger Engineering has developed a mass air conversion kit that allows the use of huge injectors while maintaining complete driveability. This is the greatest thing since synthetic oil.

EXHAUST SYSTEMS

6

Once the first combustion mixture has been ignited, the exhaust takes over and plays a major role in the engine's power curve. Until recent years, the factory exhaust systems were simply conduits designed to get the spent combustion mixture out the back of the car with the least amount of noise. As the demands for more efficient engines have increased, the exhaust systems have become more sophisticated on American production automobiles. Due to the high cost of fuel in Europe, the typical exhaust system on cars manufactured there have always sported far more "engine friendly" systems. You don't have to look very far on a new car's exhaust to see things that would have been considered racing stuff a decade ago. Tubular header-type exhaust manifolds and large free-flowing mufflers are pretty standard now. The current exhaust found on a new 5.0 H.O. Mustang is better balanced and generally superior to those found on some of the best high–performance cars of the past. However, there is power to be gained in that mass of exhaust tubes.

Since the theme of this book is

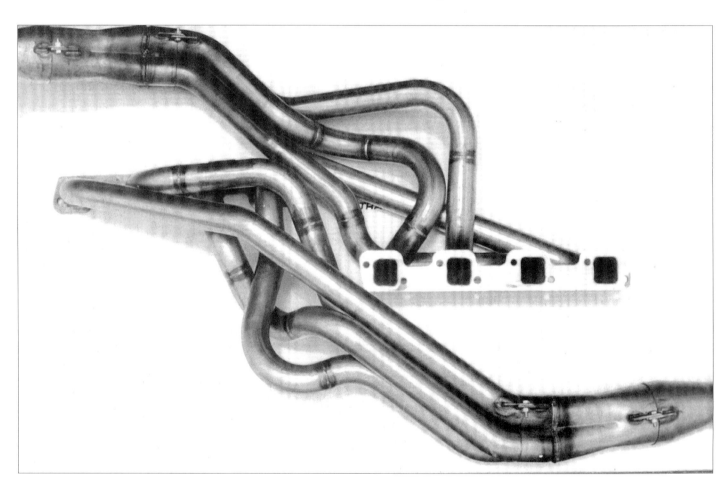

Equal length long-tube headers are required for racing applications to achieve maximum horsepower and torque. This well-made set of 1-3/4" primary tube race-only headers from Steeda Autosports will significantly improve the performance of a modified 5.0 engine, especially when running high rpm. (Photo courtesy Steeda Autosports)

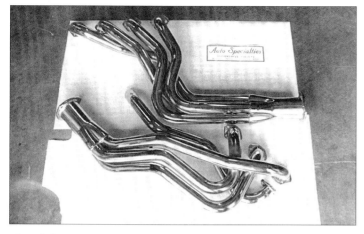

One of the most popular headers on the market is the MAC long-tube set. These headers are well made and simple to install. MAC offers a complete front-to-rear bolt-on exhaust system that can be installed without a trip to the muffler shop.

If you are trying to extract every ounce of horsepower possible from your engine, a properly located crankcase vacuum system installed in the header collector can provide a noticeable torque gain on the big end. These setups use the vacuum generated by the exhaust pulse to draw the pressure in the crankcase created by the rotating mass of the crankshaft and pistons.

improving performance on the 5.0 Mustang, we will look at the exhaust goodies that are currently available and some tricks on how to maximize the proper combinations. Today, there are a zillion headers, H-pipes, catalytic converters, mufflers and exhaust systems available to the Mustang owner. Most systems are pretty good and some are even legal. However, choosing the wrong combinations will do more damage to the performance of your car than the restrictive stock system.

UNDERSTANDING EXHAUST FLOW

The moment the exhaust valve opens, a pulse wave, traveling at the speed of sound, starts out the exhaust port. Whenever that pulse wave passes through a change in pipe diameter, a second negative or "dilution" wave is created that travels back up the exhaust pipe until it reaches an impassable obstruction (closed valve) or another change in pipe diameter (the throttle venturi opening), and reverses again. This pulse–reverse pulse process continues until the pulse energy is dissipated or converted. By designing an exhaust pipe with a length that will allow the dilution pulse to pass through the exhaust valve opening just as the valve closes, the incoming intake charge can be

snapped into the combustion chamber. With a properly tuned exhaust, the dilution pulse will continue, past the combustion chamber, moving through the intake valve opening into the intake track, and create a third pulse that will energize the incoming intake pulse. Basically this process pulls the incoming intake charge into the combustion chamber.

Tubing Length

Determining the proper exhaust tubing length for a specific engine speed can be pretty complicated, but very important to understanding how an engine responds. Although simplified, some basic rules can be applied that will get you in the ballpark. The basic formula for determining the pipe length for a given engine speed is:

Ecd = Gross Exhaust Cam Duration (expressed in degrees at .000" lift)
Epl = Exhaust Pipe Length (expressed in inches)
$Epl = (Ecd/360) \times (277,500/rpm)$

For an example, let's use a camshaft with 278° gross duration and an engine speed of 6000 rpm:

$Epl = (278/360) \times (277,500/6,000)$
$Epl = 35.72"$

This formula can be used to graph the basic pipe length necessary for a range of engine speeds. Since engine speed is used as a denominator in the above formula, it can clearly be seen that as rpm goes up (denominator increases) the pipe length shortens. The reverse is also true as engine speeds drop. Unfortunately the range of lengths are pretty significant. In the above example engine, a pipe length of nearly 86" is necessary to match the dilution pulse length to the example engine at 2500 rpm. Obviously there is considerable difference between the pipe requirements at low rpm and high rpm. This is where the word "compromise" really becomes important. It is also interesting to note that it takes a big change in cam duration to affect a change in the pipe length.

Although you can create additional dilution pulses by using stepped primary pipes, megaphones, collectors, and collector extensions, a set of headers can only be expected to function well in a vary narrow rpm range. This is why you'll see most long tube headers for the 5.0 designed with a pipe length of around 32" to 46", including the collector.

Tubing Diameter

Given the primary tube length and the engine speed, the optimum tube diameter can also be calculated for any engine.

The formula is as follows:

Ppd = Primary Pipe Diameter (expressed in inches)

Ci = Engine size (expressed in cubic inches)

Ppd = $\sqrt{(Ci \times 1900)/(Epl \times rpm)}$

For an example, let's use the 5.0 engine (302 cubic inches), running at an engine speed of 6000 rpm, that has an exhaust pipe length of 36":

Ppd = $\sqrt{(302 \times 1900)/(36 \times 6,000)}$
Ppd = $\sqrt{2.656}$
Ppd = 1.630 or 1 5/8"

Taking the calculated data we find our 5.0 engine, running a 278° exhaust lobe at 6000 rpm, requires a 1-5/8" dia. tube approximately 36" long for optimum dilution pulse utilization. Big over-simplification. Bends in the tubing, slip joints, welding protrusion and intake track design also cause reversion pulses that complicate the process. Bundle a group of cylinders together, add a collector or collector extension and things really get difficult. However, two basic rules of thumb generally apply: (1) the larger the primary tube diameter, the more narrow the powerband; and (2) the shorter the primary tube length, the higher the rpm the optimum powerband falls.

Headers that are designed for the street car are, unfortunately, generally based more on installation convenience that performance. Even those that are well designed are typically built to improve power at street operating engine speeds. True racing headers must perform in a very narrow powerband and are generally poorly suited for a street car with a stock or mildly modified engine. This is most often seen when the owner of a mildly tuned 5.0 Mustang goes for the "real power!" and installs a set of big-tube headers, only to discover his car does not run any faster in the quarter

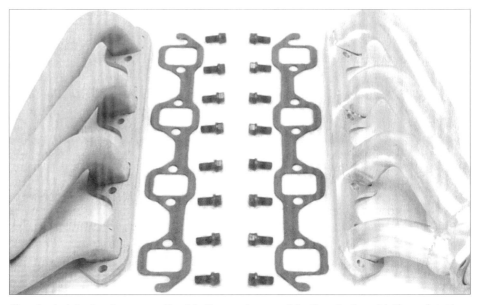

The shorty tube headers are a direct bolt-on replacement for the stock restrictive exhaust header. These things are manufactured by dozens of companies. The headers shown are the stainless (M9430-SSC) and ceramic-coated (M9430-C50) pieces from Ford Motorsport. These headers are well made and easy to install. (Photo courtesy Ford Motorsport/SVO)

mile, or worse, it runs slower. Again a balanced approach to performance is essential for optimum engine output.

HEADER SELECTION

For the 5.0 Mustang, the first step in header selection is dependent on the intended use of the car. If your car is a trailered race car, the long-tube headers are the only way to go, unless class rules specify differently. Several companies mass produce long-tube headers that provide a fair compromise for the 5.0 engine running around the 6000 rpm limit. MAC, Hedman, Hooker, Cyclone and several others all sell headers that fit this group.

Typically, mass produced, long-tube headers come in either 1-1/2", 1-5/8", 1-3/4" or even 1-7/8" primary pipe diameters. If your engine is basically stock, stick with the 1-1/2" tube size. The smaller tube size will provide better cylinder scavenging and exhaust flow acceleration than the large-tube variety. Modified, normally aspirated engines running Ford hydraulic roller lifters or the stock computer (6250 rpm redline) will usually benefit from the 1-5/8" diameter primary. Running tube

diameters beyond 1-5/8" should be reserved for the supercharged or mega-horsepower engines. The giant tube headers may look awesome, but if your engine is not on the radical side, they are a major waste.

Custom Headers—Unfortunately, for serious racers running engine speeds above 6000 rpm or for road racing applications, optimum exhaust scavenging can only be found with custom-built headers. Header selection is also complicated when using a scattershield. Fortunately, craftsmen like Ron Saddler in Houston, Texas, understand the exhaust cycle and can build custom headers that will fit your exact engine needs. Perfection is a very time-consuming process. Consequently you can expect to spend 2 or 3 times what a mass-produced header costs for a set of custom headers. However, for high horsepower applications, custom headers are mandatory. The resulting performance gains are well worth the cost.

Street Legal

Purchasing headers for the street car boils down to a matter of legality. Presently the only headers that have an

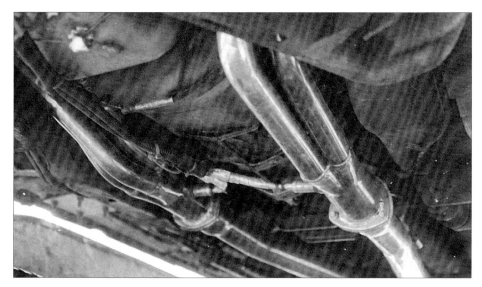

If you are running long-tube headers, it is important to wrap the oxygen sensor wires with a heat deflector and secure them up out of harm's way. The extreme heat generated by a racing exhaust system can bake the wires and cause the insulation to exfoliate.

EO exemption are the "Shorty" tube type. These come in several designs, including equal length, as well as different tube thickness, size and material. For the money, the stainless and ceramic-coated headers are the best choice. The hype about "equal length" is pretty insignificant at these tube lengths. The number and severity of the bends in the tubing are far more important. The Ford Motorsports SSC headers and the aftermarket clones of this design are probably the best bet if you want to keep your car street legal.

Texas Turbo — Although still undergoing emissions testing, Texas Turbo offers an outstanding long-tube header kit that uses ball socket couplings and provisions for oxygen sensors. The primary tubes are 1-3/4 and well made. These headers come with an H–pipe that is offered in a racing only version and a catalytic equipped version. Both H–pipes are built of 3" diameter tubing,

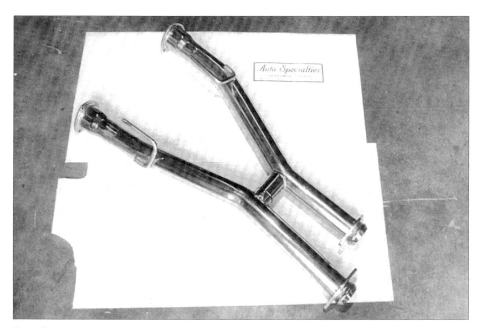

The off-road-only header pipe can provide very noticeable improvement in performance at the race track. Pictured is the racing-only H-pipe from MAC that is designed to bolt up to their long-tube headers.

including the catalytic converters. Also included in the kit are connector pipes to hook up the mufflers. I have tested these headers and highly recommend them. Hopefully this trick header kit will soon have an EO number and be 50-state legal.

H-PIPES & MUFFLERS

The H–pipe is one of the necessary evils that are seldom designed correctly on a high–performance machine. The factory unit is burdened with four (incredible) catalytic converters. You can seriously hurt yourself just picking one of these things up. Unfortunately, if your car is driven on the street and has less than 50,000 miles on it, you can not replace your stock H–pipe with anything but a factory duplicate—this is federal law.

However, if your speedometer shows 50,000 miles or more, you can legally upgrade your street exhaust system to a large diameter H–pipe (3" is good) and the Hi–Flow Thrush 3" catalytic converters. The difference in performance is nothing short of amazing. Add on a set of the 3" Walker Dyno–Max mufflers with 2-1/2" outlets connected to 2-1/2" tailpipes and you've got the best street-legal exhaust system currently available. For guys who like loud exhaust, the Flowmaster mufflers will also work well. Since dyno tests show very little, if any, difference between the two mufflers in back-pressure, I recommend you stay with the more quiet units. This will keep the neighbors and local police off your back.

For the trailered 5.0 Mustang that is required to run mufflers, the H–pipe should be made of 3" tubing all the way to the mufflers when running the "Shorty" design headers. It is important to note that a single 3" pipe will flow more air volume than two 2-1/4" pipes. Obviously, mufflers with the least amount of backpressure are the order of the day. The Flowmasters are the best choice here. Three inches in and three inches out. Instead of tailpipes, the muffler outlets should be fitted with constant radius, mandrel-bent 45° elbows that turn down in front of the axle tubes.

When running full-length headers on a Mustang that is required to run mufflers, use an H–pipe that is the same diameter as the collector. Again extend the H–pipe back to the mufflers with inlets and outlets of matching diameter. Don't forget the short elbows at the muffler outlets. I've seen numerous race cars running high–flow mufflers without a tailpipe or turndown. This is not smart. The exhaust exiting the mufflers at racing engine speeds is extremely hot. Not only does it heat up the differential, but it can actually boil the fuel in the gas tank. Most experienced road racers have lost a collector pipe extension, at some point in a race, where the exhaust blasted rearward. Along with the increased cockpit noise, drivers typically have experienced reduced engine performance and may have even been "black flagged" for a possible fuel leak. That fuel leak is generally the boiling gasoline seeking refuge on the other side of the gas cap. Boiling fuel is uncool as well as "undense," and will result in a major loss of performance.

Crossover Pipe

When fabricating the H–pipe, long, smooth radius bends are very important. Although a pipe may be mandrel-bent with constant radiuses, a bend still creates backpressure and hurts flow. A crossover pipe is also very important in an H–pipe. It must be two sizes smaller than the diameter of the H–pipe (i.e. 2-1/2" on a 3" pipe) and properly located. Properly located? Yes, followers of the hot rod faith, the location of the crossover pipe can affect performance.

Location—Calculating the correct location for the crossover pipe involves some interesting fluid dynamics formulas. However, since most hot

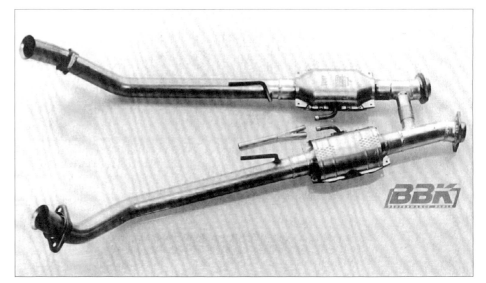

BBK's 2-1/2 inch H-pipes and equal-length headers, manufactured in-house, are popular with the street performance crowd. The headers are 50-state legal, while the H-pipe is 49-state legal with California approval pending.

The Flowmaster muffler has become the standard for durable high performance exhaust. Manufactured of heavy gauge steel, this muffler will outlast the average turbo muffler. They are famous for the throaty sound that is music to a hot rodder.

94

The finest quality racing mufflers made are the stainless steel pieces from Borla Performance, Inc. Shown here are the new generation XR-1 racing mufflers. These are tough and quiet without sacrificing horsepower.

A significant improvement in torque will occur with a properly sized and located crossover pipe. The crossover pipe should be approximately two pipe sizes smaller than the header pipe and located where the exhaust pulse changes direction as noted in the text.

rodders are more interested in racing than doing math, a simple and effective method is available to solve this often perplexing problem. Simply paint a stripe down each side of the unfinished H–pipe (no crossover pipe yet) with a non-high–heat paint (a crayon will also work). Make a couple of high-speed passes and look at the paint stripes. You will find a point where the paint is burned. This is where the exhaust pulse changes direction and is the exact location for the crossover pipe.

Collector Length

This paint trick also can be used to determine the proper length of the collector on a set of headers being run open. Instead of paint, use a crayon. Draw a stripe down each side of the collector and make a high-speed pass. Cut the pipe off about 1" beyond the point where the crayon stripe is burned. Make another high-speed pass. Check the location of the crayon burn to determine a more exact final cut. Note: If you change a major component in your engine or the rear axle ratio, you will probably have to weld on a new extension to the collector and run the test again.

When a crayon is not available (it happens), you can read the exhaust pulse in the collector to determine the proper length. Just wipe the inside of the collector clean and make a high-speed pass. Look inside the collector for a white ring. Measure the distance from the white ring to the collector opening. Cut the collector off half the distance and run the test again. Repeat the process until the white ring is exactly at the end of the collector.

EXHAUST ODDS & ENDS

One of the things that robs horsepower is a leaking header gasket. When installing headers or new header gaskets, be sure to soak the header and collector flange gaskets in water for 6 to 8 hours before they are used. This will improve their sealing ability and significantly extend their lives. Also spread a small

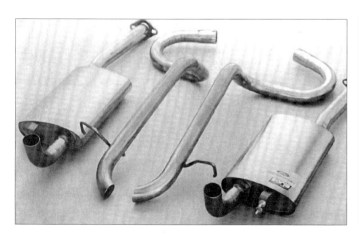

The Borla replacement muffler and tailpipe for the GT Mustang will add 15 horsepower to most high-performance turbo mufflers. These mufflers are more expensive than the standard steel muffler initially; however, they will last longer than your car.

Since all racing sanctioning bodies generally require some sort of muffler in most classes, for drag racing, the single chamber Flowmaster shown is the slick setup. These are illegal on the street but they do meet the minimum requirement for racing.

bead of Hi–Temp RTV silicone around the port outlets on the gaskets. Again to improve the exhaust seal.

When racing a pressurized intake, turbo or supercharged engine, disconnect and plug the vacuum line to the EGR valve. High boost conditions can cause the valve to surge and spoil the incoming intake charge.

One of the tricks drag racers use when running turbocharged engines with more than 6 psi of boost is to disconnect the oxygen sensors on EFI engines. Due to the slow reaction time of an oxygen sensor, a mid–throttle lean condition can occur that will hurt the E.T. There is also the danger of a reversion pulse or pop developing that can flatten the fins on the turbo's compressor wheel or even cause it to shear off at the shaft base. This is an expensive experience that will not produce a win light. ■

Keeping your car emissions-legal means catalytic converters. The premium cats are made by Thrush Industries. They come in all sizes and provide little or no backpressure.

COATINGS

No doubt you have seen the advertisements from HTC and Poly–Dyn concerning the high–tech ceramic coatings available for exhaust system components. These coatings are very durable and add a great deal to the look of the engine compartment. However, their heat insulating qualities are the prime reason for their use. Headers coated with this stuff will substantially reduce underhood temperatures.

This is not the real story though. The experienced engine builder knows what happens to new headers after they have been run and sit overnight or until the next race weekend. They rust inside. Big deal you say. Just fire the engine up and everything is cool, right? Wrong! Anyone who has ever performed engine testing on a dyno over a two-day period has seen the horsepower loss that occurs when a set of headers sits overnight and gets a light coat of rust inside. Typically you can expect a 2% to 3% loss in horsepower from the rust that forms overnight in a new set of headers. Give the rust a few days in a humid climate and things really go bad. One day you're competitive, the next you're a "backmarker." The moral of the story: If you are going to spend money on coating your headers, have the inside coated first, then if the budget permits, coat the outside. Scratch off one more variable that screws up consistency.

Wrapping headers with fireproof cloth or tape will significantly reduce underhood temperatures. This can be especially important when running nitrous where the exhaust pipes have been known to get so hot they glow red. Unfortunately the extreme heat generated by the exhaust system will generally burn the carbon from the tubing steel and extensive radial cracking will occur. This cracking is particularly prone at bends in the tubing. Although very effective for reducing heat, wrapping your headers will significantly reduce their lives. The money would probably be better spent having the headers ceramic coated. They'll certainly last longer.

COMPUTER & IGNITION SYSTEMS

7

The Ford ECU computer, called EEC–IV, is what makes it all happen in the 5.0 engine. The factory computer and ignition systems on the 5.0 H.O. Mustang are very good. They are capable of handling major modifications without a lot of attention. However, like any high–performance engine, these components do require maintenance to properly perform. As horsepower levels move past the 350 mark, the stock components begin to lose their effectiveness. Fuel ratio management, rev limits, and spark management all become a problem. Complicated though it is, the computer engine management system can easily be modified to correct these limitations.

IGNITION SYSTEM

Whether your engine is stock or highly modified, the ignition system's performance is critical to optimum engine output. The stock ignition system is generally adequate up to about 350 to 375 horsepower, provided it is in excellent condition. If your engine has more than 30,000 miles on it, or has been operated in the South where 100° summer temperatures are the norm, you will need to replace the plug wires, distributor cap and rotor.

Cap & Rotor

The factory distributor cap and rotor are manufactured of thin plastic with aluminum terminals. They are the favorite choice of the bean counters since they are cheap to manufacture. However, you get what you pay for. The factory pieces are prone to oxidation corrosion on the aluminum terminals. No doubt you've seen the chalky white buildup that forms on the inside of your distributor cap's terminals. This stuff kills your ignition spark. Even a very thin layer of oxidation significantly increases the resistance to current flow. Resistance produces a voltage drop that converts the electrical charge into heat energy. In plain language, your spark begins to change from a strong blue to a weaker yellow.

All the major aftermarket ignition component manufacturers sell replacement distributor caps and rotors. Stay with the name-brand stuff, such as

Ionization of the air inside a high voltage ignition system is often the culprit behind a high rpm misfire, though few diagnose it correctly. The cure is to have an escape for the ionized charged particles inside the distributor. Factory ECU-controlled cars come with a vented distributor cap. Be sure any replacement cap has this feature.

MSD, Accel, Mallory and Jacobs. Buy only those components that are made with alkyd resins and brass terminals. These high-grade components will significantly reduce ignition stray as plugs and plug wires begin to deteriorate under racing conditions. This is particularly important for the road-racing engine where extended exposure to heat over a long race tends to break down the plug wires.

Terminal Care—Once you upgrade your cap and rotor, it is very important to regularly (before every race) service the terminals. If there are signs of blue–green corrosion on the terminals, scrape or sand them to clean brass, then polish with a red scouring pad. Even if you do not see any corrosion, polish the terminals with the scouring pad. Often times you will notice a black tint to the terminals. This is oxidation tarnishing that happens to brass. Like the white corrosion on the aluminum, the black residue resists current flow and reduces the voltage necessary to deliver a hot spark. Polish it clean before racing.

Do not switch to the old-style one-piece distributor cap because of a lack of room. Find a way to use the wide gap cap. The ignition stray that occurs in the narrow radius cap is several times greater than the late series wide cap. This is particularly important on high-compression engines or those running forced induction. Electrical current is very lazy. It will always take the path of least resistance. Consequently, if you have a plug wire that is starting to break down or a plug that is becoming marginal during a race, the narrow cap will make it easy for the spark to jump to a less resistive path. This can be very ugly if it happens to be on cylinder 6 crossfiring to cylinder 5. A split cylinder can result.

Ionization

One of the problems early aircraft engine builders discovered was the persistent misfire that occurred in the magneto ignitions as engine speeds and altitude increased. After considerable head scratching, it was discovered that the air inside the magnetos was becoming saturated with stray positive ion particles. Since the magnetos were sealed, there was no way for the ion particles to escape and consequently the

spark was jumping all around inside. This phenomenon is also a problem for a high–performance 5.0 engine. Most high–performance distributor caps for Ford ignitions now have a small opening to vent the ion particles. Generally you will see a small oblong cap on top of the distributor cap. If you don't see it, you will need to replace your cap with one sporting this design or modify the lower cap adapter.

To provide an ion vent, you should drill two 3/8" diameter holes near the base of the distributor cap adapter. These holes should be at least 2 terminals apart. Be sure to chamfer the edges with 240-grit sandpaper to reduce cracking. This modification is generally suitable for drag racing where the race car is not subjected to the elements for very long. If you are road racing, you'll probably want to stick with a distributor cap that has the ion port. The open holes in the adapter cap can allow sand and grit to enter the distributor that could damage the bushings over a long race.

Spark Plug Wires

The factory spark plug wires are excellent when new. However, constant exposure to high temperature breaks down the conductive carbon cores. As the cores break down the resistance to current flow increases. Eventually the cores crack or become so resistant to current flow that the spark seeks a simpler path, and arcing occurs. This problem becomes particularly acute on engines that have superchargers or nitrous oxide. The high cylinder pressures provide considerable resistance to the spark bridging the plug gap. Couple this with elevated underhood temperatures and things really go bad fast.

Determining if your plug wires need replacing is not always easy. Electricity is one of those Voodoo things that can fool you. For high–performance operation, generally you can apply the

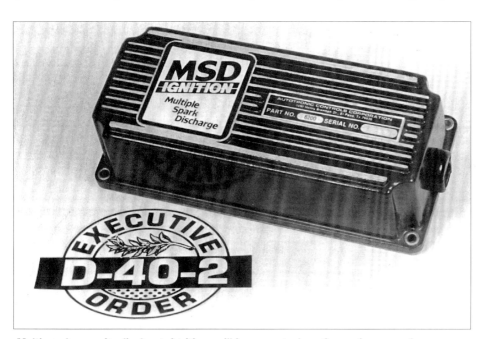

Multi-spark capacity discharge ignitions will improve stock engine performance; however, they are mandatory for supercharged or nitrous engines. Autotronic Controls Corporation is the current leader in ignition technology and makes the popular MSD 6A multi-spark module shown. (Photo courtesy Autotronic Controls Corporation)

The ultimate high-performance ignition setup for the street motor with a supercharger is shown here: MSD 6 BTM multi-spark module, Ignition Supply Monitor, RPM Module Selector. (Photo by Michael Lutfy)

following rules to make your decision:

1. If your plug wires have more than 30,000 miles on them, replace them.

2. If you can hear or see spark arcing, replace the wires.

3. If, in a pitch-black environment (moonless night without light), you can see a blue corona glow on any of the wires, replace them.

4. If, in a pitch-black environment, you touch the wires and you see a blue corona form around your finger tips, replace the wires.

5. If you hook an ohmmeter to each end of a plug wire and find the resistance changes as you draw the wire through your hand, replace the wires.

6. If your car is equipped with the factory wires and you are making more than 350 horsepower, replace them with a name-brand set of spiral-wound racing wires.

Recommendations—When replacing the plug wires on an EFI engine, it is imperative that the replacement wires be either original equipment factory wires or competition spiral-core wires. Current flowing through a wire creates a magnetic field around it. If that magnetic field is of sufficient strength it can induce current flow in an adjoining wire. This is the principle on which the alternator operates. Unfortunately, the sensors that the EEC computer depends on to operate are easily influenced by stray magnetic fields. Obviously if the sensors are affected by anything other than their

design function, the data supplied the computer will cause the wrong fuel and timing adjustments. The end result is less than optimum performance.

With few exceptions, most aftermarket plug wire sets are junk. They typically do not have the spring band connectors and the boots are rarely vulcanized to the wires. The new Ford O.E.M. wires are adequate when new. However, spiral-core performance wires are the only way to go. Typically they are made of high temperature silicone and use monel wire that is wound around a glass core, hence the reference to "spiral wound." When buying a set of these, don't listen to the hype from the local auto parts counterman about how their wires are just as good as the racing wire sets. As with any of the ignition components, stick with MSD, Accel, Mallory, or Jacobs.

For the serious racer running high-boost systems, the MSD 7 series ignition module is a must. This stand-alone ignition can be used to control timing and spark control on engine using the stock ECU or a stand-alone fuel injection such as the HyperTech system.

fire sequentially, any magnetic field-induced current flow, or *crossfire*, in the plug wire for number 5 plug can cause pre–ignition. If you have a plug wire inducing current flow in the plug wire of the cylinder that fires next, be it crossfire or magnetic induction, that cylinder will experience pre–ignition at a point equal to 90° plus the timing advance, typically 22° to 45° BTDC. That equates to the piston running head-on into an explosion at about 112° to 135° BTDC. When combined with forced induction devices like nitrous oxide or a blower, crankshafts will break or cylinders will split. Either way, you end up with a basket case of parts. Take the time to separate your wires and keep them that way.

Installation—It is very important to install your plug wires with at least a 1/2" of space between each wire and between the wires and anything metal. No matter how good your wires are, they will generate a magnetic field. That magnetic field will bleed off electrical energy onto other wires and metal objects, so keep them apart.

Plug wire separation is very important on the EFI 5.0 H.O. engines in cylinders 5 & 6. (Older 302w's use a different firing order that requires attention to cylinders 7 & 8.) Since cylinders 5 & 6

If you are running an engine with forced induction or your car is road raced, you can significantly improve the life of your plug wires by covering them with Aeroquip "Firesleeve." This is a fire-resistant sleeve used by the aircraft industry to protect fuel lines from heat and underhood fires. It can provide considerable protection from the baking

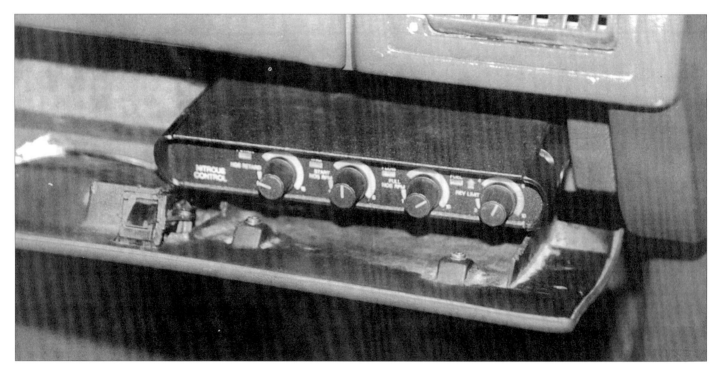

If you are running nitrous oxide, it is imperative that ignition timing be retarded as the nitrous is activated to prevent detonation. The Jacobs Nitrous Mastermind is one of the slickest controls on the market today. It allows for full adjustment when the nitrous solenoids open, the rate they open as well as ignition timing.

High voltage is a necessary characteristic of the modern racing ignition system. Joe Rivera is shown here teaching a class how to properly test a high output coil.

that occurs to the plug wires under high boost or nitrous applications. It is a must for the road-racing engine where underhood temperatures are high for extended periods. The championship-winning cars built by Jack Roush use these sleeves.

Ford sells a white dielectric grease (PN: D7AZ–19A331–A) that can significantly reduce voltage loss at electrical connectors. I highly recommend it. You've probably seen it inside a wiring connector and considered it to be a messy pain. However, it not only reduces current stray, but also helps to prevent corrosion of the connector terminals.

Multi-Spark Discharge

One of the most significant improvements you can make to your engine's ignition system is a capacitive discharge module. These systems typically generate a much more intense spark which makes for better flame propagation at ignition. The trick setup is the multiple spark discharge module. This type of ignition add–on stores energy that is used to fire the plug several times during the ignition cycle. The results are superior flame propagation and improved performance, especially on engines with forced induction or nitrous oxide.

MSD—Virtually all major high–performance ignition component manufacturers sell a capacitive discharge ignition system. However, the Autotronic Controls "MSD" modules are the best currently available. For the 5.0 Mustang, the MSD 6A or MSD 6AL (MSD 6T for road racing) with the wiring harness adapter (PN 8874) is the hot setup. This system fires the plug several times over a

20° span. Even a stock Mustang will notice an immediate performance improvement with the MSD module.

Engines running forced induction systems must have a stronger ignition system. The high cylinder pressures generated by a blower or nitrous oxide will blow out the typical combustion flame without an ignition spark enhancement. The industry standard for blown engines (supercharged or turbocharged) is the Autotronic Controls MSD 6 BTM. This module is basically the MSD 6AL multi–spark discharge module with an adjustable ignition timing retard that is activated by boost. It has a small control with a knob for setting the number of degrees the ignition will retard per pound of boost. Very slick.

Running N_2O—Using nitrous oxide also requires a hot spark. The stock

Aluminum heads and steel spark plugs do not mix well. Besides the natural electrolysis deterioration that occurs, overtorquing can cause the plugs to seize in the threads. The next time the plugs are removed, the threads in the head come with them, seriously damaging the head. Always use a good anti-seize compound on the plug threads to reduce the potential for damage.

ignition system is generally adequate for nitrous systems up to 150 horsepower. Since the nitrous system operates much like a normally aspirated engine, an ignition timing retard is necessary to optimize its performance as well as to protect the engine from detonation damage.

There are two basic types of timing retard controls available to the nitrous junkie. The simplest and cheapest approach is by installing one of the manual timing retard controls such as the MSD Timing Control module or the Jacobs Opto–Timer. Each allows you to retard your timing, via a knob, when you are ready to race (the knob can be located in the car's interior for easy access). These basic controls are generally adequate for nitrous kits up to 100 horsepower. Beyond that, you'll need a more sophisticated multi–step ignition retard control, such as the MSD Multi–Step Retard module, Jacobs Nitrous Mastermind, Hypertech Nitrous Power module, or the Crane Interceptor II.

Installation—There are two things that are very hard on electronic modules—heat and vibration. When mounting an ignition add–on module, such as the MSD 6AL, it is important to place it so there is a cooling airflow across it. Heat is deadly for electronic components, so always mount them away from hot exhaust manifolds. The best approach is to locate them in an airstream or duct air to them. The footings on the module should be insulated from the attaching structure with rubber to reduce vibration. If your module did not come with rubber mounting insulators, use the mounting insulators for a factory airbox.

Coils

The factory EFI coil produces a spark with about 30,000 volts of pressure behind it. This is over 150% of the output of a pre–electronic ignition coil. With this capability the stock coil is excellent and generally does not require replacement until horsepower moves past the 375 range. If your car is equipped with a capacitive discharge add–on module, the stock coil can handle close to 500 horsepower. Aftermarket high–performance coils typically produce 40,000 volts and should be the first choice when the coil must be replaced. Again, stay with the top high–performance ignition component manufacturers. I have had the best luck with MSD and Accel coils. However, there is very little difference between any of the top units, so go for the best price.

Spark Plugs

The factory spark plug heat range is adequate for a stock and mildly tuned engine. The plug gap should be about .045" for the high–performance street car. When a blower or nitrous is added, you will need to drop down one heat range on the plugs (ASF32) and reduce the gap to about .035", depending on the level of boost or how much nitrous is being added. This is not absolute and will require reading the plugs to determine what is actually needed. However, it will get you in the ballpark.

Installation Tips—Always use an anti–seizing compound on the threads of

The factory coil on ECU/EFI systems produces 30,000+ volts and is generally adequate for engines producing up to 375 horsepower. Above this level the stock coil will generally overheat and go south for the duration of the race. The Accel EFI coil shown here is an excellent choice for high performance or competition use.

the plugs when installing them in an aluminum head. There is a low-voltage electric current flow that is generated between dissimilar metals, particularly aluminum and steel. The fact that the head is the grounding agent for the ignition just makes the problem worse. However, it's the long periods of sitting that are most harmful. The corrosive low-voltage current flow will attack the aluminum head and create a bond between the metal spark plug and the aluminum threads. When the plug is removed for service, the bond between the threads will tend to pull the softer aluminum from the head. After a short while, an expensive and, often times, inadequate repair must be made. Anyone who has ever used an anti-seize compound can attest to the mess it makes. One small dab can somehow find its way to everything within a 50-yard radius. It can be a pain to use, but it can also save an expensive set of heads.

Indexing Plugs—One of the interesting things you learn while testing an engine on the dyno is how the little things make a difference. I had heard the direction the gap faced was important but was really surprised at just how much it affected horsepower. While dynoing a 450 horsepower Boss 302, I played with the plug gap direction. Much to my surprise, I found an additional 7 horsepower by properly indexing the plug gap!

Although each head design is different, generally the 5.0 Ford responds best when the plug gap is facing just right of center toward the exhaust valve. Setting the index requires a plug washer kit (Moroso PN 71900) and an indexing base (Moroso PN 62160). The plug washer kit contains .060", .080" and .100" copper washers. The indexing base is simply a wide radius nut that is used as a base to adjust the index. Use the procedure outlined in Fig. 7-1, p. 104 to correct your plug index.

Since the copper washer is soft, there

will be some compression and additional rotation. You'll probably have to experiment a little until you get the hang of it. The results are worth it. *Warning:* Never allow the ignition to fire without grounding the coil wire to the frame or without a spark plug installed and grounded in each plug wire. Forcing a high voltage ignition to fire without a path to ground can damage the coil or computer and can cause the distributor cap and rotor to carbon track. None of these things are good. It is best to always make sure the plug wires are connected or there is a spark plug installed in the plug wire before you fire the ignition.

COMPUTER MODIFICATIONS

The factory EEC-IV computer is capable of handling modifications that will produce horsepower up to approximately 375 horsepower on a normally aspirated engine. Beyond this level the 6250 rpm rev limit comes into play. With a nitrous, supercharger or turbo system, the stock computer will work fine as long as the proper fuel and timing retard management units are installed. The only limitation is the 6250 rpm rev-limiter. Without forced induction, you will need a piggy-back computer interface system to generate more than 375 horsepower.

Crane's Interceptor—Crane Cams' "Interceptor" has been the standard for piggy-back systems. This add-on system fits between the EEC-IV computer and wiring connector and intercepts the data from the sensors, hence the name Interceptor. Don't waste your money on the original Interceptor as it had lots of problems. It has been replaced by the new "Interceptor II" series. Like the original Interceptor, the new unit has provisions to set the air-to-fuel ratios, rev limit and ignition timing.

The Interceptor II uses a keypad to make various adjustments. Fuel can be

adjusted in 2% increments and timing in 1° steps. There are three data sets that can be programmed separately for different driving conditions. Each data set has provisions for adjusting the fuel mixture at idle, mid-throttle and W.O.T. The keypad has a liquid crystal screen that provides information on such things as air-to-fuel ratio in the exhaust, injector pulse width and timing. You can even make adjustments as you are driving the car.

For the more serious racer, there are a few electronic wizards around who will convert your Interceptor II to function from a laptop computer for a very modest fee. This conversion provides maximum adjustability, but it is serious overkill for the average racer.

Ford's Extender—Ford Motorsport has a new piggyback unit they call an "EEC-IV EFI Extender" (M12650–A50). This system was designed by Ford's computer whiz, Sam Guido. You might remember him as the guy who designed the electronic engine management system used by Brian Wolfe on his low 9-second Pro 5.0 Mustang. The new Ford Extender is the slickest thing on the market for the 5.0 H.O. engine. It is very simple, with only two switches to deal with. One sets the W.O.T. fuel mixture and the other sets the rev limiter. Fuel mixture can be adjusted from a rich ratio of 9.5 to a lean state of 14.1 in increments of .25. The rev limit can be set beginning at 6500 rpm to 9300 rpm in steps of 200 rpm. There is also a 13,000 rpm setting for engines using other means of ignition control.

Before you freak-out wondering why Ford built the Extender without multi-step adjustability and several data sets for different driving conditions, think about how the Ford EEC-IV computer works. The Ford EEC-IV computer is state of the art, bar none. When coupled with a mass airflow meter, the Ford computer has no rival in managing fuel

Indexing Plugs

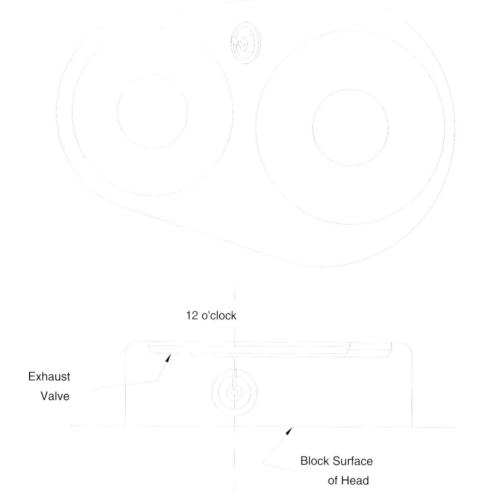

12 o'clock

Exhaust
Valve

Block Surface
of Head

1. Mark a line on the side of the spark plug's ceramic
   body indicating the open gap.
2. Screw the plug into the head and note the approximate
   degrees past the 12 o'clock position the mark is located.
3. Screw the plug into the indexing base and note on the
   index where 12 o'clock position should be in relation to
   plug in the head.
4. Select the thinnest washer that will allow the plug to
   screw in, under normal torque, and stop at the 6
   o'clock position.
5. Note on the plug the cylinder for which it was indexed.
6. Follow the previous five steps for each plug.

Fig. 7-1

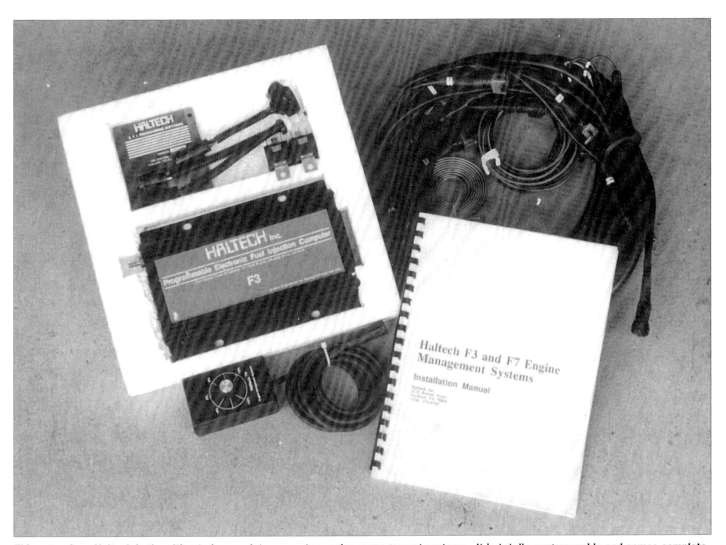

This setup from Haltech is the ultimate in complete computer engine management systems. It is totally programmable and comes complete with all wiring and controls.

at anything less than W.O.T. The stock EEC–IV's only limitations have been fuel management under W.O.T., timing retard for forced induction systems, and the rev–limit of 6250 rpm. Since racing is done mostly under W.O.T. conditions, the only fuel mixture adjustment needed is at W.O.T. The Extender covers this function perfectly. The rev–limit adjustment speaks for itself.

For those engines running super-chargers, turbos and nitrous, a timing retard module is the way to go no matter which system you choose. The Ford Extender does not have the slick crystal monitor and keypad of the Interceptor II and requires a screwdriver to make the adjustments. However, it is considerably cheaper and works extremely well.

There are those who believe they can set the fuel curve at less than W.O.T. better than the computer and mass airflow meter. It is also important to note that the Ford Extender was designed by the people who build the EEC–IV computer (Ford) and, of course, they have full access to all the PROM codes. For the money, this is the way to go. Some pretty fast people have been using this system. Gene Deputy has been running the Extender for over a year in the low 8-second world and he's an electronics engineer. Nitrous Pete and the 1993 Saleen World Challenge cars also use the Extender. Pretty good testimonials. For more details, see the sidebar on p. 106.

For those individuals with deep pockets who want the ultimate ride,

Accel/DFI has an engine management system that can handle the rigors of mega–horsepower engines. Ken Duttweiler used this approach on his 748 horsepower engine used in the CAR CRAFT COBRA 200 buildup. This fuel management system worked flawlessly at 200 mph, feeding the demands of a small-block Ford running 18 lbs. of boost.

Sensors

The Ford computer does its magic based on input from several sensors. Optimum performance can only be achieved when those sensors are functioning properly. If your car is high mileage, then you will probably need to budget for the replacement of several of them.

105

FORD'S EXTENDER

by Earl Davis
photography by Earl Davis and Mark Houlahan

This article is reprinted with the permission of *Super Ford* magazine.

"Control" accurately describes the best and worst of Ford's powerful EEC-IV engine management system. The powerful on-board computer dictates ignition timing, issues synchronized fuel delivery commands and manages several emissions systems with the speed and accuracy of a mission to Mars. As a result, fuel mileage is good, emissions are minuscule and every Ford performance enthusiast benefits from EEC's precise control, which builds horsepower, and especially torque, through efficient fuel and spark delivery. Without EEC-IV, the vintage 302 would never have evolved into the high-tech, high-performance 5.0 HO.

On the other hand, reprogramming or modifying EEC-IV software to enhance engine performance is of course desirable, but persuading the fourth-generation EEC to safely relinquish some of its control is not easy.

This is precisely why SVO developed an adjustable piggy-back computer with the help of Ford's Electronic Engineering Division—the original developers of the stock EEC-IV—and marketed through SVO's network of Motorsport dealers. Called the Extender (PN M-12650-A50), this auxiliary processor extends the capabilities of the host computer, enabling the tuner to alter the engine's air/fuel ratio and to override the preset high rpm limit. As piggy-back computers go, the Extender is fairly limited, but this can be a good thing. Operation is relatively simple, reducing the chance of making an engine-blowing mistake, and the cost is comparatively low.

Essentially, the Extender intercepts the commands generated by the EEC-IV, modifies the signal, then sends the altered signals to the fuel injectors. Those electronic commands dictate injector pulse width or dwell time; the length of time in milliseconds each injector remains open. The longer the pulse width, the more fuel delivered to each cylinder. Conversely, a short pulse width reduces fuel volume.

Naturally, adding or subtracting fuel without changing the amount of air passing through the engine changes the air/fuel ratio. From Ford, 5.0s are set to run at stoichiometric , the chemically ideal air/fuel ratio of 14.7:1 for pump gas and three-way catalytic converter-equipped cars. However, when power levels increase, this ratio is on the lean side. An ideal A/F ratio for power production is about 12:1 or 12 parts of air to one part of fuel. Maximum economy lean is around 15:1, which can be used only under light cruising conditions.

EEC-IV also controls the 5.0 engine's rev limiter. Ford sets this at 6250 rpm, which may not get the job done at the track. Plus, if you have traditional breathing mods such as heads, intake and cam, you'll need more rpm to take advantage of them. The Extender allows resetting the rev limit all the way to a Formula 1-like 13,000 rpm with the twist of a screwdriver.

The Extender is designed to work with any 5.0 Mustang factory equipped or retrofitted with mass air. That would be any 1988-94 California V8 Mustang or all Mustangs since 1989 or any EFI V8 Mustang equipped with a M-9000-A51/B50 SVO Mass Air Conversion Kit. The Extender is not compatible with the pre-1989 (1988 California) speed-density computer system, but the Extender is compatible with F-150 trucks equipped with a 5.0 or 5.8 liter engine which have been upgraded with a Motorsport M-9000-T50/T51 Mass Air Conversion Kit. And because the Extender is capable of generating air/fuel mixtures incompatible with Federal clean air standards, it is intended for off-highway use only. A tuner can dial in an optimum A/F ratio while at the track, then return to the factory setting before leaving for home.

Who needs an Extender? Pretty much anyone with a stock or modified 5.0 HO. A performance camshaft will traditionally broaden an engine's power curve, which means the engine will make more power at either end of its rpm range. However, the additional high-rpm power cannot be utilized if the non-adjustable factory rev limiter shuts down the ignition system too early. Ideally, the limit should be just above the point where the camshaft signs off.

Naturally, the same performance intake, cam, heads and headers will allow the engine to take in more air. That's why it generates more power, which is also why the stock fuel-delivery calibration will likely prove inadequate. Installing larger injectors and bumping the fuel pressure will get you in the ballpark but it will take an Extender to put you on base. The co-processor provides 16 air/fuel settings, ranging from a dripping rich setting of 9.50 to 1 to a lean of 14 to 1. The first four settings are calibrated in .50 increments. The remainder are calibrated in .25 increments to ensure the ideal calibration is obtainable. A stock engine can also be fine-tuned to deliver optimum performance, keeping in mind the level of potential is less compared to a modified engine.

Maximum engine speed can also be adjusted to any one of 16 different settings in a range from 6500 to 13,000 rpm. The first 15 settings are calibrated in 200 rpm increments up to 9300 rpm. The 16th setting then jumps to 13,000 rpm, which is essentially the same as having no limit at all.

Don't look for the Extender to satisfy all of your electronic needs, particularly if your engine is extensively modified or equipped with a nitrous oxide or forced induction system. Depending on the level of performance, these mods often require timing retard when the systems are in use. And since the Extender cannot alter the engine's ignition timing, some other timing retard device must be connected to the distributor to back off the spark advance.

Additionally, subjecting your engine to Extender's full A/F range can be hazardous to its health. Pulling hard on an engine with an A/F mixture too lean for safe operation will produce extremely high combustion temperatures, with attendant melted pistons and burned valves.

Combined with compatible performance equipment and equal quantities of common sense, the Extender is an extremely useful electronic tool. Even under average conditions, an optimized air/fuel mixture can be worth .2 to .3 seconds in the quarter-mile. *Super Ford* magazine tested Jim Glass Jr.'s '89 LX Mustang, equipped with ported heads, Ultradyne cam, 1.72 roller rockers, 65mm throttle body, 70mm DP mass air meter, MAC equal length shorty headers, two-chamber Flowmaster mufflers, 4.10 gears, Hurst shifter, Lakewood 90/10 front struts and 50/50 rear shocks, Lakewood traction bars and Weld wheels with 28 x 8 Goodyear slicks. His previous best was a 13.62 @ 101.75 mph. After testing by adjusting the Extender air/fuel ratio in small increments, and increasing the redline in 400 rpm increments, we were able to achieve a best E.T. of 13.44 @ 102.50 mph. A bit more fiddling with fuel pressure, timing and with larger slicks, we probably could have gone a bit faster.

Source:
Ford Motorsport
44050 N. Groesbeck Highway
Clinton Township, MI 48036-1108

continued on next page

FORD'S EXTENDER
(continued)

1. Ford Motorsport's Extender is a piggyback co-processor that intercepts, then modifies, the signals from the stock EEC-IV computer. All necessary hardware, including the adapter cable, are provided with the unit.

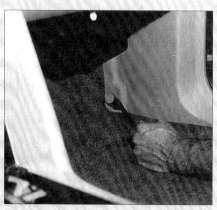

2. The EEC-IV computer is stowed behind the right hand kick panel in 5.0 Mustangs. Remove the panel by extracting the plastic "nail" with a door panel tool and the first screw in the door sill plate with a Phillips screwdriver. The panel is also held in place with a concealed door panel retaining pin. Most cars will have a piece of insulation behind the kick panel which must also be removed.

3. We chose to remove the processor for photographic purposes. The Extender instructions recommend leaving the module in place while making connections. The plastic retainer which holds the module in place is secured with a metric cap screw.

4. The computer can be slid from its compartment once the retainer has been unbolted and pulled out of the way.

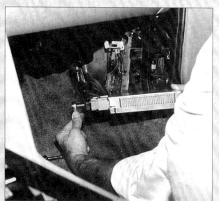

5. Disconnect the battery before separating the processor from the wiring harness! Then use a 10mm socket to remove the computer from its multi-pin plug.

6. Align and attach the double-sided connector at the end of the Extender's adapter harness to the stock processor using the same 10mm socket. The connection will slide together easily once the plug is properly indexed with the slots in the processor's plastic junction block. Do not over-tighten the connector! Use light pressure to snug the bolt.

  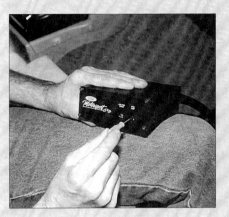

7. Attach the stock wiring harness to the back of the adapter harness in the same manner, making sure it too is not over-torqued.

8. Replace the processor if you removed it. Allow the adapter cable to exit from behind as the kick panel, then attach the other end of the cable to the Extender. Stow the Extender under the passenger's seat for easy access and tuning or mount it in the console underneath the radio.

9. Use a small screwdriver to turn the Air/Fuel and rpm upper limit rotary dials. The ignition switch must be in the off position before a new setting can be implemented.

EXTENDER ADJUSTMENT GUIDE

Switch Position	Engine Speed (RPM)	Air/Fuel Ratio
0	6500	9.50 to 1
1	6700	10.00 to 1
2	6900	10.50 to 1
3	7100	11.00 to 1
4	7300	11.25 to 1
5	7500	11.50 to 1
6	7700	11.75 to 1
7	7900	12.00 to 1
8	8100	12.25 to 1
9	8300	12.50 to 1
A	8500	12.75 to 1
B	8700	13.00 to 1
C	8900	13.25 to 1
D	9100	13.50 to 1
E	9300	13.75 to 1
F	13000	14.00 to 1

Each detent on each dial is marked with a number or a letter which corresponds with a fixed setting.

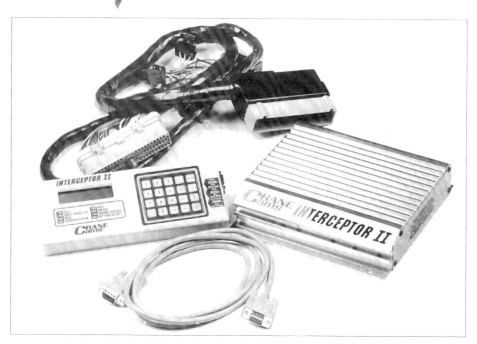

The Crane Interceptor II is a very popular piggyback computer interface that allows considerable adjustment for setting timing, rev limits and fuel mixture.

Exhaust—The exhaust oxygen sensors on the 5.0 H.O. engine are the 3 - wire variety with a heating element (the heating element allows the sensor to come to operating parameters quickly). Exposure to long-term street use or high exhaust temperatures commonly associated with forced induction systems, especially nitrous, breaks down the reactive element. The data sent to the computer becomes erratic and the computer makes adjustments that are incorrect. Unfortunately there is no easy way to test these. Generally, if your car has more than 50,000 miles on the engine, the exhaust oxygen sensors probably should be replaced. The extreme exhaust heat generated when running "on the gas" can fry your exhaust oxygen sensors. If you are a nitrous user, you probably should keep a spare set of these in your tool box.

When running a turbocharged drag racing engine with more than 6 psi of boost, most racers prefer to disconnect the exhaust oxygen sensors. Due to the lag time in the sensor, a momentary mid–throttle lean condition can occur. When this happens the engine will often backfire and damage the turbo compressor fins or cause the compressor wheel to shear off. Not good.

Coolant—The Engine Coolant Temp sensor (ECT) and the Air Charge Temp sensor (ACT) must be of equal resistance for the computer to function properly. As with any sensor that is not working correctly, when these two sensors are not balanced the computer makes adjustments that are incorrect and performance suffers. It is best to remove the two sensors and let them sit for several hours to normalize. The ambient temperature must be above 50° Fahrenheit and preferably about 60°. The hotter the temperature the more difficult to get an accurate test. Check the resistance between the terminals on each sensor with an ohmmeter. The resistance readings should be the same. If there is a difference, replace the unit that has the highest resistance and check them again. Balance is important.

When installing the ACT, be sure the sensor is indexed so the sensing element is facing the incoming airstream. Failure to do this will cause improper data output and reduced engine performance.

ELECTRONIC TUNING

After you have made the modifications to your ignition you must select an initial timing setting and adjust the boost or timing retard if applicable. Setting the initial timing on the 5.0 H.O. engine should be done with a quality timing light. Most of the timing lights on the market are junk and you will be lucky to get within three degrees of your target setting. If you can not afford a

The Digital Fuel Injection stand-alone computer is one of the best racing systems on the market today. This setup comes with a harness that connects directly to the stock 5.0 engine harness. It is also completely programmable with a laptop computer.

professional quality timing light, then borrow one or have someone set it for you who does have one.

For the stock, normally aspirated 5.0 engine, the timing should be set at an initial setting of 13°. Some engines can tolerate 14°. Experimentation is the only way to get there, especially if your engine has been modified. Don't forget to pull the distributor timing spout before attempting to set the timing. Remembering to re-install it is also important (voice of experience speaking again). If you are running a turbo, blower or nitrous, go to Chapter 9 for setup procedures.

Reading Spark Plugs

Fine-tuning the ignition and fuel pressure requires you take a plug reading, sometimes known as a "plug chop or clean cut." It is best to install a fresh set of spark plugs before attempting to take a plug reading. It is just too difficult to analyze a spark plug once it has been run under other conditions.

To perform this test, the engine is run at its maximum rpm limit, under track or running conditions (in other words, not while sitting in the driveway). Once the rpm limit is reached, the engine is shut-off at this rpm. This is known as a "clean cut."

Reading a spark plug is something learned through years of experience. Since the average racer does not have this to draw from, here are a few simple rules to follow when doing a plug chop:

•If you see specks on the electrode or plug rim, you probably have a detonation problem. Those specks are typically small bits of the piston.

•If the cement around the metal electrode has bulged out "cement boil," you probably have a detonation problem.

•If the electrode is cracked or broken, or the grounding tip has burned away,

you definitely have a detonation problem.

If your plugs indicate any of the above, take immediate action to correct the problem. Detonation is not always audible, so it is very important to check the plugs. If you are uncomfortable with reading the plugs, ask an experienced tuner. When you ask for advice, be sure to ask what they see that forms their opinion. Most will be glad to impress you with their knowledge and it's the only way you will learn. ∎

Reading a spark plug will help you determine how your engine is performing. This handy little gadget is a lighted magnifying viewer that illustrates the base of the electrode clearly.

CHIP SHOT
DYNO-TESTING 5.0 COMPUTER CHIPS

text and photos by Earl Davis

This article is reprinted with the permission of Super Ford magazine.

As the EEC-IV is a 5.0's computer command center, it makes sense to begin the search for simple, low-effort performance gains inside this mysterious black box. We know manipulating the EEC's programming, via the Extender or the Crane Interceptor, is a quick way to gain power. But the equipment and knowledge needed to hack EEC-IV can be out of reach for the average non-computer geek who wants to go fast on a budget with minimum hassle.

The aftermarket industry has responded by developing a pre-programmed, plug-in device most consumers and marketers call a chip. These non-programmable piggy-back processors are designed to intercept, interpret and re-write factory fuel and timing commands issued by the parent computer. Super Ford magazine recently dyno-tested three of the most popular performance chips—Hypertech's Power Module, Superchips, Inc.'s Superchip and A.D.S's Super Chip. The testing took place at DSS, Inc., located just outside Chicago.

Of the thousands of informational bits processed each millisecond by a stock EEC-IV computer, the commands regulating fuel delivery and ignition timing advance have the most profound effect on performance. Adding or subtracting fuel in an effort to achieve a near-perfect stoichiometric ratio will make the burning process more efficient. Adding timing also promotes efficiency by igniting the fuel earlier in the cycle. Giving the burning process a head start before the piston reaches top dead center (BTDC) allows cylinder pressure to build to a higher level. The greater the cylinder pressure, the more energy delivered to the crankshaft as the piston begins its power stroke.

The stock EEC-IV regulates fuel delivery by controlling the length of time each injector remains open. It also adds timing lead according to a factory programmed calibration table. The computer adds a preset amount of advance to the initial timing value. Advance plus initial equals the amount of total timing advance or lead. In other words, following a programmed curve, the processor will add, say 28 degrees of timing to the stock initial setting of 10 degrees, for a total timing lead of 38 degrees.

A chip reads and interprets each value. It then modifies each value using its own set of pre-programmed tables. The modified signals effectively add or subtract fuel or timing.

We began the test by first optimizing the engine's fuel and timing settings using a Kenne-Bell aluminum billet adjustable fuel pressure regulator, a fuel pressure gauge calibrated in one pound increments and a quality timing light. Our EFI dyno engine, equipped with 24 lbs-hr. injectors, C&L mass air meter and stock EEC-IV computer, delivered the most torque and horsepower— 347.5 lbs-ft. and 318.6 hp—with 35 pounds of fuel pressure and 19 degrees BTDC of initial timing. After several backup pulls to confirm our settings, the data was entered as our baseline.

Initial timing was then reset to 10 degrees BTDC as required by each of the chip manufacturers. Fuel pressure was left at 35 psi, which is within factory recommended specifications. The engine responded by dropping 10.3 lbs-ft. of torque and 12.3 horsepower, or 337.2 lbs-ft. and 306.3 horsepower respectively. After reaching this "unmodified" baseline, each chip was then installed according to the manufacturer's instructions.

The engine developed 342.6 lbs-ft. of torque and 311.3 horsepower with help from the Hypertech Power Module for an overall gain of 5.4 lbs-ft. of torque and 5 horsepower.

The Superchip made 3.3 lbs-ft. of torque and 4 horsepower over the stock non-assisted setting. Power peaked at 340.5 lbs-ft. of torque and 310.3 horsepower.

The A.D.S. Super Chip system consists of a longer octane rod, a 160 degree thermostat and a plug-in module. The octane rod mechanically advances the initial timing to approximately 17 degrees BTDC. Because the coolant temperature is systematically controlled by the Super Flow 901 dynamometer, there was no need to install the 160 degree thermostat. With the module and octane rod installed according to instructions, the A.D.S. system boosted power to 343.7 lbs-ft. of torque and 317.1 horsepower for a net gain of 6.5 lbs-ft. of torque and 10.8 horsepower. We then unplugged the A.D.S. module, leaving the octane rod in place and ran the test again. The results were the same, indicating the power increase was a result of the timing advance. The module seemingly made no difference in power output.

The performance gain generated by either of the three chips did not match the optimized baseline pull, which leads us to believe a tuner armed with an adjustable fuel regulator and a timing light can gain more power at wide open throttle than can be produced by a modified fixed-program fuel/timing table. However, obtaining those optimized results will not be easy and are potentially damaging without a sensitive dynamometer. In other words, bumping the timing up at the drag strip until the car slows down is asking for burned pistons or worse, although experienced tuners and consistent drivers can do it.

Additionally, a wide open throttle dyno test does not indicate how the part-throttle re-programmed values issued by an add-on chip will affect overall performance. Empirical evidence from chip users typically holds their engines are a bit "crisper" when it comes to throttle response, so advanced part-throttle ignition timing could make the engine respond slightly better. Also, things were stacked against the chips in our dyno test because we could optimize our particular test engine on that particular day. The chip manufacturer's had to be more conservative because their chips fit a wider variety of engines than just our one, plus they have to leave some safety margin. We could tune right to the ragged edge. Just the same, it shows what an experienced tuner can do on a dyno.

In summary, a chip is a great way for a non-technical enthusiast to gain approximately 10 horsepower and 6 lbs-ft. of torque at wide open throttle without lifting the hood. But, with some experience, we believe an adventurous tuner can achieve equal gains by investing in a fuel pressure regulator, a high quality gauge, a timing light and a little time.

Sources:

A.D.S
PO Box 348
Tyler, TX 75703
(903) 581-8357

DSS, Inc.
960 Ridge Street
Lombard, IL 60148
(708) 268-1630

Superchips
2290 N. County Road 427, Suite 112
Longwood, FL 32750
(407) 260-0838

Hypertech
1910 Thomas Road
Memphis, TN 38134
(901) 382-8888 Ext. 73

continued on next page

CHIP SHOT
DYNO-TESTING 5.0 COMPUTER CHIPS
(continued)

1. The test engine consists of a balanced and blueprinted DSS Bullet short block, a pair of pocket-ported World Products Windsor Jr cylinder heads, Texas Turbo long tube headers, Competition Cams 35-450-8 hydraulic roller camshaft with a .598-inch intake and exhaust lift and 231 degrees of duration at .050-inch lift, Jacobs Electronics plug wires, Motorsport GT-40 manifold, 65mm throttle body and EGR spacer and an ACCEL 34 gallons per hour electric fuel pump. The ignition system and EEC-IV are stock Ford pieces.

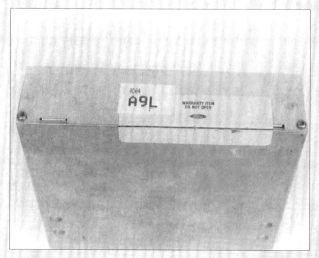

2. Two of the three chips use this service port covered by a "warranty item, do not open" label located at what could be considered the rear end of the EEC-IV processor. The gummed label must be removed before the chip can be installed. Be forewarned: Doing so may void your warranty on the box.

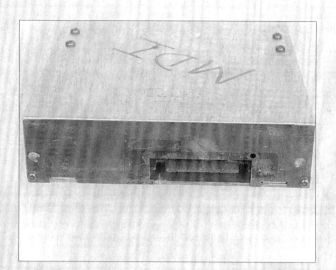

3. The label covers a window which allows access to the end of the PC board. The edge of the computer board creates a terminal end designed to be used by the factory. The metal terminals are not easy to see because they are coated with dielectric grease.

4. Superchips manufacturers a sealed one-piece module designed to mate with the service port. The application of the compact unit is by year and transmission type.

5. When the Superchips module is installed properly, the sides of the unit are flush with the top and bottom of the EEC-IV's case. The piece can be installed upside down but obviously it will not work properly.

6. Hypertech's Power Module is also fit by make, model, year and transmission type.

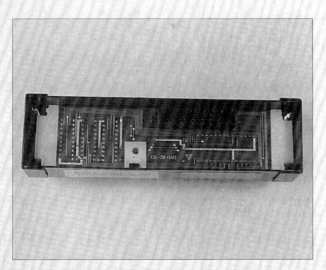

7. The computer inside the Hypertech module is exposed when the unit is not installed. Care must be taken not to dislodge the board or its plastic insulators.

8. A metal cover, held in place by two screws which replace the two end screws in the EEC-IV's case, protects the computer once the unit is installed. The EEC-IV holding fixture located behind the passenger's side kick panel will require some modification if the unit is to be stowed in its original location. A notice attached to the module warns the user that service diagnostic equipment will be given an "Error Code #15" when the unit is installed. It further recommends the module be disconnected prior to any diagnostic procedure. Error code 15 indicates a failure in the read-only-memory test and in non-chip situations can be the result of low keep memory voltage, the installation of a new processor, the first power-up of a new processor or a faulty wiring harness. An experienced Ford mechanic suggested the chip may either act as a new processor or wipe the engine's keep memory each time the key is switched off.

continued on next page

9. The A.D.S Super Chip system includes an octane rod and a 160 degree thermostat in addition to the plug-in module.

The factory octane rod is located on the distributor housing opposite the TVI-IV module.

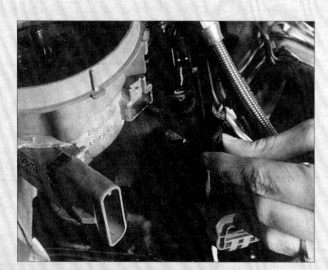

11. The rod is used to index the breaker plate inside the distributor. Installing the longer A.D.S. rod advances the initial timing approximately 7 degrees, which can also be accomplished by rotating the distributor housing. It will be necessary to remove the distributor cap and extension housing in order to replace the factory metal rod with the plastic piece supplied in the kit.

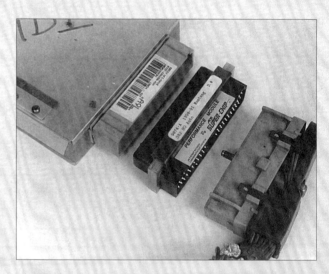

12. The A.D.S. module installs between the processor and its wiring harness. After installing the octane rod, we unplugged the module and found it made little or no difference in performance.

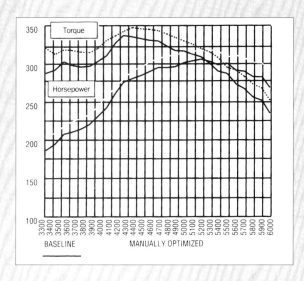

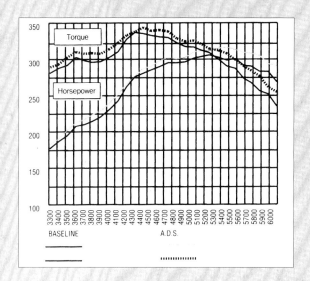

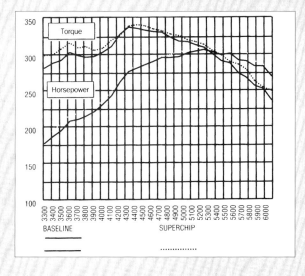

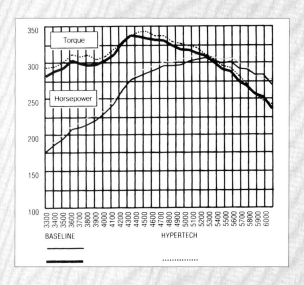

COOLING SYSTEMS

8

Every racing engine builder must deal with the increasing level of energy that is converted into heat as the horsepower generating BTU's (British Thermal Unit) in the combustion chamber multiply. The 5.0 H.O. Mustang has a single-core radiator that is perfectly balanced for the stock engine configuration. However, it takes very little additional power to the engine before overheating becomes a problem.

A smart engine builder understands that a cooling system should be designed to maintain the correct engine temperature without overcooling. Yes, you can overcool an engine and send horsepower out the radiator. Contrary to common belief, the 5.0 engine is not most efficient at 160° or even 180°. Optimum power is achieved at about a 200° coolant temperature where the coolant returns to the radiator, on an engine running stock clearances. Maybe that's why the Ford engineers build the Mustang with a 192° thermostat.

Although the optimum coolant temperature is about 200°, keeping it there is a real trick. This is why most articles written on hot rodding the 5.0 Mustang suggest the 180° thermostat. At least with the lower thermostat opening point, the small, stock radiator has a chance to keep the temperature within a reasonable range when the right foot is planted hard.

For a drag racer, the stock arrangement is probably adequate since there is generally sufficient time between rounds

In the heady rush to build more power, it's easy to forget the "little things," like keeping your pony cool. Power enhancers and engine modifications may cause the engine to run hotter than stock, which means additional cooling capacity for both coolant and oil. Optimum power is generally reached with a consistent 200° coolant temperature. (Photo courtesy BBK Performance)

The best choice for improved cooling for your street machine is the Ford Motorsport three-row radiator shown. This radiator is manufactured with three 1/2" rows of tubing to improve BTU rejection (cooling) over the stock two-row radiator.

The BTU rejection capacity, or cooling ability, is determined by the total area of the radiator, fin spacing, and tube size and number. This photo shows the tubing in a typical three-row high-performance radiator. The more rows the better the heat rejection.

to cool the engine. Besides, anything more than what is necessary to maintain the temperature through the traps will generally be excess weight. Water weighs about 8 lbs. per gallon and anti–freeze is considerably heavier. However, if your thing is racing around a tight apex turn, then a correctly balanced cooling system is a must.

A car's engine is cooled in four ways: direct heat radiation to the air and transmission; through the exhaust; approximately 30% in the radiator coolant ; and if installed, with an engine oil cooler. Each of the four heat-rejection systems plays an important role in producing optimum power output in the Mustang. For our purposes, the two most important issues in this chapter are the radiator and oil cooler.

RADIATOR SELECTION

There are a zillion radiator manufacturers that offer a larger volume radiator for the Mustang. Most are either a three–core or four–core design. However, all three–core and all four–core radiators are not created equal. Radiators are rated at their heat-rejection capacity, or "BTU Rejection" rate. The heat rejection capacity is a function of fin density per inch, square inches of area and tube size. When selecting a radiator

for upgrading your cooling system, it is very important to purchase a radiator that has 12 or 14 fins per inch and at least 1/2" tubes. This will allow sufficient coolant flow at the speeds the 5.0 water pump operates, without creating additional coolant flow drag. Since the stock water pump eats about 12 horsepower at 6000 rpm, any additional drag will only consume more of those precious horses.

The best bet is to stick with one of the Ford Motorsport radiators or one from a reputable radiator company that supports racing, such as Griffin Racing Radiators. Be sure the radiator is designed specifically for the Mustang. If you are a street or drag racer the three–core radiators should be sufficient. For the road-racing Mustang, the three–core will probably be sufficient for the stock or mildly modified engine. Road-racing engines beyond the 300 horsepower mark will generally require a four–core unit.

Coolant Additives & Substitutes

The standard additive for the radiator has always been ethylene glycol. The optimum cooling efficiency is typically at a mixture of about 75% ethylene glycol and 25% water. The ethylene glycol also

serves as a lubricant for the water pump seal and inhibits rust as well as raising the boiling point of the coolant mixture. Recently, Red Line Lubricants introduced an additive that goes beyond the benefits of the typical ethylene glycol coolant. It significantly improves the heat transfer ability of water. Called "Water Wetter," it can provide improved radiator efficiency on cars with minor heating problems. This can be especially helpful for drag racing where the stock radiator is typically used. Put three or four cans into the system for the best effect.

Regardless of which brand of additive you choose, it is important to run something to protect the inside of the block and heads against corrosion. Aluminum heads are especially susceptible to oxidation corrosion. Do not run straight water and always make sure the coolant additive is compatible with the block and head materials. Some additives will accelerate oxidation corrosion on an aluminum head. Read the instructions before you pour it.

For the deep pockets crowd, there is an alternative to water and its additives. "Meca" is a water substitute commonly used by professional racers running high-boost induction systems. This stuff is more dense than water and significantly improves the ability of the head gaskets to resist blowing under high boost operation. The drawbacks are, it requires painstaking installation (every drop of water must be removed from the cooling system), a specially modified water pump and a suitcase full of money. Make no mistake about it, this is trick stuff. However, at the current market price of $55 per gallon, you'll probably want to reserve this modification for your trailered 9-second car.

Thermostats & Flow Restrictors

The EFI engine has seen a lot of abuse concerning the thermostat. Typically a set of underdrive pulleys are added and the car begins to run hot in traffic, so in goes the 160° thermostat. Sometimes it helps, generally it does not. Contrary to common belief, the computer system does not function best at 160°. Engines operating at this temperature are thermally inefficient. A lot of drag racers go to the 160° thermostat in order to keep the computer-managed air–to–fuel ratio rich. Unfortunately what you gain in the richer fuel mixture is lost in the efficiency of the engine at that temperature. If you feel compelled to race your car at this lower temperature to fool the computer, substitute a 5,500K ohm resistor or potentiometer in place of the ECT sensor and run a 190° thermostat. This will fool the computer into thinking the water is still cold and consequently it will run the richer fuel mixture.

For a drag racing and street car, the thermostat serves to bring the car up to operating temperature quickly. It is a simple device that depends on the different expansion rates of metals for its operation. However, nothing mechanical is perfect (with the possible exception of a 427SC Cobra) and eventually the thermostat freaks out, followed shortly by the characteristic coolant surging. My experience has been that this will occur

To improve cooling on a marginal system, especially on a car running underdrive pulley sets, an add-on electric fan is the way to go. The Ford Motorsport kit shown (M8620-A120) comes with a very complete package that includes all installation hardware and wiring.

There are numerous manufacturers of add-on electric cooling fans. Typically these are sold in several sizes. Always buy the larger unit as the smaller ones will have little effect on your hot rod. (Photo by Michael Lutfy)

If you have moved your engine rearward, the parasitic and failure-prone stock fan and fan clutch can be replaced with an electric unit from a four-cylinder Mustang. This fan bolts up to the core support and radiator brackets and will provide sufficient cooling (with factory reliability) for your high-performance engine.

The best stuff to put in your radiator to improve the heat transfer between the block and the water is Red Line's "Water Wetter™". This additive significantly improves the cooling capacity of your engine and is especially helpful for radiators that are borderline inadequate.

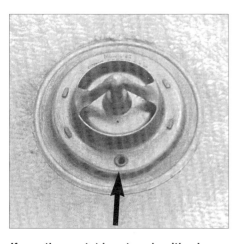

If your thermostat is not made with a burp ball check valve or hole, you should drill a 1/8" hole approximately 1/8" from the edge. This hole is important to allow the block to release the air pockets formed when filling the radiator or from gases that form in the block under racing conditions.

Thermostat Disc Substitute

Fabricate discs with center holes of:

5/8"
11/16"
3/4"
13/16"
7/8"
15/16"
1"

2.125

Materials:
(7) 2.125" discs of 16 gauge steel

Fig. 8-1

just before you absolutely have to be somewhere or in the closing minutes of a race when you are leading.

For the street car or drag racer the only choice when confronted with a dead thermostat is to replace the offending unit. However, for road racing, a thermostat is generally a poor choice. Because you will typically warm the engine before racing, the quick heat buildup benefit of the thermostat is not needed. Dependability is far more important. The trick is to fabricate several discs the diameter of the thermostat (2.125") and drill different size holes to restrict the coolant flow (see Fig 8-1). You should have a set of discs with holes consisting of 5/8", 11/16", 3/4", 7/8" and 1". Start with the 11/16" disc and change the size according to your engine's personality and track conditions. Generally on tight tracks with short straights, you will need a smaller hole to allow the coolant flow to slow and spend more time in the radiator to cool (less airflow at slower speeds). This is not chipped in stone. Drive pulley diameters, radiator size and ambient temperature all affect this, so you'll have to experiment. Just keep a log of which size you used on what engine modifications at each track.

If you are buying a replacement thermostat, look for a small ball check valve or small hole in the face of the thermostat. This is designed to allow the block to "burp" the air pockets that can develop in normal operation. It also has the added benefit of improving the filling process when replacing the coolant. If your thermostat does not have this feature, drill a 1/8" hole about 1/8" from the inside of the circular compression ridge (see Fig. 8-2). Always install the thermostat with this hole up.

For normal high–performance use, be sure to install at least a 16-lb. radiator cap and preferably a 25-lb. unit for road racing. Increasing the pressure will significantly increase the boiling point of the coolant. The heater cores on the Mustangs are famous for leaking and are allergic to high system pressures. When using a high pressure radiator cap for racing, you should bypass the heater core to avoid an expensive rupture.

Underdrive Pulleys

A car's cooling system is designed so that water spends enough time in the block to absorb heat as well as enough time in the radiator to reject the heat.

Thermostat Burp Hole

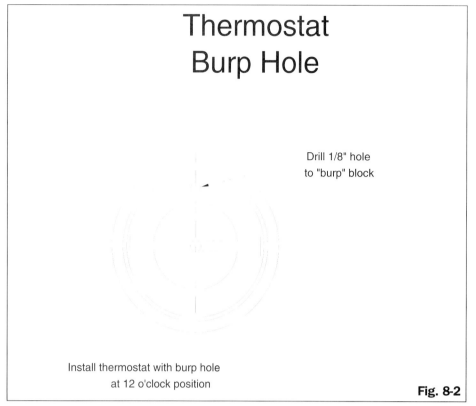

Drill 1/8" hole
to "burp" block

Install thermostat with burp hole
at 12 o'clock position

Fig. 8-2

A cheap way to reduce the parasitic horsepower loss from the water pump is to replace your water pump pulley with one from a 1986 GT Mustang. This was the largest diameter pulley installed on the Fox Mustang.

The speed that water travels through the block and radiator is generally regulated by the water pump design and pulley drive ratios. The manufacturer designs all of these pieces to minimize cost while maintaining a minimum cooling balance for the particular car/engine combination. Since everyone knows the water pump eats large quantities of horsepower, changing the pulley drive ratios has become one of the tricks to squeezing out more horsepower. Every high-performance vendor sells their own brand, even though many pieces are over–the–counter Ford parts.

Use of underdrive pulleys can be a real blessing for a racing engine. Not only do they reduce parasitic drag, they also raise the rpm level before the water pump reaches cavitation speed. Cavitation occurs when the water pump impeller is turning so fast the centrifugal force creates a cavity and prevents the pump from circulating water. Without the

BBK Performance offers underdrive pulley kits for street or racing. The street kit retains the stock serpentine belt, and presents no cooling or low rpm problems. The racing kit requires a shorter belt, and an upgrade of the radiator. It may also cause low-rpm alternator charging problems. (Photo courtesy BBK Performance)

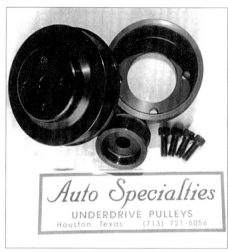

Auto Specialties
UNDERDRIVE PULLEYS
Houston, Texas   (713) 721-8056

Underdrive pulleys significantly reduce the horsepower that is consumed by the alternator and water pump. If your car is run on the street, stick with the sets that offer moderate crank pulley reduction, such as the Auto Specialties CNC machined pieces shown here. The racing set with the small diameter crank pulley will not provide adequate operation of the alternator or water pump below 2000 rpm.

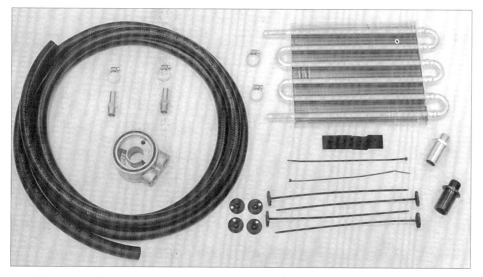

Ford Motorsport offers an excellent engine oil cooler with the Hayden thermostatically controlled oil bypass valve to insure adequate oil flow in cool start conditions. This kit (M6642-A102) is simple to install with the oil cooler adapter sandwiching between the block and the oil filter. (Photo courtesy Ford Motorsport/SVO)

OIL COOLERS

Keeping the oil temperature within its designed operational range is critical to the survival of your engine. High–performance engines transfer a great deal of heat to the oil, and often exceed the oil's oxidation breakdown point. Once a lubricant reaches the point of breakdown it loses at least 50% of its lubrication quality and is essentially junk. Most petroleum-based oils reach this point well below the average oil temperature of the high–performance 5.0 engine. Oil temperatures above 280° are not uncommon on modified engines using stock oil pans without an oil cooler.

Optimum oil temperature is between 220° and 240°, with 212° being the minimum. There are those who would argue that the oil temperature should be lower. Unless the oil temperature gets hot enough to boil water, any condensation in the oil will not evaporate. Water and oil form an interesting white foam, when whipped by the crankshaft, that does not lubricate particularly well. Granted, the condensation amounts can be small. However, it does not take much to scorch a bearing.

Maintaining an oil temperature within the optimum range will require that you either increase the oil volume or install an oil cooler. Several companies sell deep sump and wide-based oil pans for the 5.0 Mustang. Canton, Hamburger's and Moroso are the industry leaders. These pans increase the volume of the oil to 7 or 8 quarts, which provides for a greater volume to dissipate the engine heat. A 10° to 15° reduction in oil temperature can be expected. These pans are top quality , but expensive.

water circulating the engine overheats. High rpm operation mandates a change to the underdrive setup.

Unfortunately, what is good for racing is not always good for the street car. The 5.0 engine will usually overheat when run at less than 2000 rpm with the "street" version underdrive pulley kits, especially if you live in a hot climate. This is not a problem if you live in a place where there is no traffic congestion. It is the pits if you live in Phoenix, Arizona. Sometimes you can replace the large diameter water pump pulley that is typically provided in the underdrive kits, with the small diameter pulley on the early GT Mustangs or 2.3L engines, and improve the situation to a tolerable level. This will defeat part of the reason for the underdrive pulleys but it will improve cooling. Unless you can live with the overheating problem at low speeds (not to mention the lack of alternator function below 2000 rpm), I suggest you spend the money on something else for your street car.

The second option for controlling oil temperature is to install an oil cooler. Several companies offer oil cooler kits, including Ford Motorsport. Depending on intended use, the Ford Police oil cooler kit may be fine, but serious racers will need a more sophisticated setup.

The Ford water-cooled oil cooler shown on the author's SVO engine (arrow) is standard issue on the SVO and police package 5.0 Mustangs. Not only does this oil cooler arrangement provide improved oil temperature control, by using the radiator water to cool the oil, there is the added benefit of having the radiator water bringing the oil temperature up to operating temperatures quickly.

Ford Cooler—The Ford Police oil cooler kit uses the radiator coolant to cool the oil. Basically, it consists of a module that is sandwiched between the oil filter and the block. Coolant is taken from the heater return tube and routed through the cooler module and back to the water pump. This system puts additional demand on your radiator, so it will usually have to be upgraded. However, this system works very well and is simple to install. The budget-minded can find the cooler body and the special bolt on a dead 2.3L turbo engine. Regular heater hose can be substituted for the formed hoses that come in the kit.

Road Racing Oil Coolers—If you are a road racer, I highly recommend the Harrison oil cooler. Harrison primarily designs and manufactures coolers for the aviation and aerospace industry, so the quality is superb. However, there is no automotive kit, so you'll need to purchase an oil filter block plate, remote oil cooler mount and AN12 size oil lines and fittings to connect everything up. Mount the cooler in the airstream with a rubber insulated mount that you will have to fabricate. The block plate and remote oil cooler mounts can be purchased separately or as a set.

There are numerous vendors (Fram, Trans–Dapt, Moroso and Derale) who offer remote filter kits that have the block plate and oil filter mounts. If you can find one for a reasonable price, the '69 & '70 Boss 302, Boss 351, and Boss 429 Mustangs had block plates for their oil cooler that sandwiched between the oil filter and the block. With these units, there's less hardware to deal with and the construction is of high quality.

If the price of the Harrison oil cooler is a little tough to swallow, purchase a used, yellow–tagged, oil cooler from an aircraft salvage company. Just specify one from a 470 cid or larger engine, i.e. a O–540 Lycoming or O–470 Continental. Although used, a yellow–tagged aviation component means that it has been

Drag racing an automatic transmission heats the oil to tremendous temperatures. An auxillary transmission cooler can save the life of your racing automatic and provide for more consistent hookup.

certified by a qualified inspector to meet or exceed the service standards of the aviation industry. These standards are considerably tougher than the manufacturing standards of most new automotive parts, so you should be okay.

Lubricants

Do not waste your money on conventional petroleum-based oils. I know you can not turn on the radio or TV without being bombarded with advertisements on how great everybody's oil is for "today's high–performance engines." However, the 5.0 H.O. Mustang does not deserve the abuse suffered from petroleum-based oils. Synthetic lubricants are reasonably priced now, so there is no excuse.

The lubricating quality of a synthetic oil is light years ahead of the best blended petroleum-based motor oil currently available. There is just no comparison. Your engine will run cooler and generate more horsepower, as well as live longer, when operated with a synthetic lubricant. On a stock 5.0 engine, you can expect an honest 7 horsepower gain, at the rear wheels, by changing from a petroleum-based oil to a synthetic lubricant. I have seen this proven on a chassis dyno as well as an engine dyno.

Recommendations—There are numerous synthetic lubricants on the market today. Few are true synthetics. The re–constituted petroleum oils with the synthetic additives that are sold as "synthetic oil" are better than the straight petroleum-based oils. However, for the best performance and protection, stick with the true synthetics sold by companies such as Red Line Lubricants. The gains will be more pronounced. ■

Ford Police Oil Cooler Part Numbers

Cooler body:	E3ZZ–6B856–A
Hose:	E9ZZ–6B852–A
Hose:	E9ZZ–6B852–C
Adapter Bolt:	E3ZZ–6L626–A

NITROUS OXIDE, SUPERCHARGER'S & TURBOCHARGERS

9

The fastest way to add significant power to your 5.0 engine is with a power adder like a supercharger, turbocharger or nitrous oxide system. Each one of these alternatives can more than double the power output of the stock block engine. Horsepower levels approaching 500 horsepower can be attained while keeping the stock short block in one piece. The trick to maximizing the potential of your engine with a power adder is to have a well-balanced combination of the right components. Just bolting on a supercharger or nitrous kit can provide modest but impressive gains. Add a few things to improve the efficiency of your engine and things really start to happen.

Selecting one of these forced induction systems is generally a question of budgetary limits or anticipated need. Nitrous kits are the least expensive to install. However, nitrous is consumed at

Who knows what lurks underhood? Supercharging and nitrous oxide are bolt-on horsepower-producing modifications that can put a dumbfounded Z28 jockey on the trailer.

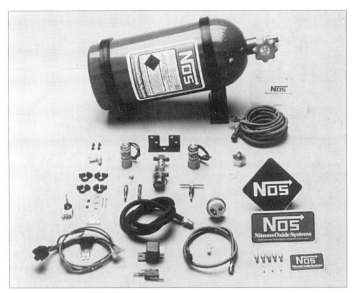

Nitrous Oxide Systems, Inc. (N.O.S.), the leader in nitrous oxide systems, has complete kits that can boost the horsepower of your engine to blower performance levels. Pictured here is N.O.S.'s basic 5.0 75 hp kit (PN 05115). This kit requires that a small hole be drilled in the throttle body to insert the nitrous nozzle.

The limitation of any nitrous system is the stock fuel delivery system. As horsepower increases so does fuel volume requirements. A simple way to upgrade your fuel system and double the horsepower of the basic N.O.S. 5.0 kit is with the addition of a Bosch fuel pump and larger nitrous jet. The N.O.S. kit shown (PN 0015) has all the hardware necessary to make this upgrade.

a rate of about 1 lb. per 100 horsepower per 10 seconds. This means the average leadfoot will need to refill his nitrous bottle at least once a week on a 100 horsepower kit. At the current price of a 10 lb. nitrous refill, you could pay for the additional cost of a Paxton or Vortech supercharger kit in a little over a year. The advantages of not having to turn the bottle on or keep it filled, just to feel the rush, strongly suggest you save your nickels and buy a blower or turbo kit. However, nitrous does have advantages, so read on.

NITROUS OXIDE

The most popular and simplest method for adding power to your 5.0 engine is to inject it with nitrous oxide. Nitrous oxide is a chemical compound consisting of two nitrogen and one oxygen atoms. This molecule can only remain in a stable liquid form if it is maintained under pressure, depending on ambient temperature. When the liquid nitrous is released into the intake system it boils and vaporizes. This process provides two power enhancers. First, the vaporization of nitrous oxide creates a temperature drop to −128° Fahrenheit.

This extremely cold temperature will cool the entire intake plenum and ports right into the heads. Consequently, a much more dense air mixture will enter the combustion chamber. Denser air means more oxygen. With the increased oxygen of a cool dense air mixture and the additional oxygen available from the nitrous oxide molecules, you get a very oxygen-rich environment. Since oxygen is the stuff that allows the engine to burn fuel, more oxygen means more fuel can be utilized in the combustion chamber. More oxygen and more fuel translate into higher combustion pressures and more of that intoxicating hp.

Nitrous Kits

There are several companies that sell bolt–on kits that can produce immediate, on-demand and short-lived power gains from 50 to 250 horsepower for the stock-block 5.0 Mustang. Probably the most recognized manufacturer of these kits is Nitrous Oxide Systems (5930 Lakeshore Drive, Cypress, CA 90630. 714/821-8319). They offer high-quality kits complete with all the components, as well as excellent installation and operation instructions. They understand

the fuel and ignition system modifications that are necessary with each level of kit they sell and advise you accordingly. In addition, they can provide invaluable information on dialing in your system. Compucar (509 Old Edgefield Rd., N. Augusta, SC 29841. 1-800-NITROUS) and The Nitrous Works also sell quality nitrous kits that are easy to install.

Nitrous kits for the 5.0 H.O. engines come in several designs. Some kits require drilling a hole in the lip of the throttle body (N.O.S.) or inlet hose (Compucar) to install the nitrous nozzle, while others offer spray bars mounted in a plate that sandwiches between the EGR plate and manifold (Nitrous Works) or installs through the expansion plug in the stock upper plenum (N.O.S.). Power levels of these kits are determined by the quantity of nitrous that is injected into the engine. This is regulated by altering the shim thicknesses in the solenoids, as is the case with the N.O.S. systems, or by changing the jet sizing much like the "pill" in the old Hilborn injector system.

Obviously, the fuel delivery system will need to be upgraded to provide the additional fuel necessary on all but the

This innovative approach to the "stock" look was developed by Joe Rivera at EFI Hyperformance in Houston. The tubing provides fuel and nitrous delivery, via correctly sized holes, through a Ford Motorsport EFI Heat Spacer (M9486-A51) between the upper and lower intake manifolds. Very sneaky.

lowest horsepower kits. Bolt–on nitrous kits are typically designed to operate "on the gas" at a fuel ratio of 8.75:1. This means a bsfc (brake specific fuel consumption) rate of about .69. At this bsfc, your fuel delivery system must be capable of delivering a minimum of 148 lph of fuel, at an elevated pressure, to handle a 150 horsepower nitrous kit on a stock 5.0 H.O. engine. This is well beyond the capability of the in–tank pumps and at the limit of the stock fuel lines. If your nitrous kit does not include the required fuel system upgrades, follow the procedures outlined in Chapter 5 for determining your fuel delivery system needs.

System Overview

Nitrous oxide injection systems consist of three basic parts: the bottle, pressure control solenoids, and nitrous/fuel delivery spray bars or nozzles. On high horsepower systems, a timing retard control is also required.

The Bottle—Generally, the nitrous oxide bottle (actually, a pressurized container similar to a scuba diving oxygen tank) is mounted in the trunk, with the valve end pointing toward the front of the car. If the bottle is mounted in the rear of a fastback Mustang, it must be covered and shielded from the sun. Dangerous bottle pressures can result if it is allowed to sit exposed to the sun's rays in an enclosed car.

Considerable effort is often taken to hide the bottle from unsuspecting prey. One of my favorite methods is to cut the bottom from a gym bag and slip it over the bottle. Aging the bag and having a dirty towel hanging out of the partially closed zipper is a nice touch. The truly sneaky individual will also install a remote bottle valve so there is no telltale trip to the rear of the car to turn on the gas.

The nitrous delivery hose, running from the bottle to the solenoid, must be carefully routed away from hot exhaust

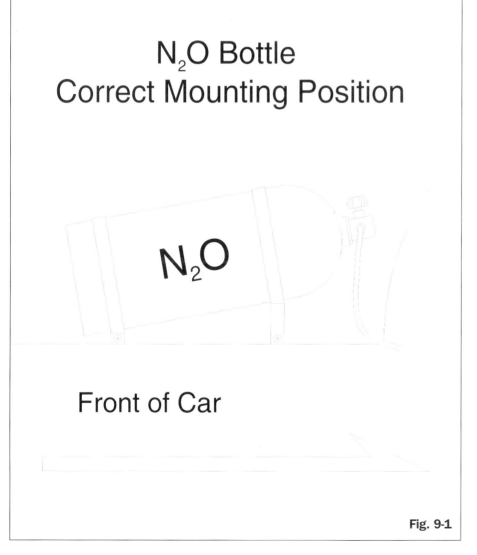

N$_2$O Bottle
Correct Mounting Position

N$_2$O

Front of Car

Fig. 9-1

systems. The Mustang has an inspection plug on the right side of the trunk (rear deck on the fastbacks), that can be used to pass the nitrous hose through. You will need a MS35489–12 (AN931–6–16) synthetic rubber grommet to seal the hole around the hose, if your kit does not include it.

Solenoids—The solenoids regulate the nitrous and fuel flow and should be mounted away from hot exhaust headers, but as close to the nozzles as possible. Since the solenoids reduce the pressure of the nitrous to injection pressures, the nitrous begins to boil and vaporize when it passes through the solenoids. Obviously the closer the nitrous to the nozzles the less heat btu's are absorbed before the nitrous reaches the manifold.

Keeping the solenoids close to the nozzles is not always practical. The problem becomes more acute when you try to hide the nitrous system. If this is your situation, mount the solenoids inside the cowl plenum and run the nitrous hoses through ordinary-looking heater hoses. Properly installed, they will be tough to detect.

The nitrous and fuel spray bars must be mounted according to the manufacturer's instructions. The nitrous bars or nozzles in the bolt–on kits for the 5.0 are generally very easy to install. Unless you are an experienced nitrous user, you should stick to the instructions for installing these things. Obviously, hiding the nitrous and fuel nozzles can be tough. Mounting the plates or nozzles to the rear of the engine, under the lower side of the throttle body or back of the plenum, is your only hope. Again, if you are into the sneaky approach, take your time and use your imagination. I've installed these systems where detection has been virtually impossible, at least until 2nd gear.

Nitrous Bits & Pieces

Most nitrous oxide kits have the basic components to function under ideal conditions. Since ideal conditions only exist in Murphy's mind, there are a few things that should be considered before you tap the button.

1. Nitrous oxide is dependent on high pressure to function properly. If your bottle pressure is less than 900 psi, you will probably run out of gas before the end of your run.

2. Cold or cool temperatures condense nitrous oxide and reduce the bottle pressure. Riding around in air-conditioned comfort in your Mustang can affect the performance of your nitrous system. A bottle warmer can heat the bottle to proper operating temperature. Additionally, a bottle warmer can be used to heat the bottle to increase the pressure when the juice starts to run low. Spend the bucks and get a bottle warmer.

3. You can find yourself in a most embarrassing situation if you run out of gas in the middle of a run. You can take the bottle out and weigh it to determine how much nitrous is remaining before making a pass. However, this is a real pain. Since nitrous systems are famous for leaking, a bottle pressure gauge is a must.

4. If you are installing a used nitrous system, use liquid Teflon, and only liquid Teflon, on the threads of all fittings. The Teflon tape has a tendency to flake off and clog the filters and nozzles.

5. Engaging the gas below 2500 rpm (higher on more radical engines) can reduce your engine to a lot of broken pieces. Unfortunately, we don't always have our brains completely functional in the heat of a tight race and sometimes forget this small point. This is not good. The smart nitrous junkie will install an rpm limit safety switch. These things connect directly to the solenoids, preventing them from opening until a safe rpm.

6. If your nitrous kit does not come with a fuel pump upgrade, then you must purchase one and install it before you make your first run. No one runs the small horsepower nitrous kits and no doubt, you won't either. Without a fuel pump upgrade you'll be very disappointed in the performance, especially when the system cycles on and

The MSD Multi-Step Retard is ideal for the car running multi-stage nitrous systems. This setup allows the ignition to be retarded in three separate stages as each successive stage of nitrous is turned on.

The glove compartment is one of the best places to store your Jacobs Nitrous Mastermind. The Nitrous Mastermind is the best and easiest to use nitrous control black box on the market. This unit allows complete control of timing and nitrous volume staging at the turn of a knob.

The high cylinder pressures generated in a supercharged or nitrous application will require the addition of a multi-spark ignition module to fire the plugs. The MSD 6 series shown (MSD 6BTM for supercharger/turbochargers) is a minimum upgrade.

off as fuel volume varies from adequate to inadequate to adequate. This is tough on drivetrains too.

Controlling Detonation

As mentioned in Chapter 7, the real trick to managing the nitrous system is controlling the detonation by regulating the timing. The stock EEC–IV computer doesn't know the difference between nitrous and gasoline and will advance the timing as if under normal operating conditions. Because of the increased flame propagation rate associated with nitrous oxide combustion, detonation will occur under normal timing. To avoid engine damage, detonation must be controlled by an add–on module. I know you can retard your timing, especially on low horsepower kits, but normal driveability suffers while you're tooling around looking for prey.

Timing Control Kits—For the 5.0 H.O. engine fitted with a bolt–on nitrous kit, MSD (Autotronic Controls), Jacobs and Hypertech sell ignition retard controls that can properly retard the timing for each level of nitrous used. If you already own one, the Crane Interceptor II computer interface can be

programmed (by you) to include a data set to manage the fuel and ignition curves during nitrous operation.

The MSD Adjustable Timing Control and the Jacobs Opto–Timer kit require manual setting of the timing retard, via a knob, before arming the nitrous. These are relatively simple units and do not provide the sophistication of fuel and timing management of the Hypertech or Jacobs Mastermind systems. The MSD module requires an MSD ignition to function. The Jacobs Opto–Timer is a stand alone system. Unfortunately, these controls are inadequate for those nitrous systems beyond the 80 horsepower level. Above 80 horsepower, a stepped ignition control should be used.

MSD manufactures a multi–step timing retard control for high horsepower nitrous applications. It is sold under the name MSD Multi–Step Retard Control (PN 8972). This is a minimum requirement for those systems producing more than 80 horsepower. This system also requires an MSD capacitive discharge ignition module. Although this system is great, it does require that you understand how to map the timing retard. With this module, you will have to install

plug–in timing retard chips to define the degrees of retard to be used. Since the timing retard is connected to the nitrous activation switch, it is only activated when on the gas. This control is very popular with experienced racers. Due to its low price and simplicity of operation, it is commonly installed by many nitrous shops to maximize the system.

The Jacobs "Nitrous Mastermind" module is the current state of art for a nitrous oxide system. This module allows the tuner complete control to map timing curves, rpm safety limiting, and the rate at which the nitrous is fed. Controlling the feed rate of the nitrous can avoid the sudden hit that is so tough on drivetrains and traction. For the serious nitrous junkie, this is the trick setup.

For the racer wanting optimum performance with minimum input, the Hypertech "Nitrous Power Module" is the hot setup. This nitrous control system is specifically designed for the 5.0 H.O. Mustang. This is a very sophisticated and well designed system that works extremely well. The Hypertech module is dormant until the nitrous is activated, at which point it switches your engine to a special program that provides specific mapping of fuel and timing for the nitrous system. It is also simple to install.

This 5.0 street machine sports a Paxton supercharger, a Nitrous Works system, a polished GT-40 intake and numerous other go-fast goodies that make it the ultimate street sleeper. (Photo by Michael Lutfy)

Paxton superchargers have been installed on Fords since the supercharged 312 cid T-Birds in the '50s. Made popular on the Shelby GT-350s in the '60s, Paxton superchargers have a long history of reliability and quality. Richard Gibson is finishing up a high-boost Paxton installation on a Saleen Mustang.

Mapping Timing

A basic rule of thumb says you must retard timing 6° for every 100 horsepower that is added. This is just a rule of thumb, but it should get you in the game. Kits that add up to 75 or 80 horsepower can generally be managed by retarding the stock ignition. It is not the most efficient way to run your engine, but it will work. This requires the timing be altered just before racing. This approach can be the pits for the street car, since you'll have to retard the timing before you go trolling for a race. If your budget permits, install a retard control.

Mapping the timing for an engine that has other modifications in addition to nitrous can be tricky. Generally you will want to start with too much retard, then slowly dial in more advance. The basic 6° retard per 100 hp of nitrous should be OK on a normally aspirated engine.

Engines sporting turbos and blowers will typically need 1° per pound of boost retard when combined with nitrous. Do not run the engine with less than 20° total advance. Even with all the power adders, the combustion flame needs a minimum amount of time to burn the combustion mixture. Too much retard and optimum performance will go away fast. It is a delicate balance that can be difficult to achieve as the horsepower levels increase. Slow, methodical experimentation and good record-keeping are necessary to achieve good results. For manually mapping your timing, follow the general rules in the chart nearby.

SUPERCHARGING

Supercharging the 5.0 Mustang is the choice for those individuals wanting consistent horsepower that is not dependent on the pressure level of a bottle. Horsepower gains of 30% to 50% are pretty normal on a stock or mildly modified 5.0 H.O. engine with the addition of a supercharger. Add a few goodies to improve the airflow volume through the intake and exhaust and 475 horsepower becomes a reality. The *Slot Car Mustang* that we ran in *Super Ford Magazine's FoxTrot Challenge* in November of 1992 was equipped with a GT–40 kit, a Ford E303 cam (Crane

Mapping Timing

The following are general rules to use when manually mapping the fuel and timing requirements for the typical bolt–on single stage nitrous kit: (This does not apply to blower or turbo engines.)

Horsepower Added	Initial Retard Timing	Timing "on gas"	TPS Setting	Fuel Pressure	Fuel Pump
50	10°	0°	.998v	40 lbs.	stock
75	8°	0°	.998v	42 lbs.	110 lph
100	12°	4°	1.0v	42 lbs.	155 lph
125	12°	8°	1.05v	43 lbs.	155 lph
150	12°	8°	1.15v	44 lbs.	200 lph

If you are an amateur nitrous user, then you should get a copy of Nitrous Pete's booklet on set up and tuning the nitrous system. It is very readable and is written for the average racer. It is available from:

P.J. Performance
12-6 Zelus St.
Tuckerton, NJ 08087
(609) 294-0243

444132), a V1 Vortech supercharger at 8 psi of boost, a Pro–M 77mm Mass Airflow meter with 24-lb. injectors, Texas Turbo long–tube headers and Flowmaster mufflers, all bolted to a stock short block. This car weighed nearly 3,600 lbs. with Ron Grable at the wheel and still managed a 119 mph trap speed through the quarter mile. That equates to about 470 horsepower. Not bad for a stock short block, especially when you consider both head gaskets were blown before the car ever ran a single lap. Obviously, supercharging has its advantages.

Aftermarket Units

Currently there are only three players in the bolt–on supercharger market for the 5.0 Mustang: Paxton, Vortech and Kenne–Bell. There are other systems on the market, but they are as yet unproven by the masses. The Paxton and Vortech superchargers are of radial compression design. Air is drawn into the middle of the compressor and thrown outward (radially) at extreme speeds (40,000 to 50,000 rpm), where the increased volume causes it to compress against the outer chamber. The overdrive ratio determines

The Vortech supercharger is a very complete and well-designed kit popular with 5.0 hot rodders. Complete with all hardware, high-volume fuel pump, regulator and ignition management system, this kit can make 500+ horsepower when combined with good heads, intake, exhaust and cam.

the boost that can be made. These two systems are very popular and are constantly competing for the majority of the hot rod market. I have used them both and found them to be excellent. Paxton offers kits that have a standard compressor basically unchanged since the '60s. They also sell one with a new high-volume 18 psi compressor. Vortech compressors are sold in standard kit form with the "B" trim compressor that is capable of producing about 11 psi of boost on an unported engine. Vortech also offers an alternative high-volume "R" trim compressor with the large compressor impeller that is capable of 18 psi of boost. It was this compressor that was used by Ken Duttweiler on the CAR CRAFT COBRA 200 project Mustang that made the 201 mph blast at the Transportation Research Center of Ohio. Obviously, it works pretty well.

The third and most recent addition to the supercharger war is the Kenne–Bell TS1000 kit, which uses the Whipple Industries' twin screw, positive displacement type blower (sometimes referred to as a "Sprintex" blower). Unlike the centrifugal compressors of the Paxton and Vortech kits, the Whipple compressor creates boost by compressing air between two interlaced screws or rotors. This is a very efficient type compressor, with a volumetric efficiency of 88%. Volumetric efficiency is the ratio of compressor volume to displaced, or exit air. This is of course so much feldagarb to most racers. However, if

The Whipplecharger supercharger from Kenne-Bell is one of the slickest kits on the market. It has a very efficient compressor ratio that produces instant boost without heating the intake charge. This application has the advantage (or disadvantage, depending on how you look at it) of using the stock pulley/serpentine belt arrangement and comes in 5, 8 and 11 psi kits. (Photo courtesy Kenne-Bell)

you are into high boost levels, the volumetric efficiency of a compressor will determine how much it heats up the air it discharges. That should get your attention. Even a novice knows that hot air is less dense and more prone to detonation. With this compressor, the exit air temperature at 10 psi of boost, on a warm day (80° ambient temperature), will only heat up to 200° F. This is a pretty low exit air temperature for any compressor operating at 10 psi of pressure. By comparison, a turbocharger operating at the same boost will probably heat the air to 215° F.

Because the Kenne–Bell uses a positive displacement type compressor, the maximum boost level is reached almost instantly. This translates into more horsepower at lower rpm than the centrifugal type compressor which depends on increasing engine speed to spool up. On systems running less than 8 psi of boost, the roots-type compressor has a definite advantage. However, my experience has been that once you exceed 6 or 7 psi of boost, with the street application, the overdrive ratio necessary to spin the centrifugal supercharger to attain the higher boost levels already has the compressor spooled up at 3000 rpm, at least with the new Paxton and Vortech compressors.

The weakest link of any belt-driven supercharger has always been the belt. The Vortech supercharger seen here has the original narrow 6-groove belt drive that often threw the belt at high rpm. In this photo, you can see the belt has already jumped one groove to the outside. However, Vortech has recently produced an 8-groove and 10-groove belt drive that greatly improves reliability.

The high volumetric efficiency advantage of the Kenne–Bell kit takes a beating when it comes to engine maintenance. Both the Vortech and Paxton systems allow easy removal of the valve covers by simply loosening a couple of hose clamps and popping off the inlet hose. With the Kenne–Bell kit, you will have to unbolt the compressor, which can be a major time-consuming process. For an engine running the stock-type hydraulic roller cam and factory rev–limit, the need to access the valves only becomes important when

something goes wrong. At that point, hassling with the supercharger generally won't make much difference. However, if you are into optimum performance and are constantly checking the valves, or your engine is equipped with a mechanical cam, you'll probably find the Kenne–Bell kit to be a major hassle.

Drive Belts

Although I really like the Kenne–Bell blower, I believe the use of the narrow factory drive belt may create problems for boost levels beyond 5 or 6 psi. These belts are pretty strong, but add a 100 horsepower drag on the belt at 8 psi of boost and things change dramatically. The single biggest limitation of a crankshaft-driven supercharger has always been the drive belt. High boost levels and the inherent harmonics of the belt at higher rpm, combined with the friction it generates, will heat the belt up tremendously and make it unstable. Heat and the stress of trying to drive a device that requires 40% to 50% of the horsepower it adds just to turn it is very tough on these belts. This phenomenon almost prevented the CAR CRAFT COBRA 200 project car from making its historic 201 mph run in Ohio. Losing a

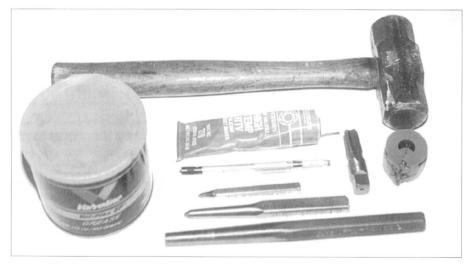

Having the right tools before you start a supercharger installation is important. Shown here are the items necessary to punch the oil drain hole in the side of the oil pan for a Vortech installation.

belt on a Vortech or Paxton compressor generally means you lose boost. On the Kenne–Bell setup, you walk if the belt dies.

The drive belt has been a problem for the Paxton and Vortech kits as well. Anyone who owns a Paxton or Vortech supercharged car knows to keep an extra belt in the trunk, including a factory accessory belt. The instability of the belt harmonics at high engine speeds makes it difficult to keep the belt on track across the pulleys. This is further complicated by the normal bending of the compressor brackets under high-boost conditions. It only takes a few degrees of misalignment and the belt is history. The narrow six-groove belt that comes in the kit does not have the strength to withstand high-boost conditions, and it is virtually impossible to keep on track when the tach reads 6000 rpm or above. The stress of the belt harmonics and the misalignment from bending of the brackets are just too much for the narrow belt. If you are planning to install a Paxton or Vortech kit, spend the extra money and get the 8- or 10-groove belt and pulleys. Although I have not seen the new 10-groove pulley arrangement, Vortech has incorporated the lessons learned with the CAR CRAFT COBRA 200 project car into their latest kits. Hopefully the drive belt problem has been eliminated.

Installation Tips

Installing a supercharger on the 5.0 Mustang is no big deal; however, it does take a considerable amount of time. Forget the recommended time for installation on the instruction sheets. They are not realistic. The average do-it-yourself hot rodder can expect to spend the better part of a weekend completing an installation. If Murphy decides to give you a hand, and he always does, the job rapidly deteriorates into a multi-six–pack affair, further extending the time of installation.

Before you open the hood of your car,

Making the hole for the oil drain nipple on a Vortech installation is no big deal. The most important things are not to punch the hole too big (make holes in small steps) and to locate it in the correct spot. If you punch the hole too low oil will not drain properly and your supercharger will probably fail.

read the instructions thoroughly at least twice. Follow the steps in the exact order specified. Get a red ink pen and check off each step as it is completed and only after it is completed. This will limit mistakes and make for a much more pleasant installation.

Tools—Make sure you have the required tools before you start. On the Vortech kits, it is necessary to use a large diameter, blunt-nose punch to expand the drain hole in the side of the oil pan you must make. Due to the proximity of the oil pump to this location, a short blunt punch is required. Generally you will have to cut off a "1/4 Line Up Punch" to get the job done. Don't kid yourself into thinking you can make the smaller punch work by wallowing out the hole. That oil pan is a lot tougher than it looks and there is not enough room for it. Besides, if the hole you make is not round and the correct size, it will leak badly. If you make it too large, you'll have the additional pleasure of removing the oil

pan. Take your time and do it in small steps until the fit is right.

The Vortech kit also requires a special thin 3/4" or 19mm wrench to tighten the bottom bolt on the idler pulley. Without the wrench, it is impossible to loosen or tighten the bolt. These slimline wrenches, once referred to as *tappet wrenches*, can be purchased at Sears or from Snap–On (PN LTAM1719).

Lubricants—Paxton and Kenne-Bell superchargers have a self–contained oiling system. This requires changing at least as often as you change your engine oil. There is a tremendous amount of heat generated by the compressor under boost. Heat breaks down the lubricant and its effectiveness. It is not uncommon for a Paxton to drop two pounds of boost when the lubricant goes bad. Always change the lubricant in a Paxton after a weekend at the drag strip or road racing circuit. The lubricant will definitely be bad. Don't waste your money putting conventional ATF in a Paxton. It's just

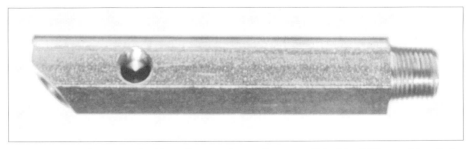
Feeding lubricating oil to the Vortech supercharger is accomplished by drilling and tapping a 1/8" pipe hole in the side of the oil pressure sender extension. This is not difficult, but like all modifications, take your time.

Before you blast off in your new supercharger installation, check the pulley alignment between the supercharger and the crankshaft pulleys. Factory machining tolerances and cam chain gears can cause slight misalignments that guarantee drive belt trouble. Correct any misalignment by machining the pulley spacer or shimming as necessary. Shown here is the 8-groove pulley drive from Vortech. If you have been having problems keeping the belt on, you will need to contact a Vortech dealer for this upgrade.

not slick enough to allow the compressor to make maximum boost. The best lubricant is Paxton's Paxta–Trac synthetic lubricant. This stuff will typically increase the boost on a Paxton by 2 lbs. over the same unit running conventional ATF. The Paxta–Trac lubricant is probably equivalent to the high grade synthetic ATF's on the market now, although I have not tried them.

For extended high-boost operations, such as road racing, autocrossing or running of the Nevada Silver State Classic, you will need to add an oil cooler to the compressor. Central Coast Mustangs (708 B W. Betterravia, Santa Maria, CA 93455. 805/925-8848) sells a slick oil cooler kit that fits the Paxton supercharger and is hassle-free. For the Vortech supercharger, the simplest

approach is to adapt one of the rugged power steering "finned–loop" coolers, found on most of the big Ford cars from the '60s and '70s. These coolers are about 2" wide and 6" tall, with 3/8" hose nipples. Either flare the hose nipples to use an AN818–6 nut to mate with an AN815 union, or install a compression coupling to adapt the oil feed lines.

Hoses—If you are running more than 6 psi of boost, safety wire all the vacuum hoses. High-boost conditions will tend to blow the hoses off.

Pulley Alignment—It is most important that you check the pulley alignment before you button things up. This is particularly important on a Vortech kit. I have yet to see an installation that did not require that a spacer be installed behind the compressor pulley to make the critical alignment. If you ignore this, you will be losing a blower belt every time you run the engine past 4000 rpm. This is the voice of experience. The problem is particularly acute on those systems using the narrow six-groove belt. The slightest misalignment and the belt exits the playing field, often taking the accessory belt with it. Use a long straight-edge held against the crankshaft drive pulley to check the alignment on the idler and the compressor pulleys. If there is not an exact match, measure the error and fabricate a spacer of the proper thickness or machine the pulley to correct the over extension, if applicable. This is a must!

Mass Airflow Meter—A supercharger can be installed on a car without a mass airflow meter. However, without a mass airflow meter you will not be able to produce big horsepower numbers without going to a stand–alone fuel management system (HalTech, Accel/DFI, etc.).

One of the problems that has plagued high-volume, high-boost setups has been the tendency for the compressor–to–mass airflow meter hose to collapse at high rpm. The horsepower instantly goes

Porting heads and intakes increases the volume of air they can carry. That increased volume equates to horsepower, but also means the boost level will drop. Increasing the boost will require a special crankshaft pulley such as the March Performance pulley shown here.

For off-highway use, Auto Specialties makes this slick smog pump replacement idler pulley for the Vortech supercharger.

134

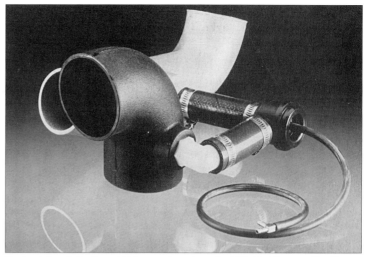

If you move the engine rearward, and you are installing a Vortech, the alternator comes very close to the swaybar at full suspension bump. You'll have to add spacers to move the swaybar down, or modify the alternator bracket to ensure clearance when the suspension is fully compressed.

Vortech has introduced this new boost control kit that is specifically designed for the 5.0 Mustang. The kit replaces the original air inlet and outlet hoses.

away. If you have this problem and you have already cleaned your air filter, you will find it necessary to fabricate a conduit using foam and fiberglass. Essentially you must carve and contour a section of closed–cell urethane foam, the exact shape and interior dimension necessary to provide a conduit from the mass airflow meter to the back of the supercharger, and then cover it with fiberglass resin and three layers of 8 or 10 oz. glass cloth. After the fiberglass has cured, chip and scrape the foam from inside the tube. Lightly sand the inside surface, wipe it down with acetone and paint a thin coat of fiberglass resin to provide a smooth surface for airflow. Fit

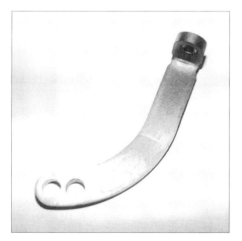

Seen here is the new hole in the alternator bracket that is required for the alternator to clear the swaybar on the Vortech system when the engine has been moved rearward.

the new conduit to the compressor and mass airflow meter with short straight sections of industrial radiator or compressor hose.

Upgrade Fuel Pump—At minimum, you must upgrade your factory in–tank fuel pump to a 155 lph pump. Skip the 110 lph pump. It will have to work at near maximum just to feed a 6 psi boost system. Fuel requirements are covered in detail in Chapter 5.

Ignition Retard—Always run a boost retard control on any supercharger installation. If your kit does not come with one, then buy it. There is no way to protect your engine against detonation, with the junk that passes for gasoline these days, without an ignition retard control. This is covered in more detail on p. 138 of this chapter.

Idle Control—If you have idle problems on your 5.0 engine with a supercharger installed, install the Ford engine idle air kit (PN F2PZ–9F939–A). The kit includes a plate that sandwiches between the throttle body and the idle air bypass solenoid. This plate provides the user the ability to manually adjust the throttle idle air bypass.

A supercharger can be installed on a stock 5.0 H.O. Mustang with impressive results, even if you did nothing more than upgrade fuel and ignition controls. Add

high-volume intakes, big port/ported heads, camshaft, and a free–flowing exhaust system, and you can more than double the horsepower output of your engine with a supercharger. However, when upgrading your engine to a high-volume intake system, you will also have to increase the overdrive ratio of the compressor to maintain the same boost level. Free–flowing intakes and heads require more air to fill their ports and consequently the boost pressure will drop. It is important to note that even at a reduced boost level, the addition of a free–flowing induction system will put more air into the cylinders, resulting in higher horsepower gains than before the change. Returning the boost to the original level will allow full utilization of the larger ports and provide optimum output. March Performance, (5820 Hix Rd., Westland, MI 48185 (313) 729-9070) sells a 7" diameter, eight-groove crankshaft pulley (PN 1052) for the Vortech installation that can keep the boost around 8 or 9 lbs. at 6000 rpm on engines running high–flow intakes and heads. The Paxton unit will require a smaller compressor pulley available from Central Coast Mustangs or other Paxton dealers.

If you intend to run high boost (above 8 psi), I strongly suggest you install head

Turbocharging has gained considerable stature with the auto manufacturers in an attempt to make V8 power from 4-cylinder engines. Shown here is the author's 2.3L SVO engine that produces 400+ horsepower with the help of a modified Garrett turbo.

Turbochargers are rated according to their compressor capacity and the exhaust housing "A/R" ratio. The A/R ratio is the ratio of the exhaust housing inlet area over the distance from the centroid of the inlet to the center of the vortex (center of inlet to center of turbine shaft). Shown here is a Garrett TO3 housing with the A/R ratio of .48 cast into the housing just above the mounting flange. The smaller the A/R the faster the turbo will spool up.

studs, preferably 1/2", or drill and tap the block to use 1/2" head bolts. The stock 5.0 block has very thin deck surfaces and needs all the help it can get to keep the head gaskets in one piece.

TURBOCHARGING

The most efficient way to add horsepower to an engine is with an exhaust-driven supercharger, or turbocharger as they are commonly

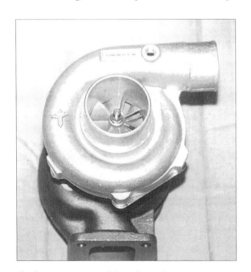

An important consideration when purchasing a turbocharger is the type of compressor impeller it is fitted with. The dual-vane impeller shown here on a Turbonetics compressor is superior to the old single-vane type. Spool-up time and surge are improved considerably with this new type of impeller.

referred to. The belt-driven supercharged engine must use 40% to 50% of the power it produces to turn the supercharger. This equates into considerably more strain on the engine, at the same flywheel horsepower, than when generated by a turbocharger. Basically, if a supercharger adds 120 horsepower at the flywheel, the engine is actually producing about 200 additional horsepower, with 40% of it being used by the engine to turn the supercharger. Since the turbocharger is driven off the spent combustion gases, it produces no additional parasitic drag on the engine.

Once believed to be too finicky for ordinary use, the turbocharger has gained considerable stature in recent years. The high efficiency of the turbocharged engine has forced most of the U.S. auto manufacturers to fit them to many of their small engine applications. Turbocharged Trans Ams, Chrysler LeBarons, and the SVO Mustang are but a few of the many factory systems that have seen street action. Horsepower on demand, without the ugly fuel economy that goes along with a normally aspirated engine with the same power output, are the turbocharger's big selling points.

Currently there are several companies

that sell turbocharger kits for the 5.0 Mustang, and numerous high–performance shops will build a custom application for your car. Of the kit manufacturers, the most recognized are Cartech, Spearco, Turbo Technology, Gail Banks, and of course, Ak Miller Enterprises. These companies have tremendous experience building turbocharger systems and offer some very well-designed kits.

Depending on your budget, you can go from an entry level turbocharger kit, that produces 5 or 6 psi of boost and generates about a 100 horsepower

If you drive a turbocharged four-banger, then this new Mass Air controlled EFI intake from Esslinger Engineering is the trick deal. This setup uses a modified Ford ECU computer and mass air meter to allow 400+ horsepower output from the 2.3L engine.

increase at the flywheel, to the high boost systems that produce 800+ horsepower. The entry level kits typically do not include an intercooler and are generally driven by a single turbo. Most of the twin-turbo kits produce about 400 horsepower as a starting point and go up from there. The only limitations are your budget and the stock short block.

Pros & Cons

The good thing about a turbocharger, as previously mentioned, is the reduced strain on your engine to generate the same flywheel horsepower a supercharger produces. The turbocharger system also does not have to deal with a blower belt that is constantly stretching and breaking. There is the added benefit of a more quiet exhaust due to the muffling effect of the turbo's exhaust impeller. Nonetheless, there are some disadvantages to consider.

Heat—The turbocharger radiates a considerable amount of heat into the engine compartment. This is very tough on hoses and electrical wiring. Also, installation is far more complex on a turbo system and generally requires a great deal more time for installation and removal than a supercharger. Some turbocharger kits make spark plug replacement on a Sunbeam Tiger seem like fun. The Spearco twin-turbo kits require the starter be pulled and the #4 spark plug removed from below.

Lag—Probably the most notorious and overstated problem of the turbo system is the spool-up time or "turbo lag" that is characteristic of single turbocharger kits. In order to handle the volume of air necessary for a V8 application, such as the 5.0 engine, the A/R ratio on a single turbocharger must be pretty large. Therefore the velocity of the exhaust gas through the housing is slower. Consequently, there is a momentary lag before the compressor reaches operational speed, or "spools up." Although very disconcerting to the

person who is accustomed to the instant response of some supercharger systems, a simple adjustment in driving style is all that is needed to adapt. One of the finest Mustangs ever built by Ford Motor Company was the 1985-1/2 SVO Mustang. I have one on which the original TO3 turbocharger has been replaced with a larger unit, allowing the original 2.3-liter four–banger to produce over 400 horsepower. The minuscule turbo lag is far outweighed by the incredible exhilaration of accelerating in a 2,500-lb. car with this much horsepower churning the rear tires.

Because turbochargers are less efficient than the current crop of superchargers, the outlet air temperatures are higher for equal amounts of boost. This characteristic mandates an intercooler be installed whenever boost levels exceed 6 psi with a turbo system.

Cost—The biggest problem of a turbocharger installation is the cost. Most entry level turbo systems producing 5 or 6 psi of boost will cost at least $500 more than a Paxton or Vortech kit in current dollars. Go for high boost or the twin-turbo kits and the price skyrockets, doubling or even tripling the entry level cost. The cost is even worse if you do not have the aptitude or equipment to handle the installation yourself. This generally sends most would-be buyers out the door to a supercharger shop. However, to get even close to the same

The biggest limitation of a turbocharger has been the instability of the impellers at high rpm. Typically the harmonics of the impeller combining with the high inertial mass generated by 100,000+ rpm bends the turbocharger's shaft. The cure is a large shaft center section such as the one on this Turbonetics turbo.

Although careful sizing of the compressor and A/R ratios can eliminate the need for a wastegate, big gains in horsepower require turbochargers that can flow more than the engine can handle. Consequently, a wastegate like the one seen here on Mario Meza's 9-second rocket, is a must to prevent overboosting and destroying an engine.

horsepower potential in a Paxton, Vortech or Kenne–Bell supercharger system, you will also have to shell out some big bucks for free–flowing intakes, larger throttle body, Pro–M mass airflow meter, ported heads, camshaft kit, and headers. When you add the necessary additional pieces and parts, the turbo is probably cheaper.

Detonation—You have already gathered by now that if detonation is a problem in a belt-driven supercharged engine, it must also be a problem in the exhaust-driven supercharged engine. This is of course true. The following section will address the needs of the supercharged engine in controlling detonation.

CONTROLLING DETONATION

The most critical aspect of any power adder is controlling detonation, as has been mentioned and harped upon throughout many areas of this book. Controlling detonation is an absolute must in any engine, but most particularly

in those engines running power adders. Detonation produces a violent collision, "knocking" between the combustion flame and the piston. If it's severe enough, and you are running at racing speeds, it can destroy the engine before you can lift your foot. Controlling detonation can be accomplished either by retarding your initial timing to compensate for the higher combustion flame propagation speed and increased air inlet temperature from the compressor, or by adding a boost-activated ignition timing retard control.

The various options available to control timing retard were covered in Chapter 7. For a supercharged engine, be it exhaust- or belt-driven, the best timing retard control for the 5.0 is the Autotronic Controls MSD 6 BTM module. This is a multi–spark, capacitive discharge ignition module with a built–in boost retard control. Included with the module is a dash-mounted boost retard knob for dialing in the correct timing retard per pound of boost. Obviously, the capacitive discharge ignition is a real plus

and an absolute necessity for those systems running more than 6 psi of boost.

If you already have an upgraded ignition, the MSD Universal Boost Timing Master or the Jacobs Opto–Timer modules are the way to go. These modules provide the convenience of being able to adjust the timing retard from the cockpit of the car. Simple and inexpensive.

Setting Retard

For the engine running a boost retard system, you should set your initial timing at about 16° to 18°, then adjust the retard control. The MSD boost retard knob is calibrated in degrees of retard for each pound of boost. Generally a .75° to 1.25° retard per pound of boost is the range in which to operate. If you have to retard your timing more than 1.25° per pound of boost, you probably need to correct another problem. Do not trust the calibrations on the knob—set it with a pressure pump.

To set the retard control, remove the

distributor timing spout and start the engine. Set the initial timing at 16°. Hook the outlet port of a hand vacuum pump to the vacuum port on the boost control module and pressurize to the anticipated operational boost. With the boost module pressurized, turn the boost retard knob until the timing is retarded 1° for each pound of boost. This is a good baseline to start from. If it is a hot day with poor air quality, use 1.25° retard for each pound of boost as the initial setting.

Make a pass, preferably on a safe drag strip, to test the setting. Listen for detonation. If you hear it, lift immediately. Dial in a 1/4° more retard and try again, repeating the process until the detonation goes away. Install a fresh set of spark plugs and do a plug reading.

If your plugs indicate any detonation, take immediate action to correct the problem. If you do a series of plug readings while increasing fuel pressure to correct a lean condition, and there is no improvement, you have a flow restriction problem. Typically the fuel lines or fuel pump are not up to the demands of a supercharged engine and will require upgrading to correct. See Chapter 5 for determining your fuel delivery needs.

Generally the retard control should not be set to retard the total timing to less than 22° total timing. Retarding the timing below 22° total will not allow enough time for sufficient flame propagation and will only hurt performance. The engine needs at least 22° total advance to build power, so don't go below this. If your engine needs less total timing than 22° you've got other problems. Most likely the air inlet temperature is too high coming off the compressor and an intercooler is needed, or the fuel delivery system is inadequate. Either way you need to fix the problem before proceeding.

Intercooling

An air charge heat exchanger, or intercooler, can be installed between the turbocharger's air discharge nozzle and the throttle body on the 5.0 engine to reduce the temperature of the incoming air. Superchargers and turbochargers agitate the air when compressing it. Consequently, the discharged air is significantly hotter than the ambient temperature. Heated air lacks oxygen density and is prone to pre–ignition or detonation. Detonation you know about. Heated air, because of the reduced oxygen content by comparative volumes, cannot utilize as much fuel as cooler air and therefore horsepower takes a dive.

With an intercooler, the supercharger's heated air can be cooled to provide optimum air temperature. A properly sized intercooler, fitted to a supercharger or turbocharger, can cause the engine to generate more power at 10 psi of boost than 15 psi. This is the reason the '85-1/2 SVO Mustang, with only a 2.3-liter engine, can produce over 200 horsepower in stock condition, running 15 psi of boost. If you are running a turbocharger or supercharger, you can significantly improve performance by fitting one to your car.

There are several companies that sell intercoolers. Probably the best units on the market for the 5.0 Mustang are sold by Ak Miller Enterprises, Cartech, and Spearco. The intercoolers they sell are large and very efficient, as well as providing only a 1/2 lb. of pressure drop through them. Fabrication of custom intercoolers for your system can be made by most of the top turbo installation shops, such as Cartech, Gale Banks, Ak Miller, and McClure Performance. ∎

Due to the low volumetric efficiency of a turbocharger, the air is heated significantly as boost increases. Generally boost levels above 5 psi (10 psi on a supercharger) will require an intercooler to keep the temperature of the compressed air cool enough to avoid detonation. Shown here is a typical mounting approach for installing an intercooler in a Fox Mustang.

INSTALLING A KENNE-BELL WHIPPLECHARGER

(Photos courtesy Kenne-Bell Performance Products)

As I mentioned in the text, the supercharger system offered by Kenne-Bell is the newest one offered for the 5.0 liter Mustang. The core of the system is a twin-screw, positive displacement blower from Whipple Industries, that effectively creates boost by compressing air between two interlaced screws or rotors. Some of its more positive features are higher volumetric efficiency, lower exit air temperature, and instant maximum boost. Its major disadvantages are accessibility to valve covers for maintenance, and its use of a single, factory-type serpentine drive belt that power all pulleys and accessories. If it breaks, as many supercharger belts are inclined to do, the entire engine stops running. Carry a spare at all times.

1. The basic Kenne-Bell Twin-Screw Whipplecharger comes complete with all brackets, bolts and gaskets.

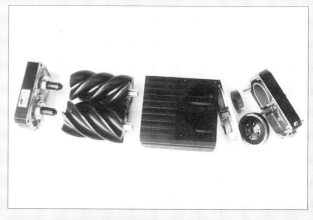

2. When disassembled, you can see the dual compressor screws that make the Whipplecharger so efficient. The screw-type compressor has the additional benefit of providing constant air output, unlike the pulsing generally associated with the Roots-type blower.

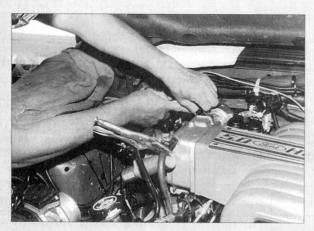

3. After you have disconnected the battery ground, drain the coolant, discharge the a/c refrigerant, remove the serpentine belt, the air inlet tube, both air conditioning hoses from the compressor and the coolant lines to the throttle body.

4. Remove all the hardware that attaches the air conditioning and power steering bracket to the front of the engine. Remove the bolt closest to the water pump from the compressor-to-head mount, loosen the other bolt and swing the air conditioning compressor out of the way.

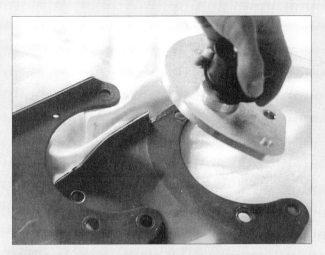

5. Modify the a/c-p/s bracket according to the template provided by Kenne-Bell. Dress any burrs on the redrilled hole and cut off the edge.

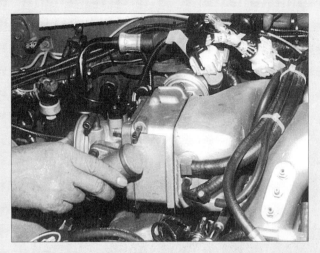

6. Remove all hoses and throttle linkage, and disconnect the TPS connector. Remove the throttle body and the throttle cable bracket. Remove all remaining hoses attached to the upper intake.

7. Remove the six bolts that hold the upper intake to the lower intake and remove the assembly. Remove the two long studs from the stock upper intake that hold the throttle body on, and install them on the supercharger. Rotate the injectors counterclockwise until the electrical connector contacts the fuel rail. Also disconnect the plug wires from the left engine bank and lay them out of the way on the right side of the engine. Clean the gasket mating surface thoroughly.

8. Install the modified a/c-p/s bracket and the power steering pump, and loosely install the a/c compressor. Install the 5/16" stud to the right rear upper intake attachment hole on the lower intake. Using the 5/16" stud as a guide, slowly lower the supercharger in place. Install the remaining two passenger side attachment bolts and the three special socket head bolts for the driver's side. A special Allen wrench is provided in the kit for this step. Torque all six attachment bolts to 24 ft-lbs.

continued on next page

9. Attach the two bolts for the a/c compressor to the special bracket and tighten all the remaining bolts.

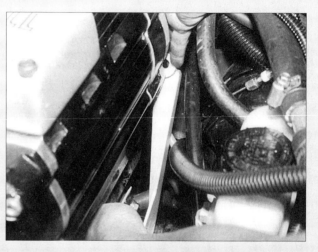

10. Install the rear support bracket to the supercharger and the rear exhaust bolt. Headers may require slight modifications or the addition of washers to get the spacing correct. Do not install so as to bind or pull against the supercharger. This bracket is only for support .

11. Install the supercharger belt. Start at the supercharger pulley, under the stock idler pulley, over the alternator pulley, over the outside of the smog pump pulley, over the top of the water pump pulley, around the outside of the crank, power steering, and a/c pulleys and then under the new idler back to the supercharger pulley. Kenne-Bell supplies a detailed drawing in the kit to help.

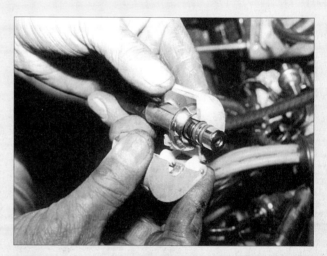

12. Using the special spring-lok coupling disconnector, disconnect the return fuel line at the fuel rail. This is the smaller of the two lines.

13. Connect the fuel regulator lines from the fuel system booster in series between the fuel return line and the fuel rail.

14. Re-install the throttle body, reconnect the TPS and EGR idle control connectors as well as the throttle cable bracket and cable. Connect the three vacuum lines to the supercharger.

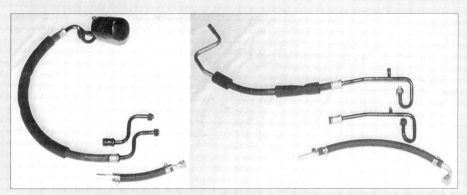

15. Modify the a/c hoses by cutting them 1-1/2" back from the metal sleeves. Install the new hose fittings and reinstall to the a/c system.

16. Re-install the left side plug wires, routing them under the supercharger's drive snout.

17. Re-check all bolts and belt installation. Fill the supercharger with the provided oil. Do not overfill. If you overfill the system, drain out the surplus. Too much oil will cause a seal failure. Not good. Turn on the ignition and check for fuel leaks. If everything is cool, hammer it!

DRIVETRAIN

10

Building high horsepower engines to go fast will not mean much if you can not get the power to the ground. The stock Mustang equipment is pretty rugged, however things start to break as horsepower is elevated. Upgrades to clutches, transmissions, driveshafts, differentials and axles all have to be considered.

It is extremely frustrating to have a drivetrain component go south at the starting line or in the middle of a race. The key to avoiding this is to be prepared. You must budget for the extra costs of getting the horsepower to the ground. The stock 5.0 clutch is barely adequate for a stock engine and clearly will not withstand the demands of additional engine modifications. This is further compounded by the lack of torque handling capacity in the Borg–Warner T–5 gearbox. Anyone who has ever heard that explosive bang and sudden deceleration while hammering it in third gear knows all too well the limitations of the T–5 gearbox.

Although it has proven itself to be quite tough, the Ford 8.8 axle will generally require upgrades to handle major horsepower increases. The old saying "If you want to play, you gotta pay" was never more true.

When planning your project it is important to keep in mind the limitation of the stock pieces to withstand increased horsepower and torque levels. The stock T-5 gearbox is adequate, at best, for stock class autocrossing or road racing. However, powershifting and the abuses of drag racing will generally result in a wasted third gear as shown above (arrow).

Elevating the horsepower and traction in your Mustang will require an upgrade to the clutch. The Ford Motorsport Heavy Duty clutch kit (M7560-A302) pictured here is the way to go on a normally aspirated engine. (Photo courtesy Ford Motorsport/SVO)

CLUTCHES

Upgrading the 5.0 clutch can be as simple as replacing the pressure plate and disc with a Ford Motorsport or Centerforce set, or it can be as complicated as a multi–disc setup. The choice is largely dependent on your budget and the horsepower output of your engine. No doubt about it, the multi–disc clutches are the trick setup. They are extremely durable and can take all the 5.0 engine can dish out. If your engine is producing more than 450 horsepower, the single disc clutches will not hold up for any extended period of time. Spend the bucks and go for one of the dual–disc setups available from all the top clutch manufacturers.

Ford Motorsport & Centerforce

For applications under 450 horsepower, the Ford Motorsport and Centerforce clutches will provide good service. Ford Motorsport sells them both. I have used both behind engines generating near 400 horsepower and found them to be reliable. At about 400 horsepower and beyond, the life of the standard disc is significantly shortened.

If your engine is putting out horsepower in this range, replace your clutch disc with one of the super heavy–duty discs, with the metallic lining on one side and an organic material on the other. Ford Motorsport sells one such disc that they claim will take 750 horsepower.

If you are upgrading the clutch in your Mustang, and your engine is not producing horsepower above 350 or so, the best buy on the market is the Ford Motorsport H.D. clutch kit (M7560–A302). It comes packaged with the heavy–duty pressure plate and disc as well as a new throwout bearing. Even if your Mustang is stock, this is a mandatory upgrade. The stock clutch will not hold up to any aggressive driving for very long.

Safety Items

I strongly recommend the installation of a scattershield and block plate. Watching a clutch go sawing through the dash of a Fairlane as I power–shifted into third gear made me a firm believer. I was fortunate. You may not be so lucky. Clutch technology has improved by several light years since my experience with the disappearing pressure plate. However, this upgrade is still very important. If you are a drag racer and plan a trip to a real drag strip with your sub-12-second Pony, the NHRA and IHRA tech inspectors will require a scattershield.

Clutch Quadrant

The weak link in the clutch system on the 5.0 Mustang has always been the self–adjusting plastic clutch quadrant. It is prone to failure when heavy-duty clutches are installed. If you are experiencing this problem, you can replace your clutch quadrant with a billet aluminum piece sold by BBK Performance (see sidebar p. 146). It is a direct replacement for the plastic quadrant and utilizes an adjustable clutch cable for precision clutch adjustment.

For a high horsepower engine running a single disc setup, the Centerforce clutch is the only way to go. Shown here is the trick setup from Esslinger Engineering for the high boost turbo 2.3L engines.

BBK's CLUTCH QUADRANT KIT

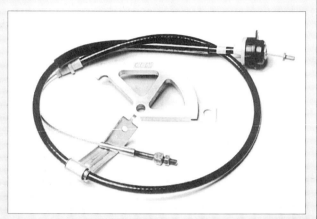

The Fox-chassied Mustangs & T-Birds equipped with manual transmissions and self-adjusting clutch mechanisms are notorious for developing clutch problems, especially if the driver likes to dump the clutch now and then or is teaching a friend how to drive a "stick." Hard shifting between gears or poor clutch adjustment where the clutch will grab at a low pedal height (such as right off the floor) are some of the more common problems that occur. But before you remove the transmission and replace the clutch, check the clutch quadrant. The quadrant is located underneath the dash panel directly above the accelerator pedal, and is composed of two plastic pieces with plastic gears that activate the clutch cable. When the clutch pedal is depressed, the gears engage and move the cable, which engages the clutch. As you might have guessed, the plastic gears wear out rather quickly and will either not stay engaged or will slip. Furthermore, the stock setup does not allow for any cable adjustment. Both of these design features can lead to hard shifting between gears, and low pedal grab.

The problem has been solved by BBK Performance Parts. They have designed a replacement clutch quadrant machined from a single piece of billet aluminum that does not rely on gears to activate the cable. The unit will fit any Fox-chassied Mustang or T-Bird with the self-adjusting clutch mechanism. The BBK cable is of a heavy-duty performance caliber, complete with a threaded end that allows for fine clutch pedal adjustment. Installation is relatively simple, with the hardest part being the removal of the quadrant itself because it must be done by feel while lying under the dashboard.—Michael Lutfy

Source:

BBK Performance Parts, 1611 Railroad St., Corona, CA 91720. 909/735-8880

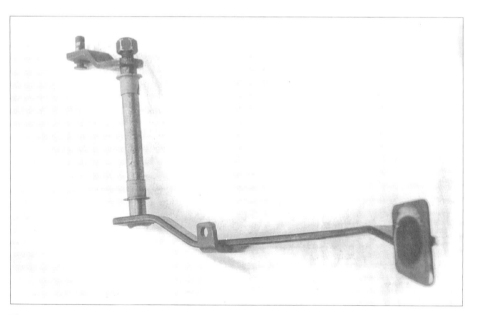

Tired of the plastic clutch quadrant blues? An alternative is to replace your self-adjusting clutch pedal and quadrant with the manually adjusted pedal from the '79/80 Mustang. Use the D9ZZ-7K553-B clutch cable and fabricate a bracket to attach a spring to pull the clutch fork away from the pressure plate.

Alternately, you can also replace your clutch quadrant and pedal with pieces from a '79-'80 Mustang or Capri. These cars used an adjustable clutch cable instead of the self–adjusting quadrant. Use a D9ZZ–7K553–B adjustable clutch cable, and fabricate an L-shaped bracket to attach a spring to pull the clutch fork away from the pressure plate when at rest. Attach the bracket to the left side middle tailhousing bolt on the transmission and run a spring to the clutch fork (purchase the spring at any hardware store). If you are running a long–finger or Borg & Beck style clutch, you will need to replace the clutch fork pivot stud with an adjustable stud from a Chevrolet Vega (PN 03973138). This is necessary to correct the clutch

Outwardly identical to the TR-3550, the Reider modified version, the TR4250, can withstand 425 lbs-ft. of torque. If you are hard on gearboxes then spend the extra bucks and get this for your mean machine.

fork–to–pressure plate angle for proper clutch actuation.

Flywheel

When upgrading your single-disc clutch, you must have the flywheel resurfaced. It may appear fine, but invariably there are hard spots that can give a new disc fits and cause it to chatter. If your flywheel has numerous hard spots (blue or raised areas on the clutch disc engagement surface) or if after machining, the hard spots can still be detected, replace it. These things don't get better and will only cause a new clutch to go bad quickly, not to mention that embarrassing chatter.

The stock cast-iron flywheel is adequate for its intended purpose. However, for the protection of your feet (especially if you are not running a scattershield), replace it with the Ford Motorsport billet steel flywheel (M6375–C302). This thing is a real work of art. Built to withstand more rpm than any 5.0 engine will ever see (17,000 rpm), this upgrade is a must for those engines turning more than 6000 rpm.

If you are a road racer, a lightweight flywheel can vastly improve corner exit acceleration speed as well as deceleration. Hays and McLeod both sell

excellent lightweight flywheels for the 5.0 engine. You will probably notice a rougher idle after installing a light flywheel. Without the mass of a heavy flywheel to smooth out the power pulses at low engine speeds, the engine will go through a series of short accelerations and decelerations between power pulses. Basically there will be the sensation of a mildly cammed engine.

If your Mustang is set up for road racing and you are going for maximum performance, you will need to fit a small-diameter flywheel and bellhousing assembly. This will allow the engine to be lowered at least 1" and moved back 2". Without the small-diameter bell-housing, the bellhousing will collide with the firewall, and ground clearance will be a problem. The most common solution to the small bellhousing problem is to use the Tilton Engineering setup. This is first-class equipment that is standard issue in IMSA, SCCA Trans Am and NASCAR. They have the lightweight small diameter bellhousing with matching flywheels and clutches, as well as the rear entry starters.

MANUAL TRANSMISSIONS

Every gear jammer knows how delicate the stock T–5 gearbox is. Transmission shops are littered with dead T–5s. The only cure is to swap for an automatic or install a strong gearbox. If you are a clutch and stick driver, there are only four bolt–in options. You can replace your weak T–5 with the Ford Motorsport M7003–X Heavy–Duty "World Class" T–5, install a TREMEC TR3550, upgrade to the 425 lbs-ft. capacity TREMEC TR4250, or go whole hog and move up to a Richmond Gear 6–speed.

If you are a stick driver in a modified Mustang you will want to upgrade to the 400 lbs-ft. torque capacity of the Tremec TR-3550. These are tough gearboxes that can withstand considerable abuse.

147

Ford's HD T-5

The Heavy–Duty "World Class" T–5 is an excellent gearbox for production level road racing and mildly modified drag racing Mustangs. This gearbox is the same as the original "World Class" T–5 (M7003–A) except it has stronger cluster 2nd and 3rd gears. Although an excellent gearbox, the 325 lbs-ft. of torque capacity limits its reliability. If you are a drag racer, the close ratio first gear (2.95:1) is generally thought to be undesirable for optimum launch. You would have to install a 4.10 axle gear to achieve the same basic first gear ratio that a standard T–5 with a 3.73 axle has.

T–5 gearboxes are prone to input shaft seal failure. Anytime you pull the gearbox you should replace this seal. If you are running a T–5 transmission, do not put 60 or 90 weight gear oil in it. The T–5 is designed to use ATF weight oil and has very small oil transfer holes to lubricate the needle bearings. The thick gear oil will not flow into these tiny holes, especially under cold conditions, and the transmission soon becomes junk. Some of the quick lube stops will often

The best guarantee you can get for longevity in a gearbox is a Hurst shifter. The precise shift patterns go a long way toward preventing missed shifts and blown trannies.

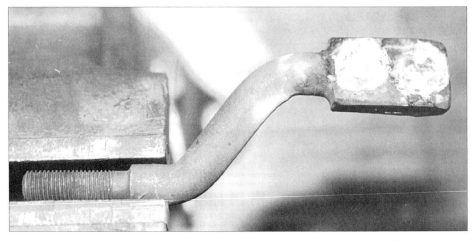

If you are stuck with the stock shifter or you are using the '85 short-throw shifter, improve your shifting precision by brazing up the holes and drilling new holes with a "P" drill bit. This will allow the lever to be bolted firmly against the shifter, eliminating the mush associated with the rubber grommets.

fill a gearbox with the heavy grease by mistake. If you have your car serviced, ask before they start work. They may get incensed by such a stupid question, but it is better to be safe than to walk.

TREMEC

The TREMEC TR3550 and TR4250 are rugged 5–speed gearboxes that represent a new standard of reliability. These are tough gearboxes that can withstand some serious horsepower. The TR3550 is rated at 350 lbs-ft. of torque, which equates to 400 to 500 horsepower. The super–duty TR4250 can handle 425 lbs-ft. of torque at 600 horsepower. This is a serious transmission. The gear spacing is well suited for drag racing, with a 3.27 low gear and a .68 overdrive 5th gear for the economy trip. If you are having gearbox trouble, this is definitely the cure.

Richmond Gear

For those wanting the ultimate streetable transmission, the Richmond Gear R.O.D. six-speed gearbox is it. This thing is a religious experience. Rated at 450 lbs-ft. of torque, this gearbox can take whatever you dish out. The first five gears are closely spaced for keeping the engine "on the pipe," while the overdrive 6th gear comes in four different ratios to match your driving

needs. Is this cool or what? It gives a gear jammer goose bumps just thinking about it.

Shifters

The TREMEC and Richmond Gear transmissions are supplied with their own unique shifters. No aftermarket shifters are currently available. Fortunately, the short–throw shifters that are supplied are excellent. For the stock or "World Class" T–5, there are only two options for shifters. The least expensive approach is to replace the stock shifter with the 1985 "Short Throw" shifter sold by Ford Motorsport (M7210–A). This shifter is installed on all new "World Class" T–5s. It is a good shifter that will provide a much improved shift pattern over the long-gated shifter found on the production T–5 transmission. Obviously the best choice would be to install one of the new Hurst shifters that utilizes the stock long shift handle. This design change from the original Hurst T–5 shifter vastly improves the relationship between the driver and the shift handle. This is particularly important if your arms are shorter than an NBA forward. If you are drag racing, skip the short-throw shifter and go directly for the Hurst. The T–5 gearbox is fragile enough without having to contend with a missed shift.

148

AUTOMATIC TRANSMISSIONS

If your Mustang is equipped with an automatic transmission, you will have to upgrade the stock A.O.D. to handle even small horsepower increases. There are several companies that offer kits that can significantly improve the shifting and reliability of this transmission. However, if you are a straight-line leadfoot, the A.O.D. should be replaced.

There are essentially three options to the drag racer wanting the consistency that an automatic transmission offers. You can replace your A.O.D. with a modified small-block C–6, install one of the racing C–4's, or spend some real money and install one of the Project Industries TH700–R4 conversions.

C-6—Before the rash of modified C–4 transmissions, the only way to get reliability from a racing Ford automatic was to use the C–6. This is a very tough automatic that can withstand monster levels of torque. Ford Motorsport, as well as B&M and others, sells first-class, race-proven parts for this transmission. It is easy to service and parts are plentiful.

C-4—The current rage for the quarter-mile addicts running automatics is a modified C–4. This includes some very fast company. Gene Deputy and Joe Rivera are two of the many who swear by it. There are several top transmission shops who modify the C–4 for drag racing. Jim's Transmissions, Rossi Transmissions and Art Carr Performance Transmission Products are currently the top contenders, although there are many others with transmissions that make it to the winner's circle.

700R4—If you want a bull-stout transmission that has an excellent .70 overdrive 4th gear, as well as a lockup converter, the TH700–R4 makes for a slick street/strip setup. Kenny Brown markets a complete conversion kit for the 5.0 Mustang for installing this transmission. If you have access to a post-'85 TH700–R4, Rossi Transmissions and Art Carr Performance Transmission Products sell adapter kits for the Ford engine. B&M also sells a slick Lock–Up Converter Electronic Speed Control that allows you to adjust the speed at which the converter locks up. Much like the Ford C–6, there are quite a few racing parts available for this transmission, including torque converters for virtually any stall speed needed. Although this transmission is built by GM, it is the best tranny currently available for the street/strip drag racer wanting the benefits of an overdrive for highway cruising.

REAR ENDS

There are only really two axle assemblies to run, the 8.8 and the brute 9-inch. The 8.8 axle assembly that is installed in all 1987 and newer H.O.

Breaking transmissions can be a real problem with a monster motor 460 in your Mustang. Although not real streetable, the Lenco will take all the abuse your mega-horsepower engine can dish out.

149

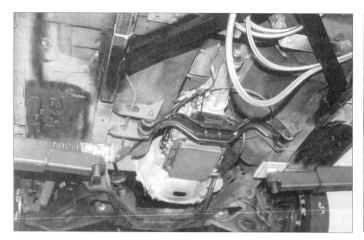

Unless you are Bob Glidden it is unlikely you can shift a gearbox as consistently as an automatic can for a quarter-mile stretch of payment. The current rage in drag racing is the modified C-4. Shown here is a popular variation from Jim's Transmissions that allows this Mustang to consistently run mid-10s.

Drag racing an automatic transmission requires a converter that is matched for the optimum power curve of your engine. The TCI unit shown here has a small diameter converter that allows the engine to run at 4800 rpm (stall speed) before engaging. Without this high stall speed the car could not launch under full power.

Mustangs has proven to be far more difficult to break than was first thought. This axle assembly sits under some very fast cars. Richard Holdener runs the 8.8 in his 180 mph Silver State-winning Mustang, as does Hal Baer in his World Challenge supercharged Mustang. The Joe Rivera-prepared 9-second Mustang of Mario Mesa also runs the 8.8 axle assembly. If you have ever seen his dual-turbocharged monster launch on the way to a 9-second run, you truly can appreciate the strength of the 8.8 assembly.

8.8 Improvements

The 8.8 axle assembly is strong but can be improved for better reliability by adding a TA Performance cover girdle and carrier bearing studs. This high-grade aluminum inspection cover provides significant support and rigidity to the axle housing center section. Additionally, it has adjustable set screws that butt against the carrier bearing caps to reduce torque induced distortion. If you are a drag racer running in the sub-12-second range, this should be a mandatory upgrade.

8.8 Axles—The stock 28-spline axles will generally go south when subjected to repeated drag race launches. This becomes particularly common when the horsepower moves beyond the 400 mark. There are numerous reputable axle manufacturers (Moser Engineering, Summers Bros., Strange Engineering and Williams) who sell competition grade replacement 28- and 31-spline axles. Unless you are limited by budget or class rules, upgrade your carrier and install the stronger 31-spline axles. They are significantly stronger and will provide much more reliable service.

Controlling the in-and-out movement of the axles on an 8.8 rear end is imperative if you are running tight-fitting slicks or rigid-mounted rear disc brake calipers. There are two common ways to deal with this. The simplest approach is to install Moser Engineering C–Clip Eliminators. This kit provides two single–roll ball bearings mounted in aluminum housings that press onto the stock 8.8 axles. You must cut a small section from the ends of the axle housing, as well as remove the factory axle bearings. Since the axle is secured by the pressed-on bearings, there will no longer be a need to use the axle C–clips. Not only does it control the in-and-out movement, but it also allows easy access to the axle without having to go through the laborious process of removing the C–clips.

This scattershield will not make your car go faster and definitely is heavier than the stock bellhousing. Yet, it can save your life and is mandatory on most modified cars at an NHRA or IHRA event. Don't leave home without it.

If you are having problems with the 8.8 rear, a bolt-in 9-inch replacement shown here from Currie Enterprises is the cure. The strength of the 9-inch Ford housing is legendary, and Currie Enterprises has made replacement relatively simple.

You can substantially improve the life of your 8.8 axle assembly by installing a TA Performance cover girdle and bearing support studs. This cover is made from high grade aluminum and incorporates adjustable posts that butt against each carrier cap. This extra support greatly reduces housing distortion that occurs when the carrier is subjected to drag race launches.

Although simple, this approach to controlling axle movement should be reserved for drag race cars. I have done extensive testing with these C–Clip Eliminators on the *Slot Car Mustang* and have confirmed exactly what Greg Moser promised. These things work great in a straight line but leak like a sieve when subjected to high cornering forces. Fear not, there is a cure for the corner racer. Replace your axles with a set of 28.75" long axles that are designed for the 9-inch big-bearing Ford housing. You will need a set of 20 Timkin bearings and two specially machined 9-inch axle tube ends. The specially machined housing ends can be acquired from Moser Engineering. Once the housing ends have been modified, the 8.8 housing is shortened on each end at the point where the axle housing increases to full

diameter. The machined 9-inch axle housing ends are then slipped onto the 8.8 housing stubs, indexed and welded in place. Additionally, you will have to replace your brake drum backing plate with one from a 9-inch housing or if you are using disc brakes, you must fit a brake caliper bracket designed for the 9-inch housing. This setup provides a very tough and reliable axle housing that can withstand the rigors of road racing.

9-Inch Upgrade—When the horsepower climbs to the point where you can run 9-second passes, it will probably be necessary to upgrade to a 9-inch Ford housing and carrier. The 9-inch is sold in bolt–in form for the late-model Mustang from virtually every axle manufacturer and then some. The strength of the Ford 9-inch is legendary. However, it's probably overkill for the 5.0 engine

modifications presented in this book. For those who have not kept the faith and have installed 460 cid monster motors in their Mustangs, the 9-inch rear is a mandatory upgrade.

8.8 Differential—The 8.8 axle assembly, as installed in the 5.0 H.O. Mustang, uses the standard Ford Traction–Lok differential. This is a clutchless type differential that depends on the outward torque applied by the spider gears to compress the drive and driven clutch discs to lock up. Under new or low-mileage conditions, the Traction–Lok is an excellent differential. Unfortunately, the rigors of racing quickly reduce the clutch discs to slippery spacers. Curing the slip problem

Need tubs and fender-to-fender slicks for your Pro Street Mustang? Zander Action Products in Houston can fix you up. These jig-built housings utilizing the Ford 9-inch carrier can withstand anything, provided you keep the horsepower below 5,000.

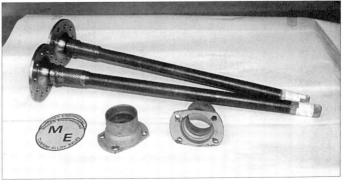

Big slicks and high horsepower spell disaster for the skinny 28-spline factory axles. Upgrade your 8.8 with a set of 9-inch axles and bearing carriers. A kit is avaiable from Greg Moser Engineering, (219/726-6689).

will entail a complete rebuild of the differential. However, when you get through, you still have a weak traction control device. Obviously an upgrade should be budgeted.

Upgrading the differential in the 8.8 requires a new carrier assembly. For the trailered drag race car the choice is simple. A steel spool should be substituted for the differential. This will insure identical application of torque to both rear wheels. The differential spool is sold by all the usual axle manufacturers. It is important to note, however, that a spool is a poor choice for the street-driven car. Not only is there tremendous stress on the axles when negotiating a turn, but the instability of the rear end through a slick or wet turn will guarantee a spin. Tooling around with a spooled rear end is a great deal like playing Russian Roulette. You just never know when things could get unpleasant.

Aftermarket Choices

The better choice for the dual-purpose street/drag racer, would be the ARB Air Locker, the Auburn locking differential,

or the new Detroit Locker. The ARB Air Locker utilizes a small air compressor to operate a pneumatic locking system inside the carrier. When the air compressor is activated, the pneumatic annular piston inside the carrier engages the locking gears and the carrier functions as a spool. When not activated, the carrier operates as a conventional open differential. This provides the best of both worlds for the straight-line addict. Installation is a bit of a hassle though, as the axle assembly has to be removed to drill and tap for the air feed line.

Auburn Differential—The Auburn differential is the most popular replacement for the Traction–Lok currently on the market. Unlike the Traction–Lok, the Auburn uses cones that lock into their seats as the torque increases to the axles. This provides for a very solid lockup that does not slip. Installation is very straightforward, requiring the usual shim juggling. This carrier is excellent for a straight-line racer and adequate for the road racer. The standard Auburn carrier is good for up to 450 horsepower.

The Auburn differential that is sold to

the average public is not designed to withstand the rigors of road racing. High cornering forces and sticky tires can cause the cones to slip. According to the technicians at Auburn, once a cone slips, the carrier is basically junk. To that end, Auburn builds a special 28-spline carrier that was originally designed for the Firehawk racing series. If you're going road racing with an Auburn, this "race-only" carrier is an excellent choice.

Detroit Locker—The best differential for the racing rear axle assembly has traditionally been the Detroit Locker. Since this differential was not available for the 8.8 axle, the Auburn has been the best option. Fortunately, there is now a Detroit Locker made specifically for the 8.8 axle. For the average racer, this is the differential of choice, especially if you are a road racer.

Thorsen-Gleason—If money is no object, the finest carrier is the one used by the F1 cars, the Thorsen–Gleason. This carrier is a very sophisticated carrier that is capable of withstanding anything a 5.0 can lay on it. However, it will put a significant dent your wallet.

Smoke from the inside tire is a clear indication that your differential has gone south. If it is an Auburn, as is the case in the photo, you may be able to sand the glaze from the cones and seats for a small revival. If you have driven it hard with the cones slipping, you may not be able to revive it.

The Auburn differential is a super heavy-duty unit that incorporates cone-type clutches instead of plates, built to withstand the most severe street, strip or race track abuse. It bolts directly in place of the stock differential with no modifications. (Photo courtesy BBK Performance)

Installing a new ring and pinion is like dealing with anything inside an engine. Keep it clean, keep it clean , keep it clean. Ford high-performance whiz Don Schulz uses a brake cleaning spray to wash out all the uglies that have collected inside a housing before fitting a new gearset.

CHANGING GEARS

One of the quickest ways to improve the performance of your Mustang is to install a set of "gears." The factory sends the Mustang to the street sporting a 2.73 axle gearset as standard issue. The exception is the SVO Mustang that had 3.45 ('84) and 3.73 ('85 & '86) gearsets (with the 7.5" gears). There is an optional 3.08 available for the 5–speed cars and an optional 3.27 gearset for the automatic-equipped Mustang. The best approach is to change the ring gear & pinion on those Mustangs equipped with the 8.8 axle or swap the complete 7.5 rear axle assembly for a Ford Motorsport 8.8 with the gear set of choice.

Recommendations—For a street car that is driven on a highway occasionally, the 3.55 gearset is normally the optimum choice. However, the 3.73 ratio is by far the best choice for the hot street setup. Gear ratios beyond 3.73 typically are better suited for the drag strip or tight road racing circuits. Generally a normally aspirated car set up for drag

If your budget does not include a new Detroit Locker or Auburn, you can improve the lockup of your Traction-Lok by replacing a driven disc with a drive plate and stacking them in series as shown in the photograph above.

Ford Motorsport offers replacement high-performance ring and pinion gearsets with ratios from 3.27 to 4.56. BBK Performance sells them along with all necessary shims and gear oil. (Photo courtesy BBK Performance)

When installing a new gearset, a small section of 2x4 can be placed across the exhaust to hold the driveshaft out of the way. This beats banging your head on the driveshaft or dealing with the transmission fluid on your driveway.

The mating surface on the carrier must be clean and burr-free. The easiest approach is to use a high-speed sander with a tough Scotchbrite® pad to deburr the surfaces.

racing can use a 4.10 or 4.30 ratio to put the car at 6000 rpm at the finish line. If your car is equipped with a blower or turbo, you will probably want to stick with the 3.73 gearset. For more help on selecting gear ratios, see the sidebar on p. 156.

Installing a gearset is not difficult, provided you have the correct pinion depth tool. I have seen numerous gearsets installed without the correct tools. Generally this is done by an experienced installer who understands gear patterns and can judge the crush requirements to achieve the proper wear pattern. I do not recommend this approach though. A lot of gearsets get ruined this way. If you do not have the tools, install the ring gear on the carrier and let someone else set the pinion depth.

Installing Gears

There are a few precautions to observe when installing a new gearset.

1. Always mark the right carrier cap and the housing next to it with a punch. This will insure the correct cap goes on the correct location on the housing. These caps are machined just like a main bearing cap in an engine and are therefore unique to that location.

2. Always use a countersink tool or large drill bit to deburr the ring gear bolt holes in the ring gear. This will help to insure a flat fit with the carrier.

3. Always spread a thin coating of fine valve seat lapping compound on a large flat surface (thick glass or steel plate) and carefully lap the backside (mating surface) of the ring gear before installing it. This is very important to provide a flat and smooth surface for the gear to seat

Like the carrier, the mating surface of the ring gear must be flat and burr-free. Counter-sink the bolt holes and deburr the mating surface with a high-speed sander.

Production tolerances being what they are, it is imperative that you check the inside of the housing, especially the carrier caps, for casting burrs that must be removed. Little pieces of this can break loose and trash a bearing or gearset.

Setting the pinion depth on an 8.8 axle requires this special tool. I know a lot of backyard mechanics install new gearsets without this, but doing so is a big gamble. If the pinion depth is set wrong, the ring gear will howl and you'll probably ruin it in the process.

With the pinion depth gauge installed, it is a simple matter of finding a pinion spacer that fits between the pinion tool and the carrier spool. Generally the fit should have about the same feel as a feeler gauge does when setting a valve on a mechanical camshaft.

onto the carrier. This may seem like overkill, but it will amaze you how often the ring gear has little burrs on the back that prevent a positive seat. When this happens the gear can work loose and then things really go bad. Take the time to do it.

4. When pulling the axles out, do not just jerk them out. Hold them up so they do not slide along the axle seals. The seals are easily damaged. You can cut one of these and probably not notice it. However, when the leak starts, you will have to go through the fun process of pulling the C–clip and axle again to replace the seal, so be careful the first time. ■

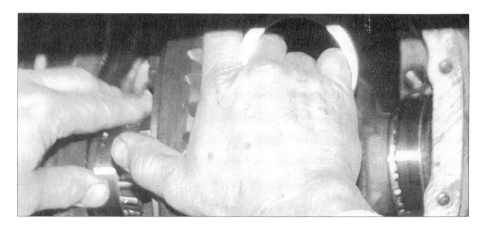

After you have set the pinion depth the last adjustment is the backlash. On the 8.8 axle this is done by changing the bearing cone spacers. Essentially you move the carrier right to reduce backlash and left to increase it. This is not difficult, just increase or decrease the opposite cone spacer for the identical amount of change you make on the other side. Typically .008" to .012" is the range you want, with things a little on the loose side for road racing.

Setting the backlash requires a dial indicator be mounted against the end of a ring gear tooth for an accurate reading. The Ford service manual says checking the wear pattern is unnecessary if the pinion depth and backlash are correct. The experienced racer knows to check everything regardless of what the manufacturer says.

Before you install the spider gear pin retaining bolt, clean the treads thoroughly, spray a cleaner inside the bolt hole (brake cleaner) and apply a thread locking solution (Loctite). This bolt has been known to work loose without the thread solution, so do not overlook this.

CALCULATING GEAR RATIOS

Selecting the best gear ratio for optimum performance is a function of tire diameter, mph, rpm and the transmission and final-drive ratios. By using these variables in several different mathematical formulas, it's possible to calculate what effect a certain gear ratio will have on rpm and fuel mileage. You can also determine which gear ratio is best to achieve various levels of performance.

The available gear ratios for the 8.8-inch rear end in the 5.0 liter Mustang are: 2.73, 3.08, 3.27, 3.55, 3.73 and 4.10. The transmission ratios for the stock 5-speed transmission are: 1.00 in fourth gear, and 0.68 in fifth. For the automatic, the ratios are 1.00 in third and 0.67 in fourth, so what works for the 5-speed will also work with the automatic. Three stock tire sizes, P215/65R-15, P225/60VR-15, and P225/55ZR-16 ('91 and up only) are available, with tire diameters of 26.0, 25.5 and 25.0 inches respectively. These figures can be plugged into a formula to help you determine the rpm you'll be turning at a certain mph with a certain gear ratio. They can also help you determine what gear ratio is needed to achieve a certain rpm at a given speed.

RPM

Suppose you want to know what rpm you'll be turning at a given mph in fifth gear if your Mustang is equipped with 2.73 gears? The formula for this is the mph times the transmission ratio, times the gear ratio, times the constant 336, divided by the tire diameter. Expressed as an equation, it looks like this:

$$RPM = \frac{mph \times transmission\ ratio \times gear\ ratio \times 336}{tire\ diameter}$$

Let's say you're cruising along at 60 mph, running the stock P225/60VR-15 tires which have a diameter of 25.5 inches. The fifth gear ratio for the manual transmission is 0.68. Plug these figures into the formula:

$$RPM = \frac{60 \times 0.68 \times 2.73 \times 336}{25.5}$$

$$RPM = \frac{37,425.024}{25.5}$$

$$RPM = 1467.64$$

With this setup, you'll be turning approximately 1468 rpm, which means good fuel economy. However, you're only about midway on the stock 5.0-liter engine's torque curve, which peaks at 3200 rpm. If you downshift to fourth gear, using the same figures above (remember, fourth gear on the 5-speed is direct, at 1.0) the rpm jumps to 2158, which gives you more power for passing.

But suppose you change gears to a lower set, say 3.73? In fifth gear, under the same conditions, you'll be turning a little over 2000 rpm at 60 mph. Downshift to fourth, and the rpm goes up to just about 2950 rpm. Because the stock 5.0-liter engine's torque peaks at 3200 rpm, you'll be pretty close to maximum power for passing at 60 mph. However, keep in mind that your fuel economy will go down as well. If you do a lot of freeway cruising and you're concerned about fuel economy, you may want to go with 3.55 gears with this example. These gears would lower the rpm for better economy, but still put you closer to maximum torque than the 2.73 gears at 60 mph in fifth gear, meaning better performance. In other words, 3.55 gears split the difference between 2.73 and 3.73 gears and offer the best compromise.

APPENDIX

Engine
Data Sheet

Assembled by: _____

Date _____

Block

Manufacturer _____		Part No. _____

Cylinder Bore _____ "

Cylinders Sleeved

1	2	3	4	5	6	7	8

Mains Bore _____ "

Align-bored?   [yes] [no]

Lifter Bore _____ "

Bore Centered?   [yes] [no]

Cam Bearings: Manufacturer _____   Part No. _____

Main Studs/Bolts: Manufacturer _____   Part No. _____

Head Studs/Bolts: Manufacturer _____   Part No. _____

Oil Pump

Manufacturer _____   Part No. _____

Blueprinted?   [yes] [no]   Blueprinted by: _____

Oil Pump Shaft: Manufacturer _____   Part No. _____

Oil Pump Screen   Manufacturer _____   Part No. _____

Plate-to-Rotor Crush _____ "   Rotor-to-Rotor Clearance _____ "

Special modifications: _____

Connecting Rods

Manufacturer _____   Part No. _____

Pin Floated?   [yes] [no]   Beams Polished/Peened?   [yes] [no]

Center-to-Center Length _____ "   Weight _____ grams

Small End:

    Size _____ "   Weight _____ grams

Large End:

    Size _____ "   Weight _____ grams

Rod Bolts: Manufacturer _____   Part No. _____

Engine
Data Sheet

Engine

Piston

Manufacturer _____ Part No. _____

Skirt Diameter _____ " Pin Hole Diameter _____ "

Pin Offset _____ " Weight _____ grams

Piston Pin: Manufacturer _____ Part No. _____

Pin Diameter _____ " Weight _____ grams

C-Clips: Manufacturer _____ Part No. _____

Design: Snap-ring ☐ Spiral ☐ Weight _____ grams

Installed Clearance _____ "

Rings

Manufacturer _____ Part No. _____

Weight _____ grams Top: Width _____ " End Gap _____ "
(per piston set)

Middle: Width _____ " End Gap _____ "

Oil: Width _____ " End Gap _____ "

Bearings Mains: Manufacturer _____ Part No. _____

Installed Clearance _____ "

Rods: Manufacturer _____ Part No. _____

Installed Clearance _____ " Weight _____ grams

Crankshaft

Manufacturer _____ Part No. _____

Main Journal Size _____ "

Rod Journal Size _____ "

Special Preparation: _____

161

Engine
Data Sheet

Harmonic Dampener

Manufacturer _____ Part No. _____

Flywheel

Manufacturer _____ Part No. _____

Diameter _____ " Weight _____ lbs.

Timing Chain/Gears

Manufacturer _____ Part No. _____

Water Pump

Manufacturer _____ Part No. _____

Impeller _____ Diameter _____ "

Oil Pan

Manufacturer _____ Part No. _____

Windage Tray

Manufacturer _____ Part No. _____

Assembly Lubricant

Mixture % ___ Manufacturer _____ Part No. _____

Mixture % ___ Manufacturer _____ Part No. _____

Mixture % ___ Manufacturer _____ Part No. _____

Head Gasket

Manufacturer _____ Part No. _____

Special Preparation:

Engine
Data Sheet

Camshaft

Manufacturer _____ Part No. _____

Intake: Opens _____ ° BTDC   Closes _____ ° ABDC   Lobe Lift _____ "

Exhaust: Opens _____ ° BBDC   Closes _____ ° BTDC / ATDC   Lobe Lift _____ "

Lobe Separation Angle _____ °   Lobe Center _____ °

Lobe Center Angle   Intake: _____ ° ATDC   Exhaust: _____ ° BTDC

Measured at _____ " lobe lift

Lifters

Manufacturer _____ Part No. _____

Pushrods

Manufacturer _____ Part No. _____

Diameter _____ " Length _____ "

Rev-Kit

Manufacturer _____ Part No. _____

Heads

Manufacturer _____ Part No. _____

Ported by: _____

Phone No: (____) ____ - _____

Volume: Intake: _____ cc   Exhaust: _____ cc   Combustion Chamber _____ cc

Seat Angles:

		Intake			
Intake	Top	____ °	Seat	____ °	Port	____ °
Exhaust	Top	____ °	Seat	____ °	Port	____ °

Valve Guides

Manufacturer _____ Part No. _____

Intake: Diameter _____ " Length _____ " Clearance _____ "

Exhaust: Diameter _____ " Length _____ " Clearance _____ "

Engine
Data Sheet

Engine

Valves

Intake: Manufacturer   Part No.

Diameter   Head   " Stem   "

Valve Angles: Top   ° Face   ° Undercut   °

Face Width   "

Exhaust: Manufacturer   Part No.

Diameter   Head   " Stem   "

Valve Angles: Top   ° Face   ° Undercut   °

Face Width   "

Valve Springs

Manufacturer   Part No.

Diameter   " Single   Double   Triple

Spring Pressure:

Intake   Seat   lbs./sq.in.   @   " installed height

Open   lbs./sq.in.   @   " valve lift

Exhaust   Seat   lbs./sq.in.   @   " installed height

Coil Bind Clearance   Intake   " @   " valve lift

Exhaust   " @   " valve lift

Spring Locators

Manufacturer   Part No.

Diameter   O.D.   " I.D.   "

Valve Seals

Manufacturer   Part No.

Engine
Data Sheet

Engine

Retainers

Manufacturer _____ Part No. _____

Design 7 ° [ ]   10 ° [ ]

Keepers

Manufacturer _____ Part No. _____

Rocker Arms

Manufacturer _____ Part No. _____

Ratio _____ : _____

Rocker Studs

Manufacturer _____ Part No. _____

Diameter _____ " Length _____ "

Intake

Manufacturer _____ Part No. _____

Runner Volume: _____ cc

Milled: Sides _____ " Ends _____ "

Gasket: Manufacturer _____ Part No. _____

Injectors

Manufacturer _____ Part No. _____

Rated Flow Rate: _____ lbs./hr. @ _____ lbs./sq.in.
Fuel Pressure

Spark Plugs

Manufacturer _____ Part No. _____

Gap _____ "

Plug Wires

Manufacturer _____ Part No. _____

Clutch Plate

Manufacturer _____ Part No. _____

Diameter _____ " Pressure _____ lbs./sq.in.

Engine Test

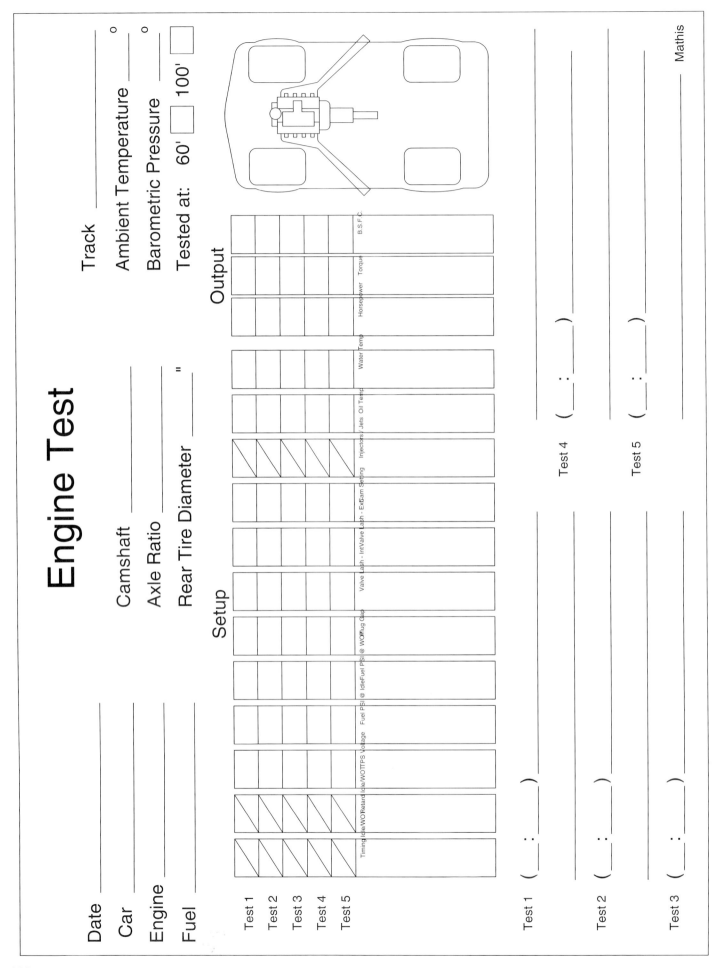

Date _____

Car _____

Engine _____

Fuel _____

Track _____

Ambient Temperature _____ °

Barometric Pressure _____ °

Tested at: ☐ 60' ☐ 100'

Camshaft _____

Axle Ratio _____

Rear Tire Diameter _____ "

Setup

	Timing Idle/WOT	Retard Idle/WOT	TPS Voltage	Fuel PSI @ Idle	Fuel PSI @ WOT	Plug Gap	Valve Lash - Int	Valve Lash - Ex	Cam Setting	Injectors / Jets	Oil Temp	Water Temp
Test 1												
Test 2												
Test 3												
Test 4												
Test 5												

Output

	Horsepower	Torque	B.S.F.C.
Test 1			
Test 2			
Test 3			
Test 4			
Test 5			

Test 1 (___) ___ : ___

Test 2 (___) ___ : ___

Test 3 (___) ___ : ___

Test 4 (___) ___ : ___

Test 5 (___) ___ : ___

_____ Mathis

INDEX

INDEX

ABOUT THE AUTHOR

William "Butch" Mathis was still in high school in 1965 when he first became hooked on Fords. It happened one night when a Weber-carbureted GT-350 rumbled into the local Dairy Queen. Since then, he has been building and racing Shelbys, Boss 302s, SVOs and 5.0 Mustangs. Although a noted CPA and federal tax authority, he is a self-taught engineer who utilizes sophisticated computer programming to design, test and evaluate new ideas. Except for a few years spent building championship-winning Kawasaki road racing motorcycles and high-performance airplanes, he has accumulated thousands of hours designing and testing engine, suspension and chassis components for the Fox Mustang. The popular *Slot Car Mustang* was one of the many test mules he has designed and built for various product evaluations. His company, High-G Performance, specializes in handling and Ford engine performance. He lives in south Texas.